W9-DGY-561

More Praise for *Grandloving*

♥   ♥   ♥

Grandloving was selected as Outstanding by Parent Council®.

"The Second Edition of this outstanding sourcebook offers wonderful ways to fulfill a child's need for unconditional love."
—**Eda LeShan, author of *Grandparents in a Changing World***

"Grandparents everywhere will have a ball with *Grandloving!* Only 10 pages into the book and I was 'hooked.' This is a fun, down-to-earth collection of easy, inexpensive ways to show your grandchild how much you love them. This would make a great gift for grandparents—or buy one for yourself, Grandma!"—**Marcia Todd, *Farm and Dairy***

"*Grandloving* answers the question 'What shall we do?' and helps grandparents fulfill their essential role with creativity."
—**Dr. Lillian Carson, author of *The Essential Grandparent* and *The Essential Grandparents' Guide to Divorce***

"*Grandloving* gives us the tools to share the gifts of love and laughter with our grandchildren...bonding forever two generations through memories of the heart."—**Joan Callander, author of *Second Time Around: Help for Grandparents Who Raise Their Children's Kids***

"Lucky are the little ones whose grammas and grandpas have this handbook that is so full of good, simple ideas."
—**Clarice Orr, author of *The Joy of Grandparenting***

"Illustrated with how-to drawings, *Grandloving* also includes the most comprehensive resource section and index we've seen. We highly recommend it!"—**Janet Haseley, *Creative Grandparenting Newsletter***

"What a fantastic collection of activities—it's a splendid book!"
—**D.J. McQuade-Lancaster, Coordinator of National Grandparents' Day**

"Anyone who thinks mothers-in-law and daughters-in-law cannot work together has not read *Grandloving*. Sue and her daughter-in-law Julie, both early childhood educators, have written an extremely helpful book for enriching relationships between children and their grandparents."—**Mary Pascall Darby,** *Mature Living*

"*Grandloving* is a thoughtful treasure to give to new grandparents or even to those who have years of grandparenting under their belts. If you are already a grandparent, or are a grandparent-to-be, don't wait for someone to buy it for you; the book will be both a wonderful treat and useful guidebook for you and your grandchildren."
—**Donna Bell,** *Parentpages*

"Sue and Julie capture perfectly that special relationship between grandparents and grandchildren in this delightfully refreshing book that is a 'must read' for every grandparent and grandparent-to-be."
—**Richard Sherman, author of** *Mr. Modem's Internet Guide for Seniors*

"I found *Grandloving* a treasure of tips and suggestions, and not only for grandparents! Aunts, uncles, friends, teachers, childless former college roommates—all of us who want to connect with kids need its help! The authors are gentle, humorous instructors—with this book's advice and its easy-to engineer activities we are truly ready for 'Funlove' between grownups and children."
—**Molly Hunter Giles, Wolfe Publications**

"Johnson and Carlson have written a peppy, upbeat blueprint to building a good grandparent-parent-grandchild relationship from both near and far."—**Wendy Taylor Carroll,** *Central California Parent*

"*Grandloving* offers more than 200 innovative and inexpensive activities for grandparents and their grandchildren that will foster and enhance a close familial bond between the generations."
—**James A. Cox,** *The Midwest Book Review*

"Every grandparent yearning for closeness will find thoughtful, enthusiastic assistance in *Grandloving*."—**Steven Trimble, author of** *The Geography of Childhood: Why Children Need Wild Places*

♥   ♥   ♥

Grandloving

Making Memories with Your Grandchildren

Sue Johnson and Julie Carlson

Illustrated by
Ronnie W. Shipman and Frederick B. Johnson

Foreword by Ann Ruethling

Second Edition

*In celebration of family
Sue Johnson*

Heartstrings Press
Fairport, New York

Published by Heartstrings Press, 20 Birling Gap, Fairport, NY 14450.
www.grandloving.com

Publisher's Cataloging-in-Publication
(Provided by Quality Books, Inc.)

Johnson, Sue, 1940–
    Grandloving : making memories with your
    grandchildren / Sue Johnson and Julie Carlson ;
    illustrated by Ronnie W. Shipman and
    Frederick B. Johnson ; foreword by
    Ann Ruethling. -- 2nd ed.
        p. cm.
    Includes bibliographical references and index.
    Library of Congress Card Number: 00-101878
    ISBN 0-9675349-8-4 (alk. paper)

    1. Grandparenting. 2. Grandparent and child.
    3. Grandchildren   I. Carlson, Julie, 1967–
    II. Title.

HQ759.9.J64 2000   306.874'5
                            QBI00-272

First Printing: September 1996
Second Printing: March 2000, completely revised
Printed in Canada
04 03 02 01 00   7 6 5 4 3 2 1

Publisher's Note: Many of the activities in *Grandloving* require adult supervision as noted throughout this book. Neither the authors nor the publisher is liable for any injuries or damages sustained while performing any of the activities in this book.

Contents

Acknowledgments   vi

Foreword   vii

Special Delivery: A New *Grandloving*!   ix

How to Use This Book   1

1. Nine Months and Counting   5

2. The Postpartum Visit   19

3. Love Across the Miles   37

4. When Your Grandchild Comes to Visit   59

5. Visiting Your Grandchild   111

6. Heartfelt Holidays and Family Traditions   149

7. More Mailbox Treasures   191

8. Caring for Your Grandchild   239

9. Wonderful Books for Grandparents   255

Notes   269

Index   270

Acknowledgments

There is no greater reward for us than updating a book that has already added joy to so many family relationships. Parenting and grandparenting this new edition of *Grandloving* to publication has not been just our labor of love. We owe our inspiration to the over three hundred and fifty grandparents, parents, and grandchildren from around the world who responded to our questionnaires and so generously shared their thoughts and wisdom. Many grandparents have taken the time to tell us how *Grandloving* has enriched their families, and we thank every one of you who wrote, called, and emailed us with your joyful stories.

We also appreciate deeply the support of family—"Opa" Rick who added his artistic talents, Grandma Kathy and Grandpa Bob, Brad, and our munchkins Nick and Charlie. We are grateful too for the hard work of our graphic designer, Laura W. Nelson, who did the interior, and the experts at Sans Serif, Inc., who enhanced the cover; everyone at the Fairport Library, especially our dear friend Sally Foster; Lane Stiles, publisher at Fairview Press, for his helpful guidance and advice; Chris Young and others at Hignell Printing, Ltd.; Sue Miller, for her insightful suggestions and continued support; and Ann Ruethling, the founder of Chinaberry Books, for her kind and heartfelt foreword.

Thank you, dear readers, for being our inspiration.

In celebration of family,

Sue and Julie

Foreword

It was about midnight, six hours after Elizabeth, our first child, was born. My husband and I were driving home from our midwife's cottage under a full moon with one of earth's newest human beings sleeping in the car seat between us. Feeling contentment and joy down to our very bones, but numbed by the intensities of the day, we suddenly realized that we were no longer two, as we had been for the eight years since we'd been married, but now three. We were struck by the powerful and undeniable awareness that in bringing forth this child we were now responsible for this 8 pound, 2 ounce person—no turning back, not ever. Awash in these new feelings, my husband turned to me and said exactly what was going through my own mind at that moment: "Wow. We REALLY did it this time!" Nothing would ever be the same again. And perhaps it was because we were simultaneously so weary and spent and emotionally high, it was as if time were standing still for us to savor the newness, the intense joy (and yes, the panic) of becoming a mother and a father.

My parents, who had attained grandparenthood for the first time with Elizabeth's birth, soon came to visit. After a twelve-hour bus ride and a five-hour plane trip (we lived in a very remote town!), they wearily yet eagerly tiptoed into our room at nearly 3 A.M. to meet their granddaughter for the first time. Elizabeth was sound asleep in her cradle. And there were my parents, silently leaning over to get a peek at her in the darkened room. I can see their silhouettes even now, nearly twenty years later. It was one of those rarefied moments that come so quietly and preciously and fleetingly when a child is new to the world. And it was in that very moment that Mom and Dad truly became grandparents.

Both Elizabeth and her brother, Evan, born three years later, are in their teens now. I'd have given anything for this book to have been available to me when they were young. Oh, I sent an enormous number of photos. I made tapes of their babblings and mailed them off to Mom and Dad. And Mom sent books and tapes of her reading those books so that Elizabeth could follow along. Our families got together about twice a year, and the children were delightfully pampered in their few days with their grandparents. But if we had known how short their time together would be, we would have tried to make even more of those connections (although, truth be told, I'm not sure I would have known how). *Grandloving* would have made these few years so much richer. Because my parents did not live to see their grandchildren reach school-age, we missed out on most of that special, relaxed connection between the oldest and youngest generations, the opportunity for my children to love someone who has lived well before them and seen so much of life. And that saddens me, because all healthy cultures know that it is our elders who can offer children the wisdom of perspective. They know that children will pass through stages and that the stages fly by with increasing speed. Grandparents know that what children need most is to be loved and that yes, they will learn to be potty trained (how many kids go off to college in diapers?) but the essence of their being is more important than any accomplishment. And so they know to take the time to show their love each moment, for the gift of age has also taught them how precious time is in our lives. The ideas and inspiration in *Grandloving* would have been a perfect fit for nurturing that relationship.

These are wonderful times to be expecting a grandchild, and I'm excited about what Sue and Julie have created in this book. With warmth and good humor, they have gathered the best tips from families worldwide. I trust that their mission of supporting and cheering on grandparents will inspire you to embark on your own journey into grandparenthood. May you create and sustain meaningful relations among all the generations of your family—and may you have warmth and joy and fun along the way!

Ann Ruethling, Founder
Chinaberry

Special Delivery: A New Grandloving!

When the first edition of *Grandloving* was published by Fairview Press four years ago, it had all the warmth and good advice that we and our over 300 contributors could fit into its pages—and all the idealism that we as *Grandloving*'s "Grandma and Mom" could feel for our newest endeavor.

More than ten thousand books—and another real grandbaby—later, our enthusiasm hasn't wavered: just as our love for little Charlie has strengthened our devotion to family, our work on this second edition, published by Sue, has deepened our dedication to grandparents worldwide. In fact, what began as a book has become our full-fledged mission to support and cheer on grandparents in their essential role.

The need for *Grandloving* is even greater today than it was when our first edition was published. By the year 2005, there will be more than 76 million grandparents: 26 percent more than there were in 1992, when Julie was pregnant with our first grandchild. Yet the vast numbers of grandparents now and to come tell only part of the story. Today more than 80 percent of grandparents have seen a grandchild and/or chatted on the phone in the previous month. Eleven percent are regular caregivers, and of the rest, 44 percent see a grandchild every week. Other research confirms that grandparents are becoming more involved in their grandchildren's lives. Yet many grandparents no longer feel that their relationship with their grandchildren is "special and relaxed." The Nanas and Papas we've met have been searching for a guidebook of heartwarming ideas to help them feel closer to their grandchildren.[1]

Grandloving has always answered that need. With over 200 activities for grandparents to do with their grandchildren or send in the mail, it provides hands-on, practical advice from a Grandma and Mom who've been there and a collection of terrific tips from other families just like yours. As you will discover, *Grandloving* is about taking the time to rock a new grandbaby, share a sideways grin with a grandtoddler, and chat with a school-age granddaughter about her dreams. In our hectic world, with many parents struggling to keep up with work and further education, grandparents are a wonderful and much-needed source of such gestures of love and acceptance. Even more important, every caring grandparent is a reminder that a precious family history is unfolding right now—and that the richness of the family story in progress depends on relaxed togetherness and fun.

This edition of *Grandloving* strives to even better answer and anticipate the interests of all caring grandparents—and to celebrate the ways in which we all can support our grandchildren and each other. In this edition, we've added activities for grandchildren as old as eight (and beyond!), armfuls of new children's books to explore, and a special new chapter for grandparents flying solo with their grandchildren—whether for a week-long visit or several years. Throughout, you'll see the same positive message of caring and joy that has inspired so many readers of *Grandloving*—from so many different circumstances and backgrounds—to make their own unique memories with their grandchildren.

♥   ♥   ♥

Join us on a journey of discovery, one that will inspire you to be the most true-to-yourself, sensitive, and fun-loving grandparent you can be. Join us for a second, updated edition of *Grandloving* that will give your grandchildren a repertoire of their own daydreams about family love and tradition that will keep you in their hearts forever.

Sue Johnson and Julie Carlson
C/o Sue Johnson, Heartstrings Press
20 Birling Gap, Fairport, NY 14450
www.grandloving.com (a free monthly webmagazine for grandparents)

How to Use This Book: Cuttings from Our Philosophical Scrap Box

Children are natural mess makers. They are masters at mudpies and perfectionists at puddle plopping. They learn about the world by *feeling,* by experimenting with movements and textures, by learning the fun of mixing colors. Open-ended explorations with paints, clays, crayons, glues, found objects, and natural elements stimulate the development of new skills and, just as important, bubbly conversations between a grandparent and a grandchild.

You can make the most of these opportunities by keeping the experience as interactive and process-oriented as possible. Simply turn your grandchild loose with the materials and keep your suggestions to a minimum. You might focus instead on making open-ended statements like "Tell me about your drawing. What's this part all about?"

Praise is like a puppy's kisses—a few licks on the cheek are the best thing ever, but more is soon overwhelming. Children, like all of us, want to know specifically what is so "neat," "super," or "wonderful" about their work, and they feel awkward receiving hyperbolic praise that they're not even sure they deserve. "I like the way your blue mixes with the yellow here," or "I see that you really took your time and had a plan!" will bolster your grandchild's self-confidence much more than the overused "That's great, honey!"

Most of all, emphasize the fun of doing rather than the finished

1

result. Join in, make "mistakes," start again, and talk with your grandchildren as you work side by side or together. Your grandchildren will feel invited to do the same in the comfortable setting you've created. But emphasizing the process doesn't mean the product can't be appreciated. Admiring a new drawing on the refrigerator door or putting up a pinecone birdfeeder is yet another way of showing your little ones how everything they do is magical in your eyes.

Containing Messes While Imaginations Take Flight

To help keep the messes and reminders to a minimum, you might (1) spread some newspapers or an old washable towel around the edges of the work surface or under the easel, (2) explain clearly the boundaries for the materials in a gentle and positive way—that they must be kept on the table, plastic, linoleum, breadboard, or wherever the activity will take place, and (3) give your little one a smock, apron, or Grandpa's old shirt to wear as a coverup. Engage your enthusiastic helper in setting up—and cleaning up! Sometimes washing up with a sponge afterward can be as much fun as creating the masterpiece.

Getting Started

The no-fuss, guaranteed-to-work activities in this book are organized into two categories: those that you can *do with your grandchildren* and those that you can *send to your grandchildren*. You'll know at a glance which is which, because you'll see two distinctive activity box corners.

The corner that features *clasped hands* of the grandchild and the grandparent indicates activities that you can do together. The border of *telephones and hearts* outlines those activities you can send to your grandchild.

Further, because each of us has favorite kinds of activities to do with our little ones, we've organized the activities by theme as well. Perhaps one of you—or both!—will get a hankering for an easy-to-make snack. Or maybe you'll be in a mood to take a nature walk and are looking for some fun things to do along the way. This guide will help you find exactly what you're looking for. Here are the activity themes you'll see as you flip to the back of each chapter.

Art. From playdough to bathtime fingerpaint, the activities we've gathered give your little ones the freedom to express their most fanciful dreams through visual art.

Construction. There's nothing like the smell of unfinished wood and the tap, tap of a little hammer to inspire your grandchild's creative side. Our super-safe variations make building fun for everyone.

Cooking. Everyone loves a homemade snack! Your little ones will love measuring, stirring, licking the spoon—and nibbling the delicious treats they create.

Let's Pretend. She's a clown, she's a tiger, she's . . . super-grandkid! This is the golden age for imaginary play, and we've got the activities to help you be a part of the fun.

Games. Remember the secret codes you used to send away for from radio programs? We've included our favorite golden oldies, as well as some unique puzzles, brain teasers, and other games to kindle love across the generations.

Music. Does your grandchild march to a wild and wonderful drummer? Celebrate the uniqueness of your little one with interactive activities that have a musical beat.

The Great Outdoors. Help your little explorer hop into his boots or clip on her sandals—whatever the weather, we've got ways to heighten every generation's awareness and appreciation of nature.

Science and Discovery. Your little rascal may not be ready for a microscope just yet, but a curiosity for learning how things work is well in place. Enrich your grandchild's understanding of the world and spark new conversations with special activities from our collection.

Staying in Touch. The miles may stretch between you, but by sending your heartfelt messages often and in unique ways, you'll feel only a snuggle away. Take advantage of our whole chapter of mailable activities to keep the love strong between visits.

"I Want to Be the Gramma"

We'll never forget overhearing three little preschooler girls play house outside in a school playground. One wanted to be the Mommy, another became the baby, and then they wondered aloud about the third. "She has to be the Daddy," said one, authoritatively. "No," said the girl whose fate was being decided. "I'll be the Gramma. I wanna have fun!" The others agreed, and they went off to recreate and dramatize the world as they knew it—sand cakes and all.

As your grandchildren grow during these magical early years, they absorb and reflect back to the world all that is around them. By shaping and enlivening your moments together and energizing your calls and letters, your grandchildren are given fresh perspectives about you as a loving and whole person. Your reward, and our dearest hope for all of you, is to see your grandchildren playing "Grandma" and "Grandpa" in a way that catches your heart and gives new meaning to all that you are.

1
Nine Months and Counting

Remember how you felt when you discovered your new baby was on the way? You can probably recall some of the joy and uncertainty you felt about the parenting adventure to come. Well, becoming a new grandparent also offers many redefining moments, and it can be equally confusing. Just like that ultrasound of your developing grandbaby on the fridge, your role in your new grandchild's life might seem a little fuzzy. You might feel unsure about whether—and how—this new little person might change your life. Maybe you're even having trouble matching up your outdated ideas about stodgy, passive grandparents with your hopes for an active, creative relationship with your own grandchild.

If you're experiencing many of these feelings now, don't worry. Your healthy anticipation of the changes to come is simply your way of preparing for a wonderful new perspective on life. In fact, we like to think of this ambiguous prenatal period as Grandma Nature's way of encouraging grandparents to reframe their family relationships and to offer their support more directly and simply. Know that your role in your growing family's life is as important now as it will be when your little grandchild is born. Like a mother's private conversation with her baby-to-be, your loving reassurance and nurturing attention during this time can be your gift to your grown child and developing grandbaby.

What the Parents-to-Be Are Feeling Now

You'll be interested to know that many first-time expectant moms and dads feel an urge to renew or strengthen the bonds with their own parents during the pregnancy. Ellen Galinsky writes about this in her book *The Six Stages of Parenthood*:

> One of the main things that mothers- and fathers-to-be think about is their own parents. . . . Evaluating, identifying, and differentiating oneself from one's parents is one of the tasks of preparing for parenthood, particularly first-time parenthood. . . . Sometimes this involves the rekindling of old feuds, other times a circling back to the parents, a desire to renew or revitalize bonds that have gone slack. . . . The wish that people have to be cared for during pregnancy is a delicate thing—if others cross the line, treat prospective parents as children once again, they often resent it. The first pregnancy makes many people feel as if they are on the verge of adulthood.[1]

Behind those more frequent phone calls and notes from your grown child could lie a hope that a new understanding will grow between you, and, if Galinsky is right, maybe a test of your flexibility and unchanging love. Responding with warmth will make the most of this unique opportunity for both generations. It really is the perfect time to put aside (or resolve) old concerns and set the stage for a new relationship—before the curtain opens and the more intensive drama begins.

Steve Trimble, father of two from Salt Lake City, Utah, wrote: "There is a sea change in relationships among a family that happens at the moment a first grandchild is born. Parents become both grandparents and parents; children become both children and parents. Everybody has different expectations about where to place the proper weight among all these conflicting priorities." These different expectations from each generation can make it seem harder than it needs to be. One helpful bit of advice we heard from many growing families is that everyone should seek to become a better listener.

> "To announce our first I tied a ribbon around my waist on Christmas Day. For my in-laws we put a box under their tree with a pink and blue ribbon on it saying, 'See you in August. Princeton Class of 2011.'"
>
> —*Sally and Reed Wilbur, Boxborough, Massachusetts*

There's a fancy name for this skill—*active listening*—and it's a trick that counselors use all the time. The most important part of being an

6

active listener is to ask meaningful questions based on what you're hearing the other person say, rather than to be absorbed in telling your own story. Slowing down and really listening to all the spoken and unspoken thoughts that someone is sharing with you takes practice. But give it a try—you'll be excited by how others will warm to you, and you'll learn more about your child's feelings about the pregnancy than you ever thought possible.

Sending and Receiving Long-Distance Love

Some of the best ideas for gifts and love messages cost very little and can help you connect with your grandbaby even before you can rock and cuddle. Use your imagination—the possibilities are endless!

A Perfect Fit for Growing Parents-to-Be

For a first-time Mom, encouraging words can be a perfect gift. As you might remember from your own expectant days, moms—and sometimes dads, too—have an insatiable appetite for absolutely everything, including books on prenatal and child care, breastfeeding (if this is an interest), and labor and delivery. (See chapter 8 for our recommendations.) Or send your own thoughts about these issues and a box of clippings you've saved from newspapers and magazines (see the activity "Snip and Send," p. 16). One of our friends in upstate New York collects sayings and advice about childrearing and offers it as a wonderful gift to families when they are expecting.

Moms-to-be will appreciate maternity clothes at any point in their pregnancies, although timing clothing to arrive right before they'll fit best is a good idea. Julie was incredulous and a bit horrified when she saw the maternity bathing suit Rick and I sent at the four-month mark; it wasn't until she called and said enthusiastically, "You'll never believe it, but that huge suit fits *everywhere* now!" that we knew we'd sent something useful. It's also nice to notice what style of maternity clothing she's choosing for herself before you package up that wild safari print dress or—even more controversial—that top with the pink and blue teddy bears.

For the dad-to-be, you might send a tiny, battery-operated reading light so that he can read in bed without disturbing his partner's sleep, or letters and articles about being a father. Even purchased books about becoming a dad can be meaningful if you take the time to add an inscription inside.

Words and Images Can Be Heirlooms, Too

Yet another way to show your daughter or son how much you care during the pregnancy is to save communications from them during this period. You might try to hold on to the notes and emails they send—or even to tape-record their phone calls home with an answering machine. Several grandmothers with whom we talked kept their own diaries during their daughter's pregnancy, and each became a priceless gift to the family after the birth (see the activity "Capturing Daydreams and New Discoveries," p. 16). Delta Fuller from Kennebunk, Maine, said, "I kept a journal from the first we knew of the baby called 'The Year You Were Born.' Seth was born in September and I kept the journal until Christmas. Christmas Eve was the last entry and the journal was a gift to the new Mom and Dad on Christmas Day." In our own family, email messages from Mom to Grandma were secretly saved and presented at the first prenatal visit. It was a gift no one else could give, and for Julie receiving it was one of the many emotional highlights of becoming a new mother.

> "To share our happy news, we asked our parents to save a certain day on their August calendar and let them figure it out."
>
> —*Hannah and Dan Rothermel, York, Maine*

If you can afford it, one way to help bridge the long-distance gap is to give your child a videocamera to capture the images of new parenthood before and after the birth (some families even film during the delivery). Lois and Jack Perlowski of Sanibel, Florida, sent their daughter a camcorder during her pregnancy. "Our hope is that they will faithfully send videos of the various stages and fun times which we miss due to distance." We guarantee that no other audience will appreciate the footage of the mom-to-be's growing belly as much as you will. (In fact, that's one video probably to leave unlabeled on the shelf!)

If both parents and grandparents happen to own a home computer, email is another way to speed messages back and forth. With a modem and a membership in Compuserve, America Online, or other communications service, you can shoot short notes or long letters to each other for as little as ten dollars a month. We found this method a super way to keep in touch during the pregnancy and an invaluable service when the newborn arrived. Email messages are less intrusive than a phone call (the message waits in your electronic mailbox) but are nearly as immediate. In addition, we tended to type along much as we speak rather than labor over words as we might have in a letter.

If you are not yet computer literate, don't be daunted; there's no time like the present to learn a truly easy new skill and rekindle your relationships at the same time. Put your turn signal on and merge onto that information superhighway—it's easy and fun!

Don't Just "Layette" on Me, Grandma!

"UPS!" hollers the delivery person, confirming the low drone of the truck outside and the thunk of package on package on the front steps. Our heroine, nearly nine months pregnant, waddles to the door and gives her electronic signature. While she considers how she's going to get these things inside without lifting more than ten pounds (her doctor's limit for this stage of the pregnancy), her eyes scan the labels. She discovers, with a half-smile, that her loving parents and parents-in-law have gone berserk again.

We know. Those miniature pajamas and T-shirts are irresistible. And somehow each new baby product you see seems like the perfect solution to some terribly important baby-care need (though, come to think of it, you seemed to do fine without many of them in your day). Furthermore, your children seem so grateful for all the things you send. But one way to make sure you're not overdoing when sending baby things is to ask what's needed or anticipate only with gifts that have sentimental meaning. Wrap up that special baby blanket of your son's for his firstborn to use, perhaps, or start sifting through your collection of books for young children for an old favorite of your daughter's. New clothing with a bit of embroidery added by you, an audio cassette of you humming or singing your favorite lullaby, or a purchased wooden toy car with a "Grampa" license plate brushed on with childsafe paints are just a few examples of how purchased gifts can take on new significance. The parents-to-be will sincerely appreciate your efforts, and you will have fulfilled your hopes of giving them something they'll cherish.

Baby Showers from Afar
Showers are often given for the mom-to-be, and if you live close to

each other the possibilities for themes and fun are endless. In our case, though, it was difficult to imagine how Julie was going to make it to the East Coast for a baby shower, given her work schedule and the prohibitive cost of plane fares. Luckily, friends in upstate New York thought of a way to have some fun, even long-distance (see "Showers from Afar," p. 17). At Sue Miller's "long-distance baby shower" in Fairport, New York, each guest brought their baby gift unwrapped for all to see—then everyone spent the afternoon tasting desserts, swapping stories about their own pregnancies and grandchildren, and wrapping their gift. Photos of the event made Julie feel a little more like she had been there, too, when she opened the big box of presents at her home in California.

We also put a twist on an old superstition. When Julie was just a few weeks pregnant, we gave her a little "good luck charm"—a simple, old-fashioned paper cutout of a womb with a baby inside (see "One Lucky Baby," p. 17). It was a copy of one that I had hanging around during my pregnancies. Something about it was reassuring to Julie—possibly just the fact that I had had one, too. And it was a subtly comforting reminder that her own mother and mother-in-law had been through the same experience and were thinking of her especially during these months.

Getting Fit to Enjoy a New Generation

Grandparents worldwide think of grandbabies with a warm glow in their hearts. Some, too, can't help but get an anticipatory flare in their backs and feet. If you're one of the latter Grandpas or Grandmas, let your grandchild's upcoming arrival be the excuse you've been waiting for to get healthy and improve your flexibility. After all, in just a few months you'll want to be able to push a diaper-bag-laden stroller, sit on the floor as your newborn grandchild takes a "sunshine bath" on the carpet, and wear a baby carrier around the house, complete with your newborn grandchild inside. Let the fact that a new generation is on the way encourage you to exercise and eat right so that you can enjoy the fun for many years to come.

A Word from Your Lower Back

Although curling up with a seven-pound infant probably won't throw your back out, now's the time to start thinking about ways to ease the strain that every grandbaby can eventually bring. Resolve now to lift from your knees, to stand fully upright when pushing that stroller, to lift young ones carefully from car seats, and to make sure that baby carrier is properly adjusted for you. Many thanks from your lower back—and your loving family.

Watch Out—Grandma's in Training!

You can also set about improving your own skills during this expectant time. Many local hospitals now have courses for grandparents that teach infant and child CPR (heart massage and lifesaving), give tours of the labor and delivery services, and provide remedial training in how to diaper. Although with the advent of diaper covers and disposables you may feel overqualified for the job, remember that there are special considerations for the littlest ones, such as keeping the umbilical area clean. You could also check out of the library a book that describes techniques for bathing a baby, giving a bottle, holding the baby in special "calming" positions, and other baby-care skills (see chapter 8 for our recommendations). Or challenge your spouse— the other grandparent-to-be—to a "remember how?" game that gets you reminiscing about this kind of hands-on loving with a baby. This playful competition is especially nice if you can follow up by babysitting for another young child together. That way you'll see how your memories match up with the even nicer realities.

Miscarriage . . .

For most families, thankfully, miscarriage is a rare occurrence—a tragedy that is unlikely to be repeated. But anytime a miscarriage happens, the hopes and dreams of parents are torn. If you felt, as did Phyllis Curtis of Ontario, New York, that the idea of becoming a grandparent gave you "feelings of immortality—of having a future life through grandchildren," you too may feel crushed by the news. Or your heart may simply go out to the parents and their sorrow. Regardless of your feelings, you are likely to find yourself in a position of being able to offer sympathy and support to the parents. If you can, you'll want to reach out to them with simple, compassionate expressions of love. You're probably aware that comments about having a "replacement" baby are not appropriate because each baby is so unique to its parents, but try to hold back from giving other advice as well. As with the joyful parts of grandparenting, if you can keep your focus on the emotional and physical well-being of your loved ones in a nonjudgmental way, you'll be the most help and you will all feel best about your relationship.

. . . and Close Calls

Judith and Ron Knight, grandparents from Pittsford, New York, endured an anxious few months with their daughter's pregnancy. Throughout, however, they worked hard to encourage the worried mother- and father-to-be. Judy stayed with her daughter and "just mothered my little girl so she didn't have to be hospitalized. I was so sure she would lose her baby." When the situation seemed to be getting better, Judy also made a point of taking her daughter out to a baby store one day. There "she became animated just looking at baby clothes. From that point on she felt better and started planning for her little one's arrival. Each day after that outing, she improved—it seemed like a miracle." We hope we can all be as attuned to the needs of our children and grandchildren during a trying time such as this. Through their devoted support of their daughter and son-in-law, Judy and Ron played an important part in the healthy delivery of their grandchild.

> "We all know grandparents whose values transcend passing fads and pressures, and who possess the wisdom of distilled pain and joy. Because they are usually free to love and guide and befriend the young without having to take daily responsibility for them, they can often reach out past pride and fear of failure and close the space between generations."
>
> *President Jimmy Carter*
> *September 9, 1979*
> *Proclamation of*
> *National Grandparents' Day*
> *[Always the 1st Sunday*
> *after Labor Day]*

Another Baby Is on the Way!

After navigating the confusing waters of new grandparenthood with a first grandchild, you'll probably feel like an experienced sailor waiting for the thrill of more high seas—or an announcement that more grandchildren are on the way. This news, if it does come, can be your call to deepen your involvement and help everyone in the growing family nurture a new pregnancy. Luckily, you've been a parent as well as a grandparent before, so you know how to give of yourself in many ways all at once. Strap on your running shoes and warm up your creative half (whether that means charming your spouse or reviving your right brain). You're going to rely on all of your combined energy, generosity, and resourcefulness in the months and years to come.

One member of the family who will definitely appreciate extra loving during a second pregnancy is your older grandchild. With humor and guidance, you are possibly the best person to give him the tender, loving care he craves. If he's younger than two, the whole concept of pregnancy is too abstract and long-term to handle; but if he is a bit older, the whole process might be confusing or distressing to him.

Before you talk to your preschooler grandchild about the pregnancy, however, it might be a good idea to ask the parents how they handled telling the "facts of life"—mostly so you won't fall off your armchair to hear the anatomically correct terms trip off his tongue. In general, however, don't worry about talking too much about the pregnancy unless it comes up. Just resolve to give your grandchild more of your time and love than ever.

"My Baby Sister Is a Barnacle?"

You'll want to be careful how you explain this little metaphor to your grandchildren, but we can't help but include it. One of our favorite authors, Anne Morrow Lindbergh, in her *Gift from the Sea*, likens the widening circle of human relationships to seashells that roughen up and take on appendages as they grow and mature. Here are her thoughts about the jump from being an intimate twosome to a larger family—an analogy we think is perfect for recasting in a more positive way the dread many children have about the arrival of a new brother or sister:

> It is true, of course, the original relationship is very beautiful. Its self-enclosed perfection wears the freshness of a spring morning. Forgetting about the summer to come, one often feels one would like to prolong the spring of early love, when two people stand as individuals, without past or future, facing each other. . . . [But] the early ecstatic stage of a relationship cannot continue always at the same pitch of intensity. It moves to another phase of growth which one should not dread, but welcome as one welcomes summer after spring. . . .
>
> Woman refinds in a limited form with each new child, something resembling, at least in its absorption, the early pure relation-

ship. In the sheltered simplicity of the first days after a baby is born, one sees again the magical closed circle, the miraculous sense of two people existing only for each other. . . . It is, however, only a brief interlude and not a substitute for the original more complete relationship."[2]

For your grandchild, as you probably realize, there is both something lost and something gained from having a brother or sister arrive. Gained is a playmate sometime much later on, and lost is some of the intimacy she enjoyed with her parents. Your grandchild will love knowing ahead of time that the two of you will always have the same special closeness no matter how many brothers and sisters follow. You and your little one can always have the occasional "brief interlude" of an intensive one-on-one adventure, as well as more ordinary moments, regardless of other family members' responsibilities. And communicating this message now will make your older grandchild feel that much more secure as "B-day" approaches.

Helping Your Little Ones Welcome the New Baby

One surefire way to give the upcoming event a positive cast is to get the soon-to-be big brother or big sister involved in making a special gift. You might try creating something that a newborn will enjoy soon, such as a mobile of tiny clay creatures (see "Suspended Imagination," p. 15)—or a flannel crib sheet or blanket that your grandchild can color with permanent fabric markers. One imaginative family we know even decorated tiny socks with faces that could entertain the new baby when she waved her feet. Simple and love-inspired, these thoughtful, easy-to-do gifts will help the older child feel more involved in the big event ahead.

Our Sneak Preview of the Wonders to Come

Ever been in line to see a movie and been encouraged to see everyone leaving the early show all excited and teary? Well, Grandma and Grandpa, think of us as your personal previewers to the grandparenting adventure ahead: we have seen the matinee, and we just know you're going to have the time of your life. Certainly there may be times when your views conflict with those of your grandchild's parents, but if you consider every difference a learning opportunity you'll soon see that positive childrearing can accommodate many styles.

Furthermore, the rewards of developing a rich relationship with little ones are so appealing they're worth any little bumps along the way: You can peek into the world of a growing child as she encounters new challenges, stroll through cherished memories of yourself as a parent, and even revisit some of the life choices you've made over the years. Most of all, we know that the enthusiasm and family-oriented approach to life that led you to pick up this book will lead you to be a positive and memorable influence on your young grandchildren. Congratulations, and don't forget your running shoes!

Suspended Imagination

The whole family will enjoy making their handmade creatures into a unique mobile for the new baby.

You'll Need
- Colored modeling clay
- String
- Wire hangers

Here's How
- Ask each family member to mold an object when they come to visit.
- Using the hangers for mobile "arms," tie and string the objects so they balance.
- Try a theme! You might try animals, nursery rhymes, or toys.

Be sure to hang well out of the way of an infant's grasp.

Capturing Daydreams and New Discoveries

Start this project as soon as you can after learning you're going to have a grandchild. This is a wonderful way to provide lasting memories for the parents and new baby.

You'll Need
- A folder in which you save letters, emails, or any correspondence from the new parents-to-be

Here's How
- Keep a notebook, jotting down notes from any verbal "baby" discussions you have with the expectant family.
- Add this to the collection of saved letters, emails, or cards.
- Present it to the new parents when the baby arrives as a diary and remembrance of the pregnancy.

Snip and Send

Keep those scissors handy and start keeping your eyes open for articles on pregnancy, childbirth, childrearing, and family issues, as well as appropriate money-saving coupons.

You'll Need
- To be alert to the interests and concerns of your new family-to-be

Here's How
- Clip appropriate articles from magazines and newspapers.
- For further ideas, you might begin subscribing to a newsletter for new grandparents (see our resources in chapter 8).
- You may not agree with all the clippings you send, but they can provide a good springboard for discussions.
- Be aware of things that new parents will need to purchase—diapers, wipes, baby shampoo—and take the time to clip and send these money-saving coupons.
- The fact that you're thinking about and "in tune" with the needs of the new family-to-be will help them feel loved.

One Lucky Baby

A simple growing baby mobile has been passed along in our family as a symbol of good luck during the pregnancy—it's easy to make and fun to send!

You'll Need
- Poster board or similar stiff paper
- Scissors or a knife, and thread

Here's How
- Follow our design or draw your own growing baby, and cut it out.
- With a heavy needle, sew a strand of thread through the top of the tiny baby's head and attach it directly above the circle. This will create the free-swinging "baby in the womb."
- Sew thread at the top for hanging.
- Suspended over a kitchen sink, it'll be a reminder that your good thoughts are constantly with the new parents-to-be!

Showers from Afar

Even if the new mother-to-be lives too far away to come "back home" for a baby shower, you and your friends can still enjoy the excitement that surrounds a baby shower, the joy of giving, and the anticipation of your new grandchild's birth.

You'll Need
- A group of friends and family who wish to "shower" the mother-to-be with baby gifts despite the fact that she lives far away.

Here's How
- Invite everyone to come with their gifts unwrapped and their paper and ribbons in a bag.
- Take turns showing the gifts—taking lots of photos for the baby's scrapbook.
- Have a "wrap it up time." The grandparents can then either send the gifts or take them when they visit.

Peek-a-Boo Book

Your younger grandchildren will especially enjoy this, and if you include some photos of yourself it'll help them remember you.

Ages: Baby to three years

You'll Need
- A small spiral notebook—spiral-bound index cards are perfect
- Pictures or photographs of things or people meaningful to your grandchild
- Clear contact paper
- Scissors

Here's How
- Starting with the second page in the book, paste a picture or photograph on every other page.
- Cover each picture with clear contact to preserve.
- Cut each blank page into thirds horizontally, cutting from the edge of the page through to the spiral binding.
- When you "read" the book with your grandchild, turn just one strip at a time.
- Give your little tyke an opportunity to play peek-a-boo and guess who as you slowly reveal the whole picture.
- You can cut pictures out of magazines, but be sure to include some photographs of yourself!

2
The Postpartum Visit

Nicole: Good morning. (*She pulls out a newspaper clipping along with her beautifully prepared resume.*) I should probably confess to you at the outset that I found your job description somewhat vague, but I hope that my skills will match your needs.

Betty: (*Smiles graciously.*) Oh, I'm sure you're uniquely qualified. But, my dear, don't worry so much about the details. You'll come on board, and then you'll see. . . . (*Seems to lose her train of thought.*) I mean, I can give you lists of books to read, and I'll certainly tell you exactly what I did when I had your job, but words simply are inadequate to describe. . . . (*Gazes off nostalgically and sighs.*) Oh, you know what I mean.

Nicole: (*Smiles cautiously.*) Well, could you at least tell me when I would start?

Betty: In nine months. And that's good, because you'll want to prepare in so many ways. (*Chuckles magnanimously.*) But of course, you'll be surprised anyway. It's more work than you could ever imagine, but you'll be so happy you chose this job. In fact, after working it for a few months, you won't be able to picture yourself doing anything else. It's simply the most rewarding and socially important occupation there is.

Nicole: Hmm. Well, everyone is telling me that this work will change my entire outlook. What might I expect for a salary?

Betty: Salary? Oh, this job is a little light in the salary department, but the benefits, though for the most part intangible, are wonderful. (*Suddenly hurried, she shuffles through the papers on her desk and pulls one out.*) Now if you'll just sign here on the line for "Mother". . .

At a recent wedding, we were intrigued and amused by the chaplain's words to the young bride and groom. Exchanging a smile with his own wife, he told the nervous couple that they would have days when all that would keep them together would be an overwhelming curiosity about their future and, further, a fascination about what ever possessed them to marry each other in the first place. It was a funny thought—there were chuckles in the crowd—and it occurred to us that becoming a parent for the first time is similar to deciding to get married. Those first few weeks of child care, as we all know, require the same leap of faith—the same courage by parents to wonder together about the future and to allow this wonder to sustain them through the newness of the present. And if that doesn't do it, then an incredulous "How in the world did we think this was a good idea?" might tickle both parents enough to carry them through those early days.

To be sure, the first month after the birth of a first child is a tumultuous one for new parents, even if they feel better informed for the job than our mythical "Nicole"—and not many of us did in our day, or do now. No matter how many books they've read, classes they've taken, and videos on baby care they've seen, the emotions and concerns that come along with that little bundle can seem overwhelming at times to a new Mom and Dad.

Moreover, it's important that others, even extended family members, respect the privacy of the new family as they begin the important process of learning about and loving the new baby. As Ellen Galinsky writes about parenting,

> For parents, the task of accepting that the baby belongs to them—
> that they are now parents—is part of forming a relationship with
> this baby. This process can take varying amounts of time and can be
> prolonged by others who often edge in between the parents and
> child, often in the guise of helpfulness.[1]

But another kind of attachment needs to take place during the postpartum visit as well—an attachment between grandparent and child. How can all the family members work together to reconcile all these needs? If Galinsky is right, the secret is not "edging in" on the time the baby has with either grandparent or parent. The trick is perhaps to take turns rather than share each moment with the baby—and to realize that for the baby's sake, parental attachment has to come first. So hop in the back seat for most of the ride—the view is still good and you might even find ways to be helpful back there. And of course enjoy to the fullest those moments when you have a turn up front.

Listening with Love

Mercifully for grandparents, but hazardously for their relationships with their children, nature encourages us to forget the less-than-perfect moments of our own parenting days. But this is an essential time to remind yourself that this miniature addition to the family comes with gigantic needs—needs that your children might not expect.

During her first postpartum visit with Nick, Julie's mom, Kathy, from Duluth, Minnesota, made the most of one potential conflict. She and Julie both arrived at Nick's bassinet at the same moment to calm him. Kathy's first instinct was to take Nick and give Julie a chance to rest. Julie, however, announced, "Let me try, Mom." Kathy didn't know until later how meaningful her response was: "Okay. But don't worry if he doesn't stop crying right away. Sometimes it's hard to know what a baby needs." In this way, she encouraged Julie to be the one to comfort Nick and also let Julie know that despite our best efforts, infants sometimes are difficult to comfort. Especially during a postpartum stay, a wise grandparent will make the most of opportunities like these.

Adopting a New Philosophy

What are your thoughts about the "family bed"? What is your ethic about disposable versus cloth diapers? Didn't newborns in your day eat every four hours on the hour? Guess what. It truly doesn't matter. The beauty of grandparenting is that you can have little responsibility and all of the fun while you're with your grandchild. Besides, if you dusted off your own mind's parenting file well enough you would see that you, too, had misgivings about all sorts of child-rearing issues when you were in charge. One thing Julie and I have learned in our years of teaching little ones is that many kinds of parenting styles lead to happy, fulfilled children. Whether your grandchildren wear hats when taking a walk in the spring or drink milk with every meal will not make or break their childhood—they will most likely still grow up healthy and still be mischievous, fun-loving, and challenging along the way.

Grandfathers, too, may feel a tug of anxiety, or even of leftover guilt, about the care their grandchildren receive. It was unusual thirty or more years ago for fathers to be involved in diapering, feeding, and many other aspects of a baby's day-to-day care. Perhaps you want to make up for these lost experiences with the new generation in your family, but are feeling uncertain about how to get involved. Not to worry. Love—unfettered and unwavering—is the most important element of a nurturing relationship, and you are an essential part of this equation, no matter what your grandfathering "style" or previous experience. (In fact, you may be uniquely qualified if you have a snuggle technique like Nick and Charlie's Grandpa Carlson.) Just enjoy these precious moments before they slip away.

Homegrown or Imported, Grandchildren Are a Part of Us

Whether your family is growing as a result of births or adoptions, your feelings about becoming a grandparent will be much the same. There are a few aspects of adoption, however, that make the time immediately following the new arrival a bit different for everyone. Brand-new parents of an adoptive baby might feel less prepared for the arrival of the baby without a pregnancy to get them in that frame of mind. On top of that unsettling notion, many adoptive parents don't have much advance notice of the baby's arrival, or may have steeled themselves against planning because of earlier disappointments.

Grandparents, too, may find themselves bouncing a bit in the emotional turbulence that comes along with adoptions. But you can still be among the most supportive family members once the new baby has arrived. Remembering back to your days as a new parent will draw out memories of how you, too, felt inadequate at times even though you may have had the "whole pregnancy to prepare." And having been an involved listener during the often long wait for an adopted baby, you can appreciate in a special way the joy and wonder the new parents feel as they hold their little one for the first time. Most of all, your tenderness toward the

No matter how many books they've read, classes they've taken, and videos on baby care they've seen, the emotions and concerns that come along with that little bundle can seem overwhelming at times to a new Mom and Dad.

new baby will be the best welcome any child can have into a family. Grandchildren are a blessing no matter how they arrive.

Your Essential Role

"Don't expect to be entertained. Bring food—lots! Don't expect a clean house. And don't stay long—anticipate leaving earlier than scheduled without feeling unloved." So wrote Sarah Hill of Summit, New Jersey, a parent of two little ones. We couldn't agree more. In fact, in our experience, your role during the postpartum visit is to encourage your child as a parent, help with household chores as much as you're able, and be independent. Your child will almost certainly ask for help with the new baby if it's wanted, but we found that it made for a smoother transition for the new parents if grandparents keep a low profile. Bring your Clancy or Michener novel, go to bed early (at a hotel or bed and breakfast if quarters are tight), be flexible, and be the genie who makes everything work smoothly behind the scenes. Trust us—your efforts will be deeply appreciated, and you will have given your own child a wonderful gift: your confidence in him or her as a parent.

With so few wakeful cuddle moments with the newborn during those first weeks, we suggest that each side of the family visit at different times so that everyone can feel included. Parents, for their part, can help make that first visit with each set of grandparents successful by being good communicators and by sharing the baby as much as is comfortable for them. One mom from Fairport, New York, Sue Eberhardt, suggested that a nursing mother express a little milk so the grandparents can feed the baby. Other parents, however, may want to be responsible for all feedings, and this is also all right. As long as parents try their best to make their needs clear, and grandparents try to be receptive and understanding, infinite variations on the theme are possible and will make for a successful new relationship.

What to Pack

What should you take with you for the first postpartum visit? You'll want some soft, cotton shirts that won't irritate the baby's skin. (Make sure you can wash every piece of clothing that you take, because babies love to make you change clothes!) Leave your perfume or aftershave at home, because new moms and dads like their babies to still smell like "theirs" after cuddling with you. Take a good book, appropriate outdoor gear, and some walking shoes so that you'll feel independent. And don't zip up that suitcase until you've packed your best hearing aid—whether electronic or that mental reminder to listen. You'll want to be as responsive as you can to the signals every member of the family sends your way.

Another great idea for a special something to take came to us from Allison Graham, of Perinton, New York. She thinks that grandparents could adapt an idea her Dad, Paul, dreamed up. When she was born he bought a new pink tie, and he wore it when he brought her home from the hospital. He has worn that same pink tie for all her big events over the years—her confirmation, recitals, graduations, and so forth. They even plan to remake it into a bow tie for him to wear at her wedding!

Some Great "New Family" Gifts

If you've been dying to give a traditional gift to the baby, you can take a receiving blanket (no one has too many of these, it seems), cotton newborn clothes that have easy access to the diaper (Julie arranged her newborn clothes for Nick by number of under-the-leg snaps—the fewer, the better!), or a welcome savings bond. But we'd like to encourage you to be more creative. Judy and Dan Hays, from Fairport, New York, wrote: "One of the first things we gave our new granddaughter was a little picture book with pictures of her and her family including us, her mom and dad, her uncles, and her dogs. Then her mom and dad would show it to her and tell her who everyone was." New parents love passing down traditions to the new baby, such as lullabies sung to them as children. Rick and I collected the music and lyrics of our favorite lullabies and had a copy shop bind them (see "Passing of the Tunes," p. 31).

Other wonderful gift ideas we learned from grandparents in the United States and abroad were to make a toy bag and include a toy that your child once used; wrap up a small item that your child had had, such as a spoon, rattle, cup, baby teething ring, or bracelet; present flowers in a vase you received when your child, the new parent, was born; pass along your child's baby book; and give a family tree as far back as you know. Our family took this "family tree" idea one step further. My father planted a climbing rose outside our front door when our second child, Bryan, was born. Before moving to our new home, we layered the rose to form an offshoot plant to take along with us. We have nurtured this rosebush for thirty-two years and hope one day to pass it along to a child of Bryan's. (If you try this, consider planting the tree or bush in the front yard rather than the back so that if the young family does have to leave it behind they can at least see it when they drive by.)

Julie Dickens, a new mother from Victor, New York, suggested for the baby "a letter to the child (for later reading) explaining the grandparents' excitement at his or her arrival." Anything that shows how thrilled you are to be a grandparent and how you want the baby to feel included in the larger family circle will be warmly received. And it goes without saying that your time and enthusiasm are the most precious gifts of all.

Making a Time Capsule

All of our ideas for commemorating the birth of a new grandchild center on the notion of preserving something special for the newborn and his family. An exciting way to do this is to create a "time capsule" for the baby (see "A Time Capsule of Treasures," p. 33). You might enclose photos of the newest addition's family members cooing over him. Pop in that day's newspaper and a cassette tape of the day's news on the radio. Document the "hip" words of the day, and what your family enjoys doing for fun. On a more personal level, you might ask each family member how they feel about the new baby— and write down their exact words in a small booklet. All of this can be contained in a simple or fancy container that will not be opened until someday much later—perhaps at a high-school or college graduation, special birthday, or even when he brings his own first baby home from the hospital.

Sharing the Fun with Older Grandchildren

If the new baby has older brothers or sisters, they will enjoy the job of unwrapping the baby gifts and "trying them out" by playing with them first. They will also delight in opening their own small gift from you that shows you appreciate their new role in the family. It will be fun for the older siblings, too, to hear you refer to the baby as "their baby" and to see your amazement at all they can do in comparison to the new addition.

Easing the Transition for a New "Big" Brother or Sister

What a shocker. Your grandchild had waited eagerly, in various stages of awareness, for several months. Everyone had been talking in excited voices about the new baby to come. Your grandchild's family had been busy "preparing" your little one for being a new brother or sister with books and videos. He or she had visions of generously taking turns with the Duplos or of pushing a giggling baby around in the stroller. Unfortunately, these images are not based in reality—at least not for many, many weeks (and remember how long a week was when you were a little person?). Instead, a tiny, needy baby is suddenly taking up time and emotional and physical energy from everyone around, especially Mom and Dad. It's no wonder that many new siblings share with their parents and caregivers feelings of hurt and occasional anger toward a new baby, feelings that are valid and helpful to talk about. But what can be done to make this crisis into a more positive experience?

> Each grandchild's birth changes us so fundamentally that we will always take a bit of their light with us as we live our lives.

Enter Grandma and Grandpa, nature's shock absorbers. Especially if they have already nurtured a loving, active friendship with the first grandchildren in the family, they are perfectly positioned to be a well-rested, caring sounding board for a little one's concerns. Grandparents can snuggle up with that older sibling and look over baby pictures of when he or she was little. They can bring small gifts for the new big brother or sister to pass out at nursery school or playgroup in celebration of the big event. They can also provide much-needed comic relief and can take little ones out of a busy house and into the world again—or as our Nick used to say as a toddler, they can "turn the key . . . vroom!" Zip out to a new playground or a favorite ice cream parlor, go see the children's petting area at the zoo, or take in a children's movie. Try your best to widen your grandchild's world again so that the baby becomes just one of many parts of an exciting life.

Of course you'll want some cuddle time with the new arrival, too. One way to include the older child in this time is to read a book to both children, with the older child responsible for turning pages (your hands will be busy cradling the newborn). (See chapter 9 for books that are ideal for this time.) Or compare features and abilities of the newborn with the older child's. Even if the older child is adopted and the newborn is "locally grown," you can still foster a sense in young children that everyone belongs together. "Look at how beautiful her eyes are," you might say, "just like yours!" The most fun part will be reminding the older child how capable he is—how far he has come from his own days as a newborn.

If you're feeling steady on your feet, and it seems like a good idea to the Mom and Dad, you can also carry the newborn in a sling or front carrier and thereby free up your hands to do more with the older child. Be conservative about how much you try to accomplish, though—even young Moms and Dads can find it draining to carry one child and chase another.

Activities Just for Big Boys and Girls

The first days of being a new big brother or sister are much like the first days of any new job. Your grandchild will feel excited about the change, anxious to learn the new routines, and eager to feel capable in his or her new role. Often young grandchildren in this position will regress a bit (especially in their toileting and sleeping habits) as they adjust to this new arrangement.

Luckily for everyone in the growing young family, loving grand-parents can help a grandchild's new "career" as a big sibling get off to a great start. The trick is to build on what makes that older grand-child special. You might try making family-member "footprints" by tracing the outlines of everyone's feet on pieces of paper, cutting them out, and decorating them for display. Taking measurements of people, beds, and even clothes might also give your older grandchild a feeling of being a part of the natural process of growing and maturing—and it's fun to use a ruler, too!

Helping your young grandchildren celebrate the arrival with a project that really extends their abilities and requires close one-on-one grandloving can also be an antidote to sibling rivalry. You might try putting out a "newspaper" describing, reporter-style, the changes in the family—with a photo or two on the front page. (You could make it a "surprise" for the new Mom and Dad.) Or you could encourage your grandchild to play "doctor" to a recovering Mommy with a pretend stethoscope and paper tablet for "prescriptions" (you can write these down for your grandchild if need be). You might even give your young grandchildren their own "babies" to tend—a doll, perhaps, for a toddler or two (see "Everyone Needs a Baby," p. 36), or a newborn herb or flower garden for an older preschooler. Appreciating the maturity of new big brothers and sisters helps them develop a positive feeling about their new roles in the family, and ensures that the family stories around this memorable time will include the fun antics of a loving big brother or sister.

Helping Your Older Grandchild Make a Present for the Newborn

One way to bridge the distance between this appreciated big brother or sister and the tiny baby in the house is to harness that little artist's energies into making a creative gift. A young grandchild can help you make a soft washcloth mitt puppet for bath time (see "Puppets in the Bath," p. 225), or can cut or tear bold, simple pictures from magazines for the baby to look at. (You could display these as a "wall" of pictures above or beside the changing table or in a baby-safe photo album "book.") Challenge your little one to come up with his own ideas—you'll be surprised at the imaginative responses you'll get!

A Parting Gift: A Grandparent's Kit for Couchside Loving

It's not really a big surprise, but the latest early childhood research tells us that older siblings adjust much better to a new baby's arrival if they can maintain some important connections with their most steady caregiver. For many families, this means that your older grandchild will need lots of loving from Mom to feel good about the new situation. But we all know that Mom is just about the last person who has energy enough for new ideas and group cuddles during this busy time. Well, how about a rescue from Grandpa and Grandma? We think that one of the nicest gifts grandparents can leave for a new family is a collection of quiet, snuggly activities that a new "big" brother or sister can do while sitting with Mom on a couch or bed while she feeds the newborn or takes a phone call. You might tuck in some new stickers or some "press and peel" plastic figures; a few books (board books for your littlest readers will allow them to turn their own pages); a sock or hand puppet; or one of those neat little toys that has buttons, zippers, and all the rest for "dressing." Anything that is new to the grandchild and that can be done quietly while next to Mom will be just right. (This makes a great long-distance gift, too, if you can't be there for the first weeks!)

An Appreciative Audience

Ever wonder if all these efforts are really noticed by the exhausted Mom and Dad? Just read on. Jen Shaw from Salt Lake City, Utah, wrote us about her Mother: "My mom came to stay during the week after my second child was born . . . and she made everything work! One of the most important things my parents do for my children (and for me) involves spending time together doing 'kid things.' Once a year they watch the children for an overnight, and it's always a memorable evening for the boys and a dreamlike chance to get away for us." Each family will have its own traditions, of course, but when grandparents pitch in with an earnest willingness to help wherever and however they can, the whole family benefits.

Postpartum Blues, Grandparent Style

For most of us, postpartum blues hit hard about twenty-four hours before we have to leave our precious new bundle. We know that the young family may be eager to "try their wings" without our guidance, and we also know that work and other obligations may make it important for us to leave. But there's no getting around the glum feeling of saying goodbye to a blossoming young family. So much has happened in the weeks leading up to and including our visit, and we feel so lucky to have been a part of the growth and enrichment of our loved ones, that it feels like a terrible anticlimax to return to our lives as they were. Luckily, though, we can take solace in knowing that we truly are not the same people who arrived at our little one's doorstep. Each grandchild's birth changes us so fundamentally that we will always take a bit of their light with us as we live our lives. As we sow seeds in our garden or take a renewed interest in a loved one's concern, we know that the expansive joy we feel for the world around us springs from the enchantment of our newest grandbaby.

> The beauty of grandparenting is that you can have little responsibility and all of the fun while you're with your grandchild.

Everyone Loves Being Welcomed Home

We've made it a tradition to welcome home our grown children and grandchildren with handmade signs. Why not give the job of welcoming home the new baby to the new big brother or sister?

Ages: Two to eight years
You'll Need
- Sign material—shirt cardboard, poster board, or easel paper
- Paints, crayons, or cutouts and glue

Here's How
- Talk about what it was like when your older grandchild was welcomed home—who was there, what did the baby wear, what were some of the special gifts that arrived, did someone send flowers, did neighbors bring in food?
- Encourage your older grandchild to make a welcome home sign for Mom and the new baby. Photographs of family members could also be used on the sign.

Toy Bag or Box Treasures

Collecting, washing, and sorting through old toys is great fun for your older grandchild and helpful to you!

Ages: Two to five years
You'll Need
- To help unearth the old baby toys from storage
- To make a plain muslin toy bag or find a cardboard box
- Fabric crayons or fabric markers to decorate the bag, or baby wrapping paper to decorate the box

Here's How
- With the help of your grandchild, wash and sort through the toys, choosing those the baby will use.
- Your grandchild could then decorate the toy bag or box to hold the hand-me-down toys.

Shhhhh . . . Baby's Sleeping!

If your grandchild makes this sign, she'll be more inclined to heed it!

Ages: Two to five years
You'll Need
- A shirt cardboard or paper of similar weight
- String or yard for hanging the sign
- Crayons, paints, or cut-out pictures and glue

Here's How
- Explain that there will be times when the baby is sleeping—times for an "inside quiet voice and gentle play."
- To help everyone in the family know when the baby is napping, have your grandchild design and make a sign that can be hung on the baby's door.

Passing of the Tunes

There's no better gift than to pass along the lullabies and songs you sang to your children.

Age: Newborn
You'll Need
- A good memory, or helpful resource book (see p. 267)

Here's How
- Write down the words of lullabies and songs you sang to your children when they were little.
- Put these in a folder or booklet and present them to your new grandchild.

You'll be glad you "jogged your memory" ahead of time, so you'll be ready when rocking that bundle of love.

Arms of Love

If you can't be there to hold that precious darling, send some "stuffed" arms of love!

Ages: Newborn to one year

You'll Need
- One yard of fabric
- Needle and thread or sewing machine
- Polyester stuffing
- Velcro (optional)

Here's How
- Cut out two pieces of fabric like our diagram, long enough to encircle your grandbaby.
- With right sides together sew the two pieces together, leaving an opening in the middle.
- Turn right side out, stuff with the polyester, and close up the opening.
- If you'd like to have the "arms" totally encircle your precious little one, sew velcro pads on the "hands"—one pad on top of one hand and the other pad on the inside of the other hand.

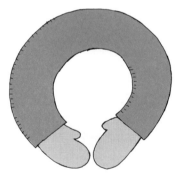

Remember not to leave an infant alone in this sitting up position.

A Time Capsule of Treasures

Start collecting things on the day your grandchild is born to make a time capsule that he can open at a special later date.

You'll Need Items Like These
- A newspaper from the day your grandchild was born
- A radio recording of the current song hits of the time
- A videotape of the day's news broadcast
- The birth announcement
- Coins from the year of your grandchild's birth
- A current family photograph
- A letter you've written to your grandchild describing how excited you are about his arrival

Here's How
- Collect everything and store in a safe place.
- You might share what you are doing with your children, but keep it a secret from your grandchild.
- To commemorate a special day, pass along your surprise.

Create a Treasure as You Record the Day

Amid the excitement of a new baby, you may be the only one with the time and forethought to record all the happenings on the day your grandchild is born.

You'll Need
- Pencil and paper
- A keen eye and ear for all that happens and is said

Here's How
- Play the role of reporter.
- Start with that long-awaited call telling you that your grandchild is on the way. Document the details—who called, when, what you were doing at the time, what was said, what the weather was like, and so on.
- Continue to report and record in this way throughout the day. Yours will be the "lead story" for years to come!

Big Brother/Big Sister Badge

Help your grandchild prepare for the arrival of a new sibling, and reward his or her efforts with a special badge.

Ages: Two to five years

You'll Need
- Projects she can do to help get ready
- A check-off list
- Your premade special big brother/big sister badge

Here's How
- Make a list of projects your grandchild can do. Perhaps he might like to:
  - Get out and clean his old baby toys.
  - Decorate a new photo album for the new baby.
  - Learn some simple songs to sing to the baby.
  - Make a mobile to hang over the crib or cut out colorful pictures to paste up over the changing table.
  - Help Mom and Dad with chores such as folding the laundry, putting away the diapers and baby clothes, or watering the garden.
  - Make announcements to pass out to his friends.
  - Put a picture of himself in the baby's room.
  - When your list has been checked off, reward your grandchild with the special badge you have made just for the occasion.

Words of Wisdom

No one but you can share the clippings you found meaningful when your children were small.

Age: Newborn
You'll Need
- A day to clean out your desk, closet, trunk—wherever you kept those "treasures" of wisdom you clipped while raising your children

Here's How
- Make copies of these inspirations.
- Put them together into a folder for the new parents.
- Add a letter saying something like:

"Over the years while searching for answers on how best to raise our children, we clipped articles, poems, cartoons, and things that were meaningful to us. These little bits of inspiration are not intended as guidelines for you, but rather as an incentive for you to become a 'clipper' of writings that catch your spirit and touch your souls! Often ideas escape us in times of stress. You'll find that occasionally perusing your special box will unearth words of wisdom or encouragement just when you need it the most."

Note: Remember, these clippings are offered in the spirit of help and assistance, not interference. Tell the new parents that if they'd like to "cancel their subscription" to your "clipping service" they can just return one and you won't be offended.

Everyone Needs a Baby

If you're a grandparent with some sewing ability, you might want to consider making a life-sized soft infant for your older grandchild when the baby sibling arrives.

Ages: One to five years
You'll Need
- Infant's stretch suit—zipper-front type is best
- A baby's hat and polyester stuffing
- An old nylon stocking
- Embroidery thread the color of infant's eyes and yarn the color of infant's hair

Here's How
- Start with an infant's stretch suit and sew the wrists closed.
- Have your older grandchild help you stuff the suit with the polyester stuffing.
- While the suit is being stuffed, you can stuff the foot of the nylon stocking until it resembles a head shape.
- When the head is stuffed, you can sew on a face with thread and then sew on loops of yarn for hair.
- After you sew the head securely to the body, your grandchild can top it off with the hat!

The soft infant doll, the same size as the real baby, will be a "safe someone" for your older grandchild to take care of, to snuggle with, and to vent any jealousies and frustrations on.

3
Love Across the Miles

"How is school?"

"Okay."

"What's new?"

"Umm . . . here's Mommy."

All right, confess. You've had this conversation before, or one a lot like it. If you haven't yet been the discouraged grandparent, you can remember being the bored child on the other end of the line. It's the phoniest phone call ever, and you seem destined to repeat it endlessly. Or are you? Get your pencils out, grandparents. We're going to give you the tools you need to make your relationship with your grandchild actually improve between visits.

Phone Calls: Long-Distance Snuggling

Dan Rothermel, of York, Maine, wrote to let us know that "the tradition of Saturday morning calls that my parents started and we make sure to continue (by calling if they haven't) keeps us connected. It's regular and reliable. It's a call that is not about a crisis but is an update." One of the most enduring and rewarding rituals you can begin with your family is just this sort of "warm fuzzy" call—one that is at a time convenient to everyone, doesn't necessarily last long, and gives you a way of touching base regularly with each member of your clan.

Your littlest chatters will look forward to your calls with eager anticipation. Even a grandchild as young as six months enjoys hearing voices over the phone, and by the time your little one is a year old, he'll be grabbing the receiver to listen to you—and probably playing touch-tone "music" in your ear. Creative parents, with encouragement from you, might place your picture by the phone so that little ones can "see" you during the call. At this stage, the most important aspect of your phone calls will be your happy, interested voice and the way in which you use easy words to carry on a one-sided conversation. Questions can be fun, but you can't expect a relevant reply from the little gigglers in your family. Moreover, as your grandtoddlers mature, they will enjoy hearing the same questions in successive phone calls. With the same gusto usually reserved for that favorite bedtime story read just the same way night after night, your youngest grandchildren will love the familiarity of your repeated phrases and songs—and best of all will learn to associate them with you.

Sometime during your grandchild's second year, those phone monologues you've been carrying on will become dialogues—but not the sort that you have with adults or even older children. Toddlers will happily burble out phrases that come to mind, but these snippets of conversation often have no relation to what you've been talking about. One of the greatest joys of listening to a child this age is to realize that you are getting the unedited exclamations of a growing thinker. As a way of showing your happiness with their new skills, you might try building on the little stories they tell by saying something like, "And then what happened?" or "That was a big surprise! What did you do next?"

Two- and three-year-olds have their own rules about conversations, too. The most apparent one is that their needs and interests come first. This view is only natural, because at this age your grandchildren are just beginning to learn that other people can have a different outlook than they have. (In fact, while teaching nursery school, we used to smile at the two-year-olds who would play "story time" with their friends and think that just because they saw the pictures, their friends could, too!) Some typical interests of your grandchild during this time are food, toys, pets, recent outings, and songs. As a way of tapping into these interests, why not sing the "ABC" song together over the phone at the end of your talk (or as your entire conversation)? Ignore the doubletakes your grandpartner spouse might do at your end of the phone—he or she will see the light soon enough—and use your most interactive, child-oriented conversation starters to get your young preschool-age grandchildren talking.

As your grandchildren grow into school-age, many more possibilities open up. Gun Denhart of Portland, Oregon, suggests for this age "reading a book nightly over the phone, while a grandchild holds a copy of the book, too." Our kids have enjoyed getting into the act as well, by performing simple pieces on the piano, reading stories created at school or at home, and describing inventions and adventures.

Little Events Seem Big to a Wee One

If it's been a while since you've talked to your grandchild, you might be astonished at how sensitive they are to the nuances of other people and to the subtleties of day-to-day events. It can seem amusing to us as experienced as we are, but the drama, excitement, and fun of these ordinary details are very real to your little one. Judy Smith, a Grandma and educator from Seattle, Washington, suggests that grandparents take advantage of their little talker's fresh perspective by "telling stories of the little things that might seem interesting to your grandchild." We couldn't agree more. Focusing on the activities of your family pet or on the latest snowstorm is exactly the kind of conversation that children appreciate most.

You'll be excited to know that by doing this you can help your grandchild learn to speak and think more clearly. Jeanne Machado, an early childhood expert, gives this practical advice for those of us who want to play with and love grandtoddlers and twos in the most meaningful way:

> Getting the most from everyday experiences is a real art that requires an instructive yet relaxed attitude and the ability to talk about what has captured the child's attention. A skilled adult who is with a toddler who is focused on the wrapping paper rather than the birthday present will add comments about the wrapping paper. Or at the zoo, in front of the bear's cage, if the child is staring at a nearby puddle, the adult will discuss the puddle. Providing words and ideas along the child's line of thinking, and having fun while doing so, becomes second nature after a few attempts.[1]

Machado's example could be easily adapted for a phone relationship. Try this conversation between a Grandma and her three-year-old granddaughter on for size:

"Hi, Monica."

"Hi."

"I hear you had pizza for dinner. What do you like on your pizza?"

"Apple and cheese!"

"Oh, my. Did you know that my dog Rex likes cheese?"

"Me too!"

The humor in this conversation is fun for both generations, and it blossomed simply because the grandparent—in this case a Grandma—asked questions and interjected new child-oriented ideas that showed she cared about things her young granddaughter enjoys. It's not hard to follow her example. First try to pick up on whatever your grandchild seems to find interesting—or ask your very young grandchild's parents for ideas. Then simply make your chats come alive with heartfelt questions and enthusiasm.

Becoming a Helpful Listener to Older Grandchildren

Steering away from "yes/no" questions and asking about your grandchild's life in an inviting way, with opening phrases like "Tell me about . . ." (rather than "How was") and "What was it like?" (instead of "Did you like it?") is a wonderful first step toward better communication with your older grandchild. Your next step might be to keep a little pad by the phone after your grandchild is old enough to remember events from week to week—in the three-and-a-half to five age range—and ask them about past concerns and triumphs. How is that scraped knee from last week's bicycle crash? Is it still hard saying good-bye to Mommy at nursery school? Knowing these and other aspects of your grandchild's daily life, including, for instance, the names of your grandchild's best buddies and classroom teacher, will mean a lot to your little one. Keeping track of these details shows that you're listening and that you really care.

"Bye, Bye, Gruppa!"

You won't have any problem knowing when your older grandbabies are through talking with you—if they're anything like our youngest, Charlie, they'll just toddle away from the phone to do something new. But learning how to close a conversation with a preschooler can be trickier. Mixing directness with a good dose of kindness will help you. Just simply say, "Thanks for our great chat—I'm going to say good-bye now, and we'll talk again soon!" But if you find yourself on the other side of this coin—if you're not yet ready to go when you think your preschool-age grandchild is ready to hang up—know that long pauses on your grandchild's end often do not mean they're ready to move on. In fact, sometimes preschoolers just need a little extra time to think of an answer or a comment. One of the great advantages of being a Grandpa or Grandma is that you may be the one who has the most patience to wait encouragingly for a reply. This simple act of allowing your grandchild to take all the time he needs is a remarkably rare and supportive one for your little one.

Parenting While on the Phone: A One-Armed Juggling Act

Although it is very special for children to get a call from Grandma or Grandpa that is devoted just to them, realistically many of your phone conversations with your grandchildren will include talks with a parent, too. The rules are so different when little ones are around that it's best to give the young parents' perspective some advance thought. It's hard to remember the hectic pace of parenting one or more young children (thank goodness!). But you can decide now that you will graciously bow out and offer to call back (or have the parent call you another time—collect if necessary) if in the background a child is crying, dishes are clinking, and the parents are trying to talk to each other between comments to you. Make it a habit of asking if you're calling at a convenient time. New parents, too, who may not have the hubbub of busy children in the background as a handy excuse—and who may still be in the throes of a "do it all" mindset—may be reluctant to excuse themselves, but will appreciate your sensitivity. And we all remember how notorious toddlers and preschoolers are for making mischief when their parents are on the phone; depending on the day, these parents perhaps need only the quickest of calls from you.

In the event you often do make special phone calls only to your grandchildren, you might want to keep in mind this comment from Hannah Rothermel of York, Maine: "I think my mother-in-law must have been a Grandma in a former life—she's so good at it. She writes letters just to the kids, and asks them what they like and think and want (she doesn't always go through us). Yet she's very careful not to 'go over our heads.' [She lets] us be the parents." With a little foresight and good communication with your grandchild's Mom and Dad, you can have a wonderfully independent relationship with your little ones and still support their parents' important roles.

No More High-Tech "Hangups"? Well, That Depends . . .

Jim and Lyn Rawlingson from Paraparaumu, New Zealand, recommend purchasing "a telephone speaker so that the whole family can hear our voices"—an idea seconded by Cookie and David Bates who wrote from Spring Hill, Florida. Does your grandchild's family have a phone that can be programmed? Are you willing to have a personal 800 number? These simple devices can make it easy for a grandchild to call you without help and will add another dimension to your calls by getting your little one more involved. From our experience, it's a thrill to know that one button on the phone pad is all that stands between you and a conversation with your grandchild. We also like the convenience and versatility of many of these new inventions. If you're at all interested, we encourage you to drop by your local electronics store and take a look at what's available, including the new visual phones and electronic mail systems that include a voice message. (Now if we could just think of a device to stop little fingers from gleefully hanging up on us!)

> "Grandparents can do more for us than anyone else in the world: they sprinkle stardust in our eyes."
>
> —*Alex Haley,*
> *author of* Roots

Rewind, Fast Forward, Play: Grandma's Telling a Story

We know, we know. You're not a professional storyteller, and you never even had any illusions about attending broadcasting school. Come to think of it, even your singing voice, which was passable in the fourth-grade chorus, now sounds like a World War II bomber in heavy turbulence.

Wait. You don't have to be a professional, or even a good amateur, to make terrific audiotapes for your grandchild. Your voice, whether confident or shaky, is the only one you've got, and it couldn't be more special to your littlest family members. Read a story, sing a song, sing a story, read a song—any combination will do. You might also read (or rap!) a nursery rhyme, talk as you make a favorite recipe (you can send the recipe and a tasty sample in the same package), read off a list of "I love you because" statements, or even make a tape of sound "riddles" (see the activity "Cassette Connections," p. 52). If you simply use your imagination, you can make a wonderfully inexpensive and personal gift for your grandchild.

When making an audiotape of a read-aloud book, it will be fun for your grandchild if you say why you like the book, or that "this was your Mommy's book, and she loved it when she was your age." Children love hearing about themselves and their parents as babies, because it gives them a more historical perspective—a sense of belonging. It's also a good idea to say "time to turn the page now" or to develop your own signal, such as a bell (or even your dog's bark!), for this purpose.

Grandparenting in Cyberspace

No, you don't need a driver's license to merge onto the information superhighway—just a sense of adventure and the confidence that comes with knowing that as this technology has become more popular, it's become easier for even nontechnical types to use.

You also, of course, need access to a computer, and so does the part of the family with whom you'll communicate. Then it's a matter of buying some communications software and a communications service such as Compuserve or America Online.

Are you still with us? Let's just say that a knowledgeable salesperson will get you set up in no time, and if you can afford the initial costs, the continuing benefits are huge. For one thing, emails never interrupt. Imagine being able to send a quick message to your faraway family members and have it almost instantly received, but not have to wonder whether you've contacted them at a bad time. At their convenience, they log on and reply to your message—or print it out for the grandchildren to keep.

Email messages are also wonderful because they encourage a casual writing style that can help build a closer relationship than a letter. Speed is the reason for this, we think. It's just so easy to type up a message, and so gratifying to have it delivered immediately, that you will find yourself writing more frequently and about more everyday events. You might find, as we have, that email provides the perfect balance between a warm and personable call and an unintrusive, but more formal, letter.

Just the Fax, Bumpa!

If you want to be really hip, you can invest in a fax machine or fax modem that allows you to send whole images over the phone lines and into either another fax or your extended family's computer to be printed, colored on, or simply displayed. In our family, pictures "drawn" by grandchildren are passed to the computer memories of the grandparents, and little "slide shows" of scanned-in photographs become computer screen savers and backdrops on the computer screen. If you're a family of more savvy computer users with sound cards in your computers, you can even send your voices back and forth (Nick's toddler giggle is now the "error alert" on our computer). If you don't have a fax, try sending and receiving through your local copy shop or other fax support store. The possibilities are endless, and they can make a long-distance relationship seem at times as close as next door.

Now Playing: Grandparents on Film

Videocameras are another item that more and more families find they can't live without, though purchasing and using one can be rather expensive. There's nothing like the image of your first grandson teetering to the slide on his new "walking legs" or your first granddaughter's gleeful laugh in the tub to warm your heart. The newer videocameras help even the most amateur of filmmakers produce quality home movies.

Grandparents can make the most of a videocamera in their own home by sending videos of themselves doing things that will entertain and enrich their young grandchildren. For the littlest grandbabies, grandparents can film themselves playing peek-a-boo from behind a chair or couch, saying "So Big" with arms stretched upward, and singing "Twinkle, Twinkle, Little Star," "Head, Shoulders, Knees, and Toes," and other classic children's songs. Slightly older children, say ages two and three, might enjoy a video "tour" of a long-distance grandparent's home, especially before a visit. You can even prepare your grandchild for a stay at your home by showing them the park, library, and other places in the neighborhood they'll be visiting with you. Or give those nearby little ones a rainy day alternative to Disney with your own video production of a children's classic tale—they'll love it! (See "The Stars of the Show," p. 55.)

Long-distance grandparents will find other ways to make a videocamera bridge the gap. Their home and environment might have things that the grandchild's doesn't—for example, a grandparent might make and videotape a snowman and snowangel for a child who lives in the South or grandparents living near the ocean could videotape themselves building a sandcastle for a grandchild who lives inland.

Videotapes, made with either rented or owned videocameras, can be an important part of documenting the growth and development of all members of the family, and you'll find you treasure these moving images as much as your cherished family photos. Some families we know make a point of asking grandparents questions about their lives to make an interview library for all to share. (See "Memory Movies," p. 189, for some questions to ask.) Perhaps you'll like the idea of becoming immortalized in this way, too.

Special Delivery: Grandloving by Mail

Many of us are looking for easy, inexpensive, and creative ideas to stimulate conversations and play between grandparents and grand-children—whether you live near or far away. Well, here's a selection to get you thinking. All you'll need is a nine-by-twelve-inch manila envelope (or smaller), a stamp or two, and a willingness to personalize these ideas whenever and however you can. If you're really inspired after reading this chapter, we encourage you to flip to chapter 7 for additional ideas that you can use every week of the year.

Did you know that every day someone goes to your grandchild's home, ready to deliver something that you thought to make and send? Most grandparents don't think of postal carriers as personal messengers, but they should. Our Nick and Charlie literally jump for joy when the mail arrives, and are always excited to be a part of opening envelopes—especially any addressed to them. Even your littlest grandbabies deserve a special delivery of a letter or package now and again, if only to tickle their parents. Or do like little Anna McKenzie from Hampton, New Hampshire, does with her Grandpa: when she learned he used Morse code in the war, they started corresponding like secret agents. (For more code ideas, see "Secret Club Codes of Yore," p. 54.) If you'd like to encourage a preschooler grandchild like Anna to send things to you, just enclose some self-addressed, stamped envelopes and postcards for an easy reply.

> It's often not what you send that's important, but the fact that you send something regularly.

It's often not what you send that's important, but the fact that you send something regularly. From Fairfax, Virginia, Linda Hansen wrote, "Establish a routine for letters and packages—Robert even thinks delivered pizza comes from Nannu!" She also wrote, "Robert has a dog, Cassidy. Every package—no matter how small—that goes to him includes dog treats for Cass." Betty Barnes of Fairport, New York, shared a great idea: send clippings of photos from newspapers and magazines as a springboard for stories between the generations. We even know of one Grandma who sent her "junk" mail along to her toddler grandchildren. The brightly colored ads had a great appeal, and the fact that a letter came every day from Grandma was the most wonderful treat of all.

Once you really get into the habit of sending off frequent mailings to your little one, you might find, as we have, that it helps to purchase a package of address labels for your grandchild. Give half to him and keep the other half for yourself—a quick lick sure beats addressing!

Good Things in Little Boxes

It's a natural. Children are intrigued by boxes, they love themes, and they adore activities that are reserved for special times. Voilà the "activity box"—a bunch of related items that together can make a hectic or difficult time fun. Lois Perlowski of Sanibel, Florida, sent us a perfect illustration of this idea. She plans to send to her young granddaughter a "Granny's (in my case LoLo's) Rainy Day Box. In it will be a multitude of little activities (cards, stickers, magic markers, tiny books, and so on) for times when the child is sick or bored. In another year I'll send Sierra a box for 'Dress-up Time' filled with glitzy [fake] jewelry, boas, hats, purses, dresses and gloves."

Hmm. We can hear the wheels turning out there—we know you have ideas of your own that will be perfect for your grandchildren. But before you jump up and get started collecting items to send, consider making the box itself work part of the magic. An easy "feelie box" can be made by adding an old sweatshirt sleeve to reach through—toddlers will be captivated by the idea of guessing what's within by touching the surprise inside. Or make a little mailbox by cutting a slot in the box and filling it with envelopes, stickers, and a canvas tote to assist your little "mail carrier." A kitchen theme could also be a special treat. Help your two- or three-year-old grandchild stock his cardboard "fridge" with small empty food boxes, and watch his imagination take flight. If you're still stumped, know that every mother of a toddler will love a box of special little playthings for her little mischief-maker to use when she's on the phone.

Bookin' Along with Grandpa and Grandma

Books are such a treasure that we couldn't resist dreaming up some ideas for how you and your grandchild can make and exchange books through the mail. Whether you start with a bunch of plain papers stapled together or a formal "blank book" purchased from a bookstore or gift shop, the unique spin you put on your cooperative creation will make it a prized record of your thoughts and times together. Think of it as a "time capsule" of your relationship that can be enjoyed throughout your life—and your grandchild's.

Books with a theme. Here's a foolproof way to get you and your preschooler grandchildren giggling—ask them what ingredients they would put into their cookies. Applesauce? Pepperoni? Oatmeal? Whatever imaginative response you get, try jotting it down with others in a shared recipe book. You might want to put a favorite "real" recipe on one side of the book and your grandchild's whimsical version on the facing page. Pictures she draws of the two of you cooking together will make perfect illustrations.

Margaret Grubbs of Silver Spring, Maryland, shared with us: "Once I made a book for Billy when he was just learning to write his name. Each page had one short sentence and in each the word 'Billy' was written in a different kind of lettering. One was made by gluing chenille pipe cleaners onto the page, another was made of letters cut from sandpaper. I don't remember the rest, but the text was: Mommy loves Billy, Daddy loves Billy, Gramps loves Billy, and so on, through all the cousins, pets, friends, to the last page, which said, 'Everybody loves Billy.' " (For another version, see "My Family Loves Me," p. 53.) Personalized books can also feature drawings or cut-out pictures of new words a toddler is just learning to say, or photos of family members with their names written underneath.

Another great book idea for preschoolers came to us from Sara Kirkpatrick in Auckland, New Zealand. You might make and send "an adventure book made of photos and the story of when the grandparent and child last visited together," she suggested. Tales of Grandpa and grandchild fishing off the dock for a "whale" or punching down bread dough with Grandma "before it grew over the bowl and ran away" can take on epic proportions when described through the eyes of your preschooler grandchild. Your job will be to write it down before the freshest, funniest version slips away.

Although your littlest grandbabies probably aren't yet bookworms, they too will appreciate books made just for them by a loving Grandpa or Grandma. You might want to scrounge in your fabric basket or workshop for materials to make a book of textures; your little ones will delight in the new sensations. Or try pictures of common objects, cut from magazines and "laminated" with clear adhesive paper, which make drool- and nibbleproof pages ideal for your teething grandchild. Your imagination's the limit and your interests should be your guide—the most important thing is that you're making something special for those little people in your life.

A journal for each grandchild: Sharing your thoughts and hopes. You've just had a lovely time seeing a neighbor whose three grandchildren were visiting, and something about the mischievous sparkle in the two-year-old's eyes reminded you of when your eldest grandchild was that age. Before you even take off your coat, you take a moment to pull down from the shelf the journal you've been keeping for your eldest grandchild since her birth. With a smile on your lips as you remember her funny antics then and now, you write a short note about how you thought of her today. This is the essence of journal writing with and for a grandchild, another suggestion given by Hannah and Dan Rothermel.

This little journal is not for you to look at alone, however—instead, let your grandchildren rediscover theirs each time they visit (or every time you visit them, if you can take it along). Your young grandchildren will delight in learning what you've written since the last time you were together, and you will have the satisfaction of having created the most personal keepsake you can for each of your little ones. You might even develop a picture "signature" to end each entry—and use it as well in your letters and notes. A hand-drawn cartoon face of Grandpa or Grandma, or another unique sketch, will become a way even infants can learn to associate you with their journal entries and all the loving packages and messages you send.

Learning to send your love by phone, email, fax, and mail is, for many of us, a bittersweet part of being a grandparent. At times, it might even seem a thankless job, with grandchildren too young to communicate their thanks and parents too busy and distracted to help your grandchild respond with frequent letters and calls of their own.

It's true that the payback for all your work often is intangible, but it sure feels right when it happens. The next time you see your grandchild after a long separation, you'll be rewarded with a flash of recognition, big smile, and happy shout of "Opa!" or "Bubbie!"—which will warm your heart and make all your efforts feel worthwhile. Even your stranger-shy grandtoddlers and twos will peek up from their parent's shoulder sooner than you might expect—and will be joking with you before you know it. It's for these times, and for the hope that you can be an essential part of your grandchild's life no matter how distant your homes, that we know you will continue to package the best of your love and send it in ways that delight and intrigue your youngest grandchildren.

Secrets in Wax

Send your huggable honey a love note or drawing meant only for her eyes!

Ages: Two years and up
You'll Need
- Wax paper
- Sheet of white paper
- Pencil

Here's How
- Lay the wax paper on top of the white paper and draw or write on it with the pencil, pressing the wax lines into the paper underneath.
- Label the right side of the paper—the side that has the wax impressions.
- Pop it in the mail with the instructions to brush a thin coat of paint over the labeled side of the paper to see the message appear.

Smiles from under the Spaghetti

Make a collage of photos of you and your grandchild into a placemat, so you can be there for her every meal!

Ages: One to six years
You'll Need
- Photos of you and your grandchild
- A piece of paper about 12" x 15"
- Glue
- Clear contact paper or access to a laminating machine

Here's How
- Create a collage of the photos on the large paper. Glue them down securely.
- Cover both sides with clear contact paper or laminate to create a durable, washable placemat.

Get ready to hear stories of your little one trying to share a bite with you—wherever you are!

Bedtime Stories from Afar

Though miles away, you can still enjoy reading to your grandbaby. Best of all, your precious little one will learn to recognize your voice.

Age: Newborn to eight years
You'll Need
- Some children's books—see our chapter 9 for ideas
- A tape recorder at both your house and your grandchild's

Here's How
- Sit back in a comfortable chair, relax, and pretend your grandchild is sitting in your lap or next to you.
- Turn the recorder on and read just as if you were telling the story to that special grandchild. Say things like "This was your Daddy's book," or "I'm turning the page now."
- This recording makes a wonderful companion to the book itself. You might try sending both together so your grandchild can "read" right along with you—turning the pages as you do.

Chief Correspondent

Someone has to help keep the family connected! This activity might even lead to a family reunion.

Ages: All
You'll Need
- A folder in which you keep correspondence from and memos about family members
- Access to a copier or computer printer

Here's How
- Ask your family to share their "news" and photos of a first tooth, those first steps, first words, the ballerina's debut, the grandson's first fish, the first day at school, and so on.
- Turn these events into headlines and articles for your monthly newsletter.
- Make a copy for each family unit and mail out your family-gram.

Sounds Like Somewhere I've Been

Turn some of your familiar house sounds into a fun long-distance game.

Ages: Two to eight years
You'll Need
- A tape recorder

Here's How
- Tape familiar sounds in your home that your grandchild should recognize such as:
  - The dog barking
  - The phone ringing
  - The car horn
  - The dishwasher running
  - A favorite CD playing
  - Rain on the roof
- See how many of your sounds your grandchild can identify.

Good Night, Grandma and Grandpa

Pictures of you snuggled on your bed or in a rocking chair together with your littlest loved one can be wonderful to laminate on a "good-night board."

Ages: One to five years
You'll Need
- Pictures of you and your grandchild
- A cardboard backing such as a shirt cardboard
- Laminating material
- String

Here's How
- Arrange the photos on the cardboard.
- Have them laminated and punch two holes in the top to hold a string hanger.
- Send to your littlest grandchild with the note that you'll be "there" every night to give a goodnight hug and kiss. You'll no longer be "out of sight, out of mind"!

Your grandchild will also enjoy laminated photos at bathtime, where he can serve you "tea in the tub."

Cassette Connections

If you can't be there in person, your precious darling can at least become familiar with your voice!

Ages: Newborn to eight years
You'll Need
- A tape recorder
- Your imagination

Here's How
- For the newborn through one-year-old grandchild: Recite nursery rhymes, sing lullabies, read favorite short stories, make a personalized "speak and say"—the dog says woof, woof; the cat says

meow, meow; the train goes toot, toot; etc.

- For the younger toddler grandchild: Play "Simon Says"; sing "Hokey Pokey," "Bingo," or other favorites; read stories; talk about colors; tell a story; etc.
- For the older grandchild: Continue to read stories. Now you can begin to gear your recordings to specific interests of your grand-child and to things you've experienced together. They'll love hearing stories about themselves or their parents!

My Family Loves Me

This simple family photograph book will, like the Velveteen Rabbit, probably become too love-worn to be an heirloom, but it's a priceless treasure nonetheless!

Ages: Six months to five years
You'll Need
- A photo of each member of the family—ideally your grandchild will be in the pictures, too
- Paper on which to mount the photos—4" x 6" works well with 3" x 5" photos
- Clear contact paper or access to a laminating machine
- Ribbon

Here's How
- Glue one photo onto each page.
- Caption each photo: "Oma loves Nick!" "Opa loves Nick!"
- The book we did for Nick had a picture of him with each family member, so that he could see himself in Aunt Bubba's lap or on Uncle Bryan's shoulders.
- Laminate or cover each page with clear contact paper.
- Assemble into book format with the ribbon or with a professional binding machine.

Secret Club Codes of Yore

Chances are when you were a kid, you joined a special club through an old-time radio show. One of the biggest attractions—the secret club code you received in the mail—is something you can recreate for your own little ones.

Ages: Four years and up

You'll Need
- To share the secret code with your favorite little decoder
- Then be sure to follow up with LOTS of messages

Here's How
- Start by writing out
  – A B C D E F G H I J K L M N O P Q R S T U V W X Y Z
  where "–" indicates a space between words.
- Then starting with any letter of the alphabet—such as M—write the code row underneath your first line. Code M would look like this:

– A B C D E F G H I J K L M N O P Q R S T U V W X Y Z
M N O P Q R S T U V W X Y Z – A B C D E F G H I J K L

- To write a message use the second line (Code M). Substitute those letters for the letters in the first line that you would normally write.
- Unhrmsg–! (Have fun!)

The Stars of the Show

Help your grandchild remember who you are, as you enjoy playing center stage. Videocameras can be rented if you don't own one.

Age: Six months to eight years
You'll Need
- A sense of silliness and a willingness to lose your inhibitions
- A videocamera and videotape
- A friend or tripod

Here's How
- For your six- to eighteen-month-old grandchild, you could:
  - Play peek-a-boo from behind a chair.
  - Sing nursery rhyme songs or play finger games.
  - Play "so big" or pat-a-cake.
- For your older grandchild, you might:
  - Try acting out animals and ask them to guess "who you are."
  - Take them on a "tour" of your house so they'll recognize it when they come to visit.
  - Introduce them to your dog or cat.
  - Take them on a "walk" around your yard, etc.
  - Record yourself doing exercises and invite them to join you!
- Send the videotape to your grandchild, and wait for the rave reviews!

A Puzzle Just for Me

Turn blank puzzles from the store into personalized love notes.

Ages: Two to eight years
You'll Need
- To buy blank puzzles at the toy store

Here's How
- Write a secret love message on it, then divide it into pieces.
- Older children might enjoy receiving parts of the puzzle in two or three consecutive letters.

It's a "Houzzle"?

Can your faraway little one remember the layout of your house? Try this fun homemade flannelboard puzzle. It's not only a challenging game, but also a unique way to remember experiences they've had with you at your home.

Ages: Three to eight years

You'll Need to Send
- A layout of your house that you draw on interfacing material and cut out into rooms

Here's How
- Draw the floor plan of your home on the interfacing.
- Cut each room out and send it in an envelope for your grandchild to reassemble.
- You can also send pretend furniture made from flannel or remnant interfacing so your "interior designer" can play "Grandma and Grandpa's house."
- While challenging your grandchild's memory, you'll also be refreshing her memories of visits to your home.

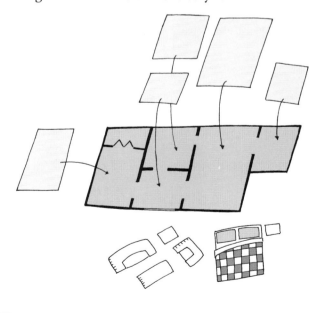

Ahoy, Matey—There's Treasure Ahead!

While you get ready to leave your grandchild's home, hide a treasure for some long-distance fun.

Ages: Two years and up
You'll Need
- Some small "treasure" that you know your grandchild will enjoy
- To make a treasure map when you get home and send it!

Here's How
- Hide the treasure in your grandchild's house just before you leave.
- From your house, send a treasure map with clues to help your "pirate" find the prize. The clues can be given over a longer period of time depending on the difficulty of finding the treasure and the age of the child. Keep it simple for the younger toddler.
- Add to the fun by sending a bandanna to be worn when hunting for the treasure!

Forget-Me-Not

Send a package of forget-me-not flower seeds in the mail for an on-going project you can share.

Ages: Two to eight years
You'll Need to Send
- Forget-me-not seeds

Here's How
- Early spring is a good time to send the seeds.
- Suggest that your grandchild fill an empty egg carton with dirt and plant the seeds in it.
- Water the seeds and cover with plastic wrap or a clear plastic bag to hold in the moisture and help the germination.
- The carton is just the right size to fit on a sunny windowsill.
- When the weather is warm, have your little one transplant the seedlings outside in a partially shaded spot.
- When the flowers bloom, suggest a blossom be picked, pressed, and mailed to you so you'll know you haven't been forgotten!

Jokes and Riddles to the Rescue

The sillier you are, the more your grandkids will love it. Pop this one in the mail when your communications need some jazzing up!

Ages: Two to eight years
You'll Need
- Riddles and jokes. These might help get you thinking:
  - What do you call a sleeping bull? A bull dozer.
  - Why is a pancake like a baseball pitcher? Both need a batter.
  - What gets wetter the more it dries? A towel!
  - What can you put in your left hand that you can't put in your right hand? Your right elbow!

Here's How
- Send the joke or riddle in an envelope clearly marked #1.
- Follow it the next day with the answer in an envelope clearly marked #2.

Together Stories

Books can be dear friends in childhood and beyond. Personalizing your grandchild's first books will give them extra appeal.

Ages: Three years and up
You'll Need to Send
- A story you've written in which you've left blanks for your grand-child to fill in

Here's How
- Something your grandchild is interested in will make a good topic—Nick's fascination with Winnie-the-Pooh led to a story that began, "The wind was whistling and whipping the trees around yesterday, and guess who blew in flying high on a _____ balloon? Winnie-the-_____. I invited him to come join us for a _____." Write one or two sentences per page, leaving room for your little one's illustrations.
- Have your grandchild fill in the blanks (her folks might have to do the reading and writing to record her words).
- Have her mail the booklet back to you so you can follow up with a sequel!

4
When Your Grandchild Comes to Visit

"Have one child at a time if possible." Mary Gordon of Wolfboro, New Hampshire, gives us words to live by—but in this case she is referring to the number of grandchildren to entertain in your home. Few grandparents realize how quickly a little hurricane of activity can overturn family heirlooms while flashing an endearing smile—and only a very unlucky few remember the trials of encouraging a young child to sleep in an unfamiliar bed or become accustomed to a strange dog or cat. Fortunately, the following tips can make the difference between a visit that is relaxed and fun and one that feels like an Olympic event.

Long-Distance Visits

For many of us, grandchildren and their families come to see us less often than we would like because they live far away. If you're in this situation, you probably feel as though nothing can compensate for the loss of day-to-day closeness with your grandchildren. Parents often lament this distance as well. "I have a keen sense of loss that my children will know my parents as exciting occasional visitors of mythic proportions rather than as the wonderful but very human people they are," wrote Jen Shaw of Salt Lake City, Utah. "I try to schedule visits as frequently as possible so that my parents, the grandparents, are as much a daily part of my children's lives as they can be."

One happier aspect of living in a separate town from your grandchildren, however, is that any time with them becomes very special. From Ontario, New York, Phyllis Curtis wrote, "One positive factor in having grandchildren far away is that we have intensified, quality-time visits not only with grandchildren but with their parents (our children). Chuck and I both dislike the common expression, 'The best thing about grandchildren is that they go home.' We disagree. [Although we] couldn't take care of them full time, . . . 'going home' is NOT the best thing about grandparenting!" It's interesting, isn't it, that sometimes a visit from a much-missed and faraway grandchild can be just the reminder we need to slow down and appreciate all the big and little people we love so much.

Getting Ready

Your timing couldn't have been better. One week before she is to arrive at your home, your photos have arrived at your granddaughter's house, and she and her father are cuddled up at bedtime looking over the snapshots of you and other family members, pets, and places she might see. What a warm and approachable way to be reintroduced to loved ones she now associates with phone calls and letters, and what a great welcome to your world.

Making a small album doesn't have to be difficult. The simplest version can be made with construction paper, plastic bags, and a stapler. In fact, it's so easy that you might feel ready to try your hand at a more creative photo calendar or peekaboo photo itinerary of outings and events to enjoy together. Susan Jones of Rochester, New York, confirms our idea that making an effort to rekindle the friendship before the visit helps everyone have more fun when the visit begins. "Show the child photos or tapes of grandparents before making calls or visits," she offered as a suggestion to all grandparents. Doing so will make your actual reunion more comfortable and will help you have more rewarding, personal experiences with your grandchild that much sooner.

Clearing Your Datebook, Clarifying Your Priorities

Martha and Dick Crawford, of Pittsford, New York, contributed this little gem: "We cancel all but the most necessary of our own day-to-day activities so we can spend as much time as possible with them. We keep their pictures, gifts they've given us, and 'treasures' they've left from previous visits out, so they know they are in our thoughts when they're not here with us. Naps and quiet times are important. We all tire easily when there's a change in our normal routines."

Okay, you say to yourself, but what about showing off the new baby to your friends and family? Well, we can relate to your desire to tour with your little ones, but your grandchildren will probably get tired of all the fuss after the first such trip (and if you have an assertive five-year-old in the lead, they might stage an outright mutiny). But there are still ways to have a little fun in public showing off your special visitors. For example, you might try a grandchild-oriented visit to the neighborhood grocery store. There your grandchild can either ride along in the cart and enjoy watching the colorful boxes go by or help you choose a few things from the shelves and cross them off your list. You're bound to see as many neighbors and friends there as if you'd taken a chance at finding them at home, and your grandchildren will probably be happier about the experience. The point is that developing a meaningful relationship with your grandchild during infrequent visits requires a bit more creativity and responsiveness on your part than you might expect. Staying grandchild-oriented is the key.

> "Be well rested beforehand."
>
> —Liz Kirkpatrick, Kerikeri, New Zealand

Baby (and Child) Equipment: The Right Stuff for Your Grandchildren

You'll never believe what you can buy for young children these days. A recent flip through an upscale baby products catalog amazed us with the sheer variety and price of many of the items. Luckily for grandparents, however, much of this equipment is more fun than essential. If you're like us, you're a minimalist at heart, especially now that you have years' worth of memorabilia to store. So here are our favorite useful (and foldable) pieces of equipment for grandparents. (See Consumer Reports' *Guide to Baby Products*, referenced on p. 266, for safety considerations.)

What Grandbabies Need

Love. Lots of snuggles. Coos and peekaboos. And from the store, depending on the age of your grandbaby, you might want to buy diapers and wipes, a waterproof changing pad, bibs, a portacrib, high chair, bath seat, baby monitor, and age-appropriate toys. (For some infants, a baby swing or rocking chair will also be critically important.) Here are just a few of our favorite purchased toys for each developmental phase during that first year.

0-3 months. Mobiles, black-and-white books, and things that rattle or squeak.

3-6 months. Overhanging "gyms" (We like the FisherPrice version best, because you can change the pieces around), board books, texture mats, jumpy seats that hang in a door frame (after four months).

6-9 months. Friendly puppets (you might want to check out the unique and beautiful Folk Tails puppets), textured books.

9-12 months. Bubbles (try Gymboree's formula; the bubbles last and can be used inside), simple books of all kinds, squirting bath toys.

Toddler Essentials

Your toddler grandbabies will still need a crib and a high chair (or booster seat), will benefit from a non-skid bath mat, and will still love cuddling in the rocker. But if you take advantage of a grandtoddler's natural curiosity and love of anything grown-ups use, you'll find that store-bought toys are much less essential. Toddlers' greatest passions include filling and dumping, getting wet, hiding things and themselves, swinging, and climbing, so arrange your home accordingly and let them go (with your watchful attention so no accidents occur). You might save a few strong cardboard boxes to make safe hideouts, and be willing to take out your pots and pans for a little drumming session (see the activity "Music, Music, Everywhere," p. 94)—or your plastic containers for stacking and nesting fun.

A Preschooler's Wish List

Preschooler grandchildren have fewer unique needs than your younger grandchildren. They can eat what everyone else eats, although care should still be taken with chokable foods. They can also sleep in a "grown-up" bed (although for a little one who's just getting acquainted with a big bed, you might want to buy a bed rail or cushion possible falls with an inflatable mattress or pillows). They'll also adore playing dress-up in your closet and making hand-drawn placemats for dinner—or even cooking some of the dinner alongside an adored Grandma or Grandpa. But high on a preschooler grandchild's wish list, whether spoken or unspoken, will be a night-light or flashlight (or both) and a waterproof pad for the bed (so that any accident won't be a big disappointment to you).

What's Cool for "School-Agers"

School-age grandchildren will be excited to be somewhere new, and although they'll still treasure that flashlight you provide, they'll use it less for scaring away "monsters" than for shining it under the covers to read Dad's old comics or look through Mom's forgotten scrapbook. You can set the scene for discovery and fun by giving your young grandchildren some fun family memorabilia to explore. You might put a basket by the bed with an old crystal radio, some early reader books that your children enjoyed, or a funny trend from days past (Mom's pet rock would be perfect!). Top it off with a new journal and pen to encourage your grandchild to jot down his or her ideas and stories—for their own children and grandchildren to enjoy.

The Big Day Arrives

Finally the car pulls in the drive, or the plane taxis up to the airport. You're excited beyond words, and maybe a little teary thinking of other greetings and departures. How can you make this the best visit ever? Sometimes getting off to a great start can make all the difference.

Gentle Greetings for First Meetings

It's a grandparent universal. You see that little bundle or giggling dynamo after a long separation and you feel an almost irresistible urge to rush right up and give your cuddliest hug. What could be wrong with a little squeeze from Grandpa or Grandma? It seems so harmless, and your heart is certainly in the right place. But imagine how you'd feel if a giant, eager person who didn't see you so often came rushing up to you after a harried day or so of traveling. Unfortunately, expecting a big hug and kiss in return is unrealistic (though magical when it happens!). Moreover, your understandable eagerness can truly upset your young grandchildren and delay that magical moment when they run into your arms of their own accord.

Instead of approaching your grandchild quickly, you might try a slower pace. A simple warm smile can work wonders to make a successful first connection with your grandbaby. With a toddler or preschool-age grandchild, you can experiment with crouching down to his or her level. Talk about the trip, about something you both see nearby, or about a small toy you've brought along just for this purpose. During one of our family's recent visits, oohs and aahs about the bags coming off the baggage carousel at the airport made a perfect conversational bridge between Nick and two of his loving grandparents.

Pets

Ideally, parents will be able to help you prepare your grandchild for visiting with your pet (by, for example, teaching the child the difference between stuffed and real animals), but in any case, pets and young children make for one blind date that requires plenty of chaperoning. Pets need time to warm up to a new person in the house, especially one who can command the sort of attention your grandchild does from you. Older dogs and cats may not appreciate the noise and chaos your small grandchild brings into the home, and younger pets may have not yet developed the self-control to simply move away from a child who doesn't yet understand the difference between a pat and a pinch. One nice way to help your grandchild and pet become buddies is to whip up some "Doggone Good Goodies" (see our recipe on p. 87).

You might be surprised to realize that your role in this new relationship is to protect both your pet and your grandchild. A child should be strongly encouraged to move slowly toward a dog or cat and to pat it gently. (Children who like to pinch or poke can be shown how to stroke the animal with only two outstretched fingers.) If the pet moves away, protect it by not allowing the child to chase it, and praise both the pet and your grandchild if they find a way to interact gently. We've found airline crates to be invaluable as a safe haven for our dogs when things get too busy and chaotic.

As you may know already, an infant or toddler must never be left alone in the same room with a pet, even one who seems trustworthy—the outcome could be tragic. Preschoolers and older grandchildren need supervision as well, but you will know soon after they arrive how the relationship is going and whether you need to be directly involved in their play or only a close observer.

If the relationship turns out to be a good one, you might try putting the animal in its bed when your grandchild is asleep and releasing it to play when the child wakes up. We've found that this way the animal associates the grandchild with fun.

Making the Fun Last

Your grandchild is going to be so excited to see you that your first hours together will be a blur. But don't call your eye doctor, because pretty soon things will slow down, and maybe more than you had hoped. What will you do then? Read on—we've got some great ideas that will save your sanity and make your grandchild think you are the best thing since fruit roll-ups.

Open-Ended Activities Inspire Unique Creations

The greatest thing about having young, exuberant people in the house is that their imaginations can't be stopped. Give that little one a piece of plain paper and a roll of tape and before you know it, it will become a boat, a hat, or a modern design that says "Beep!" Given this creative energy, it's funny that often our worries, if articulated, would sound something like "How can I keep my grandchild occupied and interested here at my home?" In fact, our task as grandparents is easier than this (though it may seem awkward at first): we just need to assemble a few items to fire our grandchildren's natural excitement for learning and then give them room to explore. Like every great dinner party, an evening or weekend with a grandchild requires simply a generous host, a few conversation starters, and an understanding by all that guests can make their own fun.

One good starting place for all this open-ended creativity is a special place for each grandchild that can be explored during each visit. "Grandma kept a variety of outrageously decorated hats for us," wrote Mary Jackson-Smith from Mt. Horeb, Wisconsin. You might make over a toy box, drawer, cupboard, closet, room, bookshelf, or even a laundry basket. In the box, put any age-appropriate toys that your child (their parent) might have used, along with others you've purchased or borrowed from friends. Or try this idea from Susan Jones: "I turned the guest room closet into a special hideaway where [my grandson Collin and I] read stories and played." When he was three she and her husband, Nicholas, made an "office for him in the family room with a children's table set, old phone, and files."

A child-sized chair or desk (which can be made from an overturned box, with one side cut out), like the one Susan describes, makes a terrific work space for your preschool-aged grandchild. And you might be surprised at how much your older grandchildren love to work on art projects that involve very little mess. Some examples of things that you could have out for your preschool-age grandchild include: paper (with or without a simple design drawn or photo-copied on it by you), envelopes, stickers (purchased, or try looking through your junk mail for some), washable crayons or markers, bingo "dot makers," paper punches, and tape (for children under five you can peel off the tape for them and offer it in pieces).

For a special desktop treat, try making some easy playdough (see "Knead It, Roll It, Squish It," p. 74) or offering some crayons reshaped in old muffin tins or cookie molds.

If you're really ambitious, you might try designing your own toys and activities that your grandchild will remember and anticipate see-ing again at their next visit. Margaret Grubbs, of Silver Spring, Maryland, wrote, "I made three dolls the size of a four-year-old child. Everyone likes to play with them and they never see dolls that size anywhere else." Margaret also devised a "special tea set for the chil-dren to serve everyone after dinner." And Linda Knox, of Lynnwood, Washington, has used an activity her mom invented: all the grandchil-dren sit on a bottom step, while Grandma or Grandpa asks fun ques-tions. Each correct answer means the child can move up a step. Whoever reaches the top first, wins!

Miniatures for Preschoolers to Collect

There's something about the teeny-tiny that is fascinating for young children, and after your grandchild is definitely safe around small objects (around age three) you can take advantage of this interest by giving them small objects to collect and play with. Add sequins to your homemade playdough, or let your preschoolers sort your button box. Allow them to choose among favorite small and inexpensive items in your home that they can carry along with them as good luck charms, or collect something outdoorsy together, like rounded rocks or shells (which are especially nice memory makers). You can even dig out your fabric scrap box for some collages. You'll be surprised at what three-, four-, and five-year-olds can create with household "junk" such as paper-towel tubes, shoeboxes, corks, newspaper, milk cartons, plastic containers and lids, magazines, egg cartons, and paper bags.

Cooking Together: Warming the Tummy, Warming the Heart

Many people remember special foods when they think of a beloved grandparent. Lucy Coonan, of Fairport, New York, says about her visiting grandchildren: "I always make soup!" Whether they're of savoring Grandma's holiday cookies or of tasting Grandpa's home-brewed rootbeer, memories like these evoke intense and vibrant memories in us all. Julie can't taste Scandinavian crumb cake without thinking of her late Grandma Carlson, and Nick and Charlie are rapidly associating their Grandma Carlson from Duluth, Minnesota—her Mom—with superb apple pie. Foods are wonderful connections to a family's shared history. (See pp. 108–10 for some simple and delicious recipes your grandchild can do with you.)

To make these treats even more special, you might try making some of your favorites with your toddler or older grandchildren the next time they visit. Cooking can be a wonderful generation-spanning activity that is at least as educational as it is fun. Mixing, measuring, and following a recipe are all cleverly subtle ways to teach skills that your grandchild will use in school. But more important, there's something about cooking that helps your grandchild feel part of a grownup, essential activity. Your preschool-age grandchild's eyes will light up when he learns he is about to make ants on a log or personalized pancakes (see "Happy Face Pancakes," p. 88 and "Kitchen Kaboodle," p. 86)—take our word for it!

The first trick to cooking with a young child is to decide beforehand that you will make a mess (then when you do, the fun won't stop). Next, you should assemble all the materials you need in one place. Your grandchild will probably need your help counting cups of flour and pouring heavy things, like cooking oil (and depending on the age of the child, spreading with a knife can be difficult), but otherwise they are incredibly capable and like to be made an essential partner in every aspect of the process. To guarantee a good time for all, keep up a friendly patter while you work and be willing to be silly—there's nothing wrong with making bread dough mustaches along the way.

Sharing a Parent's Childhood Past

There's one kind of story that your grandchild will always love, and it's the kind that you can tell the best. It might be called "How

Mommy Got Dressed for the First Time—and Forgot Her Underwear," or "How Daddy Built a Birdhouse with Grandpa When He Was Your Age." Whatever the title or topic, tales about your grandchild's parent when he or she was small are stepping stones between all three generations that keep the memories alive (and maybe enlivened a bit in the telling!). "My kids love to hear stories about us (Mommy and Daddy) growing up," confirm Sally and Reed Wilbur of Boxborough, Massachusetts. Whether it's at bedtime or as you're waiting at the stoplight, you'll find that anytime is right for a story about Mom or Dad—especially those that reveal how we all make mistakes now and then.

Leaving Some "Empty" Spaces for Relaxing Together

After your first planned activities and outings, you might find yourself going at a dizzying pace, hoping to keep your grandchildren entertained with as many memory-making experiences as possible. Ironically, though, parents and grandchildren alike adore grandparents for our wisdom to take our time and savor even the little moments of our lives. So if you find yourself leading too many expeditions and a crazy number of projects, try this little trick: turn around and follow your grandchildren. You'll find that their adventures, whether it's playing "hot lava" with the couch cushions as islands or building a fantasy world with blocks, will provide shared experiences that warm the heart and often relax the spirit. (And if you're still tired, try being a *really sick* patient in a spirited game of doctor—with toilet paper bandages to wrap your poor "paralyzed" legs!)

> Toddlers' greatest passions include filling and dumping, getting wet, hiding things and themselves, swinging, and climbing, so arrange your home accordingly and let them go.

"Yuck—What's That?"

The battle lines are drawn. Each person has a small plastic rectangle of a placemat, on which the weapons are placed: fork, plate, and catapult. The first warning cry comes from Toddler Harry, in the right corner, who says, "Oooh, what's that?!" Four-year-old Rachel starts to giggle, and pretends she's going to let that pea fly right across the room. Dinner has begun.

As you may remember from your own parenting experiences, feeding children can seem on good days like negotiating peace in the Middle East and on bad days like all-out war. Each of your grandchildren loves and hates certain foods, depending on personal taste—and probably also on who's sitting next to them or serving up dinner. Children love to push the buttons of the people who feed them.

The only winnable solution is to do a "Gandhi." Refuse to be goaded into battle. Or take the advice of Jean Rothermel, from Fair Lawn, New Jersey, who says, "We have always had the rule that no one has to eat anything they don't like at Grandma's house, but they eat what they take!" Serve the lovely meals you've planned, but hopefully with a smidgen of something you know each grandchild will like because you've asked beforehand. To ease your mind about nutrition, ask your grandchild's parents for advice about the tastiest way to make sure your little one gets the essentials—the answer might be as simple as a chewable vitamin each day. Along the same line, you'll want to be vigilant about foods that can choke a child: hot dogs, nuts, popcorn, raw carrots, and uncut grapes are the riskiest.

A few additional tips can take the mayhem out of your mealtime. Offer choices of foods to those finicky toddlers or two-year-olds. And try to have some main meals planned and frozen ahead so you won't be locked into the kitchen but can instead spend more time together. (Planning ahead has the added advantage of lowering your frustration level when your hard work goes uneaten—it's hard to get worked up about a lasagna that you made a week ago.) Judy Smith, a grandmother of five from Seattle, Washington, puts it best: "Don't worry about how they eat—or how much they eat!"

"The House that Smelled": A Short Story with a Happy Ending

Once there was a toddler, and his name was Munchkin. He loved his bottle, especially when he was teething, and his Oma loved him. Every time that Munchkin talked, or wiggled, or laughed with his bottle in his mouth, his bottle would leak a little bit on Oma's rugs and furniture. A dribble here and a dribble there, a splash here and a sneaky puddle there. No one noticed much until a few days had passed, and then Oma's house began to smell sort of like an old cow. Oma thunked her head and said, "Now what?!" Mommy and Daddy thunked each other on the head and said, "Now what?!" Finally, after a bit more concern and unhappiness, a solution was found: a bib for Munchkin and a wrap-around washcloth for the bottle that kept all the drips inside.

The moral of this story is that grandchildren don't have to ruin precious things if parents and grandparents work together to find a comfortable solution. It can be awkward at first, especially with new parents, because they can feel as though their parenting style is being challenged. If you take a friendly and open approach, however, you'll find you can often resolve the problem to the satisfaction of even that precious owner of the gooey fingers—your grandchild.

Sometimes heading off trouble is the best way to save hurt feelings—and your couches. Hannah Rothermel from York, Maine, shared with us another good suggestion: "Confine eating/drinking to certain areas." We also suggest that you all work hard to make sure that messy monkey gets a thorough washing of hands and face before leaving the table. Believe it or not, once people are together on vacation without their familiar routines, this can be overlooked. Good luck, and try to think of any irremovable spot as a healthy reminder that, after all, grandchildren are only learning and parents aren't perfect.

Capturing the Best Parts of Your Visit

No matter how you wish it weren't so, the end of a short visit will start to loom ahead of you after the first few days have passed. How can you celebrate the middle of your visit and hold on to the memories that you make together?

One super way to capture some of the best moments is to start a project that you can add on to day by day. Perhaps this will be a record of the visit—Jean Rothermel keeps a diary (see "Every Day Together Is Special," p. 109). Or maybe a mural will suit your style. On your mural, you might include aspects of each day's activities, as well as use different art media (for example, one day use markers or crayons to draw yourselves at the park, another day glue sequins, buttons, or feathers to your drawing). You can even make an illustrated storybook with a new page for each day's experiences.

(You'll also want to take photos and, if you have a videocamera, home movies to enjoy later. But we knew you didn't need to be reminded to do this!)

To Be Continued . . .

The wonderful thing about visits between grandparents and grand-children is that they never really have to end—the in-person part just changes. So put away those tissues, grandparents. Although you might live far away, long-distance communication can keep you close. (See chapters 3 and 7 for ideas).

One of the nicest ways to get this long-distance connection off to a great start is to slip notes in your grandchild's socks, shirts, books, and so forth before they're packed up to go. This way, they'll have surprise messages from you to discover for weeks to come. The important thing is to realize that each day brings a new opportunity for closeness with your little one—distance will never keep you apart.

Mixing Magic

Grandpa, your shaving cream can come to the rescue for that curious little toddler grandchild.

Ages: One to two
You'll Need
- Shaving cream
- A zipper-lock plastic sandwich bag

Here's How
- Learning to push the button on your shaving cream can will be half the fun, as your grandtoddler puts some billowy white fluff in the plastic bag.
- Add a few drops of food coloring from your cupboard and close it up.
- Let your little guy do the mixing to spread the color all around . . . remind you of turning the margarine yellow back in the old days?
- This is a good time to add two colors and try a little color mixing.

Want to "See" What We'll Be Doing?

Prepare your eager visitor with a visual calendar of all you have planned for her visit.

Ages: Two to eight years
You'll Need
- Photos or drawings of all the places you plan to go together.
- Pictures of all those who will be at your home, including cousins or neighbors with whom she might play.
- It can also be reassuring to include a few photos of your house and the room where your sweetheart will be sleeping.

Here's How
- Make a BIG calendar. In each square, paste a photo or drawing to show your grandchild what you'll be doing together that day.
- Be sure to send this a week or so in advance, so the anticipation can be part of the fun!

Love Soup

Collect notes and objects that show your grandchild she's always in your thoughts.

Ages: Two to six years
You'll Need
- Brief love notes (see below)
- Small found objects (such as a feather, sea shell, or magazine clipping) that remind you of your little sweetie
- Large soup pot
- Ladle

Here's How
- When you are apart and have thoughts about your grandchild, jot down the date, time, and what you were doing when you remembered her.
- You can write an occasional love note to her between visits, too!

- Fold or crunch these notes to make them perfect for your little one to scoop.
- Also toss into your large pot some objects that brought your sweetie to mind, and attach a similar explanatory note.
- Keep these notes and objects in your "love soup" pot, and when your grandchild comes to visit, let her scoop the notes up one by one with the ladle for you to read.

Perfect Paints

Homemade paints are fun to use but especially fun to *make!*

Ages: One to eight years
You'll Need
- 3 Tbsp. sugar
- 1/2 cup cornstarch
- 2 cups cool water
- Food coloring
- Liquid dishwashing detergent (the kind used for hand-washing dishes—*not* the kind used in dishwashers).
- Medium size pan
- Small covered jars for storing the paints

Here's How
- Have your grandchild mix the sugar, cornstarch, and water in the pan. It will then be your job to heat the paint mixture on low on the stove, stirring until it is smooth.
- Pour the mixture into small jars. When it's cool enough to handle, let your grandchild add a little food coloring to each jar.
- Add one drop of detergent to each jar and stir well.
- These paints can be used for either fingerpainting or brush painting, and if covered will keep well.

Be sure to keep little fingers away from the stove!

Knead It, Roll It, Squish It

Warm play dough you've made with a grandchild provides for wonderful tactile experiences. Turn your kitchen into a pretend pizzeria, garden, or construction site and enjoy the imaginative world your grandchild creates. Our favorite recipe doesn't require cooking on the stove and has the bonus of smelling great!

Age: Eighteen months to eight years
You'll Need
- 1 cup boiling hot water
- 5 teaspoons oil
- 1 cup flour
- heaping 1/2 cup salt
- 2 teaspoons corn starch
- One package unsweetened drink mix (such as Kool-Aid)

Mix all. Allow the dough to cool before deciding it's too sticky—and before allowing your grandchild to work with it.
- A flat surface such as a large cookie tray or table top.
- Kitchen utensils: a garlic press to make "hair," straws, popsicle sticks, forks, a potato masher, a rolling pin for the older child to use, cookie cutters, a spaghetti server, an egg cutter, etc.
- Toys: child's hammer, small plastic animals, nesting blocks, etc.

Here's How
- Turn your grandchild loose and let him enjoy molding and playing with the soft dough.

 # Stick to It!

Paste and glue hold a real fascination for little ones and can keep them occupied for longer than you might imagine.

Ages: Two to five years
You'll Need
- Glue or paste: any nontoxic brand is fine. Or make some by mixing together 1/2 cup flour and enough cold water to make a creamy mixture. Boil this on medium for 5 minutes stirring

constantly. Cool and add a few drops peppermint or oil of wintergreen. Keep this covered in the refrigerator.
- Paper
- Objects to paste: cotton, ribbons, yarn, toothpicks, scraps of paper,
  seeds, feathers, leaves, cereal, etc.

Here's How
- As with all art projects for grandchildren, the fun is in the process,
  not necessarily the picture. So provide the paper and the paste, and
  let them create.
- An older grandchild might have fun using the cotton to cover a
  picture of a lamb, the yarn to give a dog fur, or the leaves to fill in
  bare tree branches.

Magical Colors

The magic of watching red and blue turn to purple; red and yellow
turn to orange; or blue and yellow turn to green will thrill your little
ones.

Ages: Two to five years
You'll Need
- Either paints or food coloring in red, blue, and yellow
- Three empty custard cups

Here's How
- Start with a small amount of red and add a small amount of blue.
- Mix red and yellow in the second cup, and in the third stir together
  blue and yellow.
- Be sure your grandchild has the fun of being the magical mixer
  who creates the purple, orange, and green!

A wonderful way to supplement this activity is to read the book
Mouse Paint by Ellen Walsh (see chapter 9).

Beautiful Bracelets

Combine this with a walk in the woods, or a nostalgic trip through Grandma's sewing basket with your grandchild, and you're sure to find some interesting things to put on your bracelets.

Ages: Two years and up
You'll Need
- 1" or 2" wide package or masking tape
- Found objects: feathers, leaves, shells, flowers, lace, yarn, buttons

Here's How
- Make several layers of tape into a bracelet with the sticky side out.
- As you go on your hike or hunt through the sewing basket, stick your treasures onto the outside sticky side of your bracelets.
- This is a No-Fail project and no two will ever be alike!

 # Hands or Feet of Dough

You may recall making these when you were a kid—pass along the fun of making an heirloom hand or footprint!

Ages: One to eight years
You'll Need
- 4 cups flour
- 1 cup salt
- 1 tsp. alum (drug or grocery stores carry this—check in the spice section)
- 1 1/2 cups water
- Large bowl
- Rolling pin
- Poster paints and clear nail polish or clear shellac

Here's How
- Have grandchild mix ingredients in the large bowl - hands work just fine and provide a good "feelie" experience.

- Squeeze and knead, adding a little water if necessary, until dough is smooth.
- Roll out a thick circle of dough on a floured counter or board and have grandchild make a hand or footprint in the middle.
- Help your grandchild sign and date the heirloom. A straw can be used to punch a hole in the top for hanging.
- With a spatula, carefully transfer the mold to an ungreased baking sheet and cook at 275 degrees for thirty minutes. Again carefully turn the mold over and bake for another 1 1/2 hours or until dry and hard.
- Paint around the print so that it stands out. Grandma or Grandpa can help preserve the project with a sealant of clear nail polish or a little clear shellac.

Note: This dough can be refrigerated for several weeks. It can also be colored with food coloring and used for everything from holiday decorations to jewelry or name plaques.

Keep the nail polish and shellac away from the little ones because it is poisonous. Also be sure to keep grandchildren away from the stove.

Squish-and-Wiggle Painting

All ages will enjoy this unique string-painting technique.

Ages: Eighteen months to eight years
You'll Need
- A string about 10–14" long
- A plain piece of white construction paper
- Paints

Here's How
- Have your grandchild fold the paper in half.
- With the paper opened again, lay the string inside the paper so that one end sticks out.
- Drop a small amount of paint inside the paper and then fold it back in half, enclosing the paint and most of the string.
- Now comes the creative part—have your grandchild squish the paint around by pressing on the top half of the paper as he pulls the string out with his other hand. Straight pulls and wiggly pulls will give different effects.
- It's fun to then add a second or third color before your grandchild "names" his creation!

Rainbow "Rags"

Your older grandkids will love the magic of tie dying on fabric!

Ages: Four years and up

You'll Need

- 100% cotton T-shirts, pillowcases, or natural-fiber fabric to make everything from puppet stage curtains to placemats
- Commercial fabric dyes—or make your own with food coloring or crepe paper soaked in water
- A bowl or pan for each color
- Rubber bands or string

Here's How

- This project can be messy, so either do it outside or lay down lots of newspaper!
- Remember to mix the three basic colors—red, blue, and yellow—to make green, purple, and orange.
- Wash and dry the T-shirt or fabric.
- Let your grandchildren create their own scrunches, folds, or twists in the fabric and secure these shapes tightly with a rubber band or string.
- They'll have great fun dipping the tied bundles in the paint and letting them soak until the color is as deep as they wish.
- Wring out the material. With the rubber bands or string still in place, wash and rinse the fabric alone in a washing machine. Add a few tablespoons of salt to a washer full of cold water to help fix the color.
- Remove the string or rubber bands, and hang the fabric to dry.

 # Spaghetti Painting

Your grandchildren will love the feel and creative expression this terrific activity provides!

Ages: One to eight years

You'll Need
- Cooked and rinsed spaghetti
- Food coloring
- Shirt cardboards or other stiff paper for backing

Here's How
- Mix some water and food coloring in bowls—using one bowl for each color.
- Add some cooked spaghetti to each, let the spaghetti absorb the color, then drain.
- Give grandchildren a piece of cardboard and let their imaginations take over. They can swirl the spaghetti, pinch it, draw with it, write with it, and maybe even eat a bit!
- As it dries, the starch in the spaghetti will make it stick to the cardboard backing.

Dress-Up Drama

Pretending is fun and important to a grandchild's development. Besides, there's nothing quite as sweet as seeing your little ones pretend to be "all grown up"!

Ages: Two to five years

You'll Need

- An old suitcase or trunk
- Old clothes that are easy to put on. Check out the fasteners so they won't be frustrating for those little fingers; you may want to replace difficult closures with Velcro
- You might add hats, shoes, jewelry, gloves, scarves, and handbags
- Include some "treasures from the past"—perhaps a girdle, a veil, or Grandpa's bow tie

Here's How

- Show your grandchildren their dress-up suitcase and then enjoy watching their delight in trying on new "fashions."
- They'll love carrying things around in the handbags, so provide "goodies" such as combs, old plastic sunglasses, and keys to help them feel grown up.

Big, clunky shoes and oversized clothing are fun, but they pose a potential tripping hazard. Be especially careful near staircases and other obstacles.

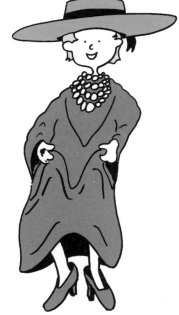

Hand in Hand

Create a scrapbook that will remind your grandchild of your love as he grows!

Ages: Newborn and up
You'll Need
- Sheets of 8 1/2" x 11" paper
- Colored pens
- Each other

Here's How
- At the top of the paper write: "I'll hold your hand a little while"
- At the bottom of the paper write: "I'll hold your heart forever"
- Trace around your grandchild's hand in the center of the page.
- Then lay your hand on top, and trace around it.

We've had fun dating these tracings, and our grandchildren have enjoyed seeing how their hands are growing. One day their hands will be bigger than ours, but we'll always be able to hold them in our hearts!

I'll hold your hand a little while

I'll hold your heart forever

Cardboard Box Creations

Cardboard boxes are indispensable for creating everything from houses and kitchens to cars or trains.

Ages: Three to eight years

You'll Need

- Cardboard boxes of all sizes and shapes
- Paints, markers, or crayons
- Paper cups and plates
- Plastic cups, plates, and containers
- Buttons, pan lids, etc.
- Brass fasteners

Here's How

- Plates or pan lids can become wheels or steering wheels, cups can become headlights, and buttons help create a realistic dashboard.

- Appliance boxes make great houses, which need little more than a cut-out door and window before your grandchildren make it their own with paint and accessories.
- Give your grandchildren the materials and marvel at their creativity!

Creative Curls

If you're a Grandpa or Grandma who loves woodworking, you might try this simple, enjoyable art project.

Ages: Three years and up

You'll Need
- Scraps of wood
- A wood plane tool
- Tacks, staples, nails, or glue
- Shirt cardboards or Styrofoam

Here's How
- Set the wood planing tool to yield thin curls of wood.
- Plane the scrap of wood until you have a pile, then turn your little builder loose.
- She can tack, staple, nail, or glue them to each other, to another piece of wood, to Styrofoam, or to cardboard.
- These can be used to make marvelous decorations.

Supervise closely with the tacking, stapling, and nailing steps.

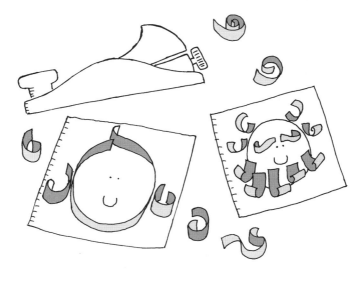

Sawdust Sculptures

Save that sawdust, Gramps, and help your next generation builder mold sawdust sculptures.

Ages: Four years and up
You'll Need
- Sawdust
- Wallpaper paste
- Poster paints

Here's How
- Your little builder will love mixing the sawdust and paste until it reaches a good modeling consistency.
- Then he can create anything—buildings, trains, animals, even puppet heads.
- If a puppet show has some appeal, suggest making the head around one end of a wooden tongue depressor. Yarn hair might be the crowning glory!
- When the sawdust is dry, your little sculptor can paint his creation with poster paints.

Keep It Going

You'll have lots of laughs and fun if you introduce your grandchildren to the old-fashioned round robin story.

Ages: Two-and-a-half years and up
You'll Need
- Your imagination

Here's How
- Start telling a story, either one you invent or one you know, and then pass it along to the person sitting next to you.
- The second person picks up where you left off, turns it into a creation of his own, and then passes it on to the next person.

This is a great activity for anytime, anywhere.

Kitchen Kaboodle

Soups and salads will become favorites if your "imaginative chefs" make them themselves. Start these cooking projects by taking your new "cooks" to the grocery store to pick out the ingredients!

Ages: Three to eight years

You'll Need for Soups

- A variety of veggies (spinach, broccoli, peas, corn, tomatoes, mushrooms, carrots, celery, potatoes, etc.) from which your creative cooks can choose
- Different pasta shapes to add
- Simple bases from canned vegetable juice, spaghetti sauces, or canned chicken broth

Here's How

- When the ingredients have been chosen, leave the cleaning and scrubbing to the younger set. Many veggies can be broken or torn into bite-size pieces, but you'll have to help with those that need cutting with a knife.
- Have your little chefs stir it all up together in a big pot. Your next job will be to supervise the cooking while the creators come up with a novel recipe name and set the table!

You'll Need for Fruit Salads

- A variety of fruits (apples, peaches, pears, melons, berries, oranges, etc.) from which your little chefs can choose
- Extras if they want them: coconut, raisins, yogurt, etc.

Here's How

- Again when the ingredients have been chosen, leave the cleaning and scrubbing to the younger ones. Help cut any fruits that require the use of a knife.
- Have your little ones stir it all up together and serve it garnished with a special name.

Top with lots of praise!

 *Remember, keep the knives and any chokable foods away from the younger set, and the little cooks away from the stove!*

Doggone Good Goodies

This could become a favorite activity not only for the grandchildren, but for the four-legged "kids" in the house too!

Ages: Three to eight years

You'll Need
- 2 cups whole-wheat flour
- 1 egg
- 1/2 cup liquid (chicken or beef broth, or gravy)
- 1/2 teaspoon each garlic salt and garlic powder
- 1/2 teaspoon onion salt
- 2 tablespoons wheat germ or oatmeal (optional)

Here's How
- Your grandchildren can stir flour, egg, and enough liquid to moisten the mixture.
- After they've added the rest of the ingredients, the fun really begins!
- On a floured board, your grandchildren can roll the dough into about twenty dog biscuits—letting their imaginations dictate the shapes.
- Put biscuits in a single layer on a large baking dish and microwave on high for 10 minutes or until firm.

*Be sure **you** take the biscuits out of the microwave, because they'll be too hot for little hands.*

Happy Face Pancakes

Do this on a morning when you're feeling a bit silly—your grandchildren will love your edible, humorous creations!

Ages: One to eight years
You'll Need
- Your favorite pancake recipe
- Blueberries, raisins, or chocolate chips for eyes
- Melon pieces for mouths or whiskers, bananas for hats, etc.

Here's How
- Create a creature or face on the griddle with the fruit, then top with the batter. When you flip the pancake your creation will be smiling up at you!
- Grandchildren will also love pancakes cooked in simple shapes you've "drawn" as you pour out the batter.
- Another trick is to "draw" a simple shape or letter with the batter, let it firm up, and then top it with more batter. When flipped, your "drawing" (in reverse of course) will be darker than the rest of the pancake.

Scrumptious Snow Balls

Half the fun is making these delicious treats!

Ages: Two years and up
You'll Need
- 1 cup peanut butter
- 1/2 cup dry powdered milk
- 2 tablespoons honey
- Shredded coconut
- A bowl and spoon

Here's How
- Measure and mix the first three ingredients in the bowl.
- Refrigerate for an hour.
- Roll in small balls, then roll in the coconut to coat.
- Enjoy!

88

All This from One Balloon

Lightweight and tiny, balloons offer even the littlest imaginations new ideas. Don't leave home without them!

Ages: Six months to five years

To keep your youngest grandbabies amused

You'll Need
- A balloon
- Some water

Here's How
- Fill the balloon with about 1/3 cup water.
- Knot the end to keep the water inside and then under your supervision let the baby wiggle and squish it around.

To entertain a fussy grandtoddler

You'll Need
- A balloon
- A permanent felt tip marker
- A string, piece of ribbon, or yarn

Here's How
- Blow it up and draw a funny face on one side and a sad face on the other.
- Blow it up and while stretching the opening share the fun of making weird squeaking sounds with your "no-longer-fussy" toddler as the air escapes.
- Blow it up and instead of tying it, let it take off like a rocket!
- Blow it up, tie it securely with a short string, and then tie it onto your toddler-grandchild's wrist. She'll enjoy making it fly around, and you'll have an easier time keeping track of her!

Please remember that deflated or broken balloons are a choking hazard and that long strings can tangle. Never leave a little one alone with a balloon.

1, 2, 3 . . . How Many Do I See?

These easy games will keep your little ones entertained even on long car trips.

Ages: Three to eight years
You'll Need
- Sharp eyes

Here's How
- Any of these games can be played with individuals or teams.
- *Country Cows:* One team takes the right-hand side of the road and the other the left-hand side. The object of the game is simple—just count the cows, horses, or whatever you choose. The first one to reach fifty wins. But if you pass a cemetery, all the animals on that side of the car must be "buried"—and that team has to start all over again!
- *Cars of a Color:* Each person picks a color and then gives himself a point whenever he sees a car in his color. The first person to see ten cars in his color wins! Another twist on this theme would be to pick one object for all to look for—a ship, a load of hay, a tanker truck. The first person to see the object gets a point and chooses the next object to be found. The game continues until the winner reaches ten points.
- *License-Plate Lookout:* The object of the game is to see who can find the most license plates from different states. This might be a good ongoing game for a long trip. Tally up the states at the end of the trip. You might present the winner with a U.S. map puzzle!

For more fun car games, see p. 242-43.

"Follow Me" Footsteps

Imagine how thrilled your grandchild will be in the morning to follow a path of little cut-out feet from her bed to yours.

Ages: Two to six years

You'll Need
- Paper and scissors
- Double-stick tape

Here's How
- After your sleepyhead falls asleep, cut out little paper feet.
- Make a trail from her bed to yours, using a piece of tape to hold down each footprint.
- In the morning, she'll know where to go for warm snuggles!

Extend this to the breakfast table or in reverse for bedtime stories!

Magical Music Drawings

Encourage your imaginative, musical grandchild to join you as you both create to the music!

Ages: Four to eight years
You'll Need
- Paper, pencils
- Music on tape, compact disc, or radio
- Watercolor paints, crayons, or markers

Here's How
- With a pencil and paper for each of you, place your pencils on your papers to start.
- Make your pencils "dance" to the music and create designs.
- Designs can be colored in with watercolor paints, crayons, or markers.

Grandpa's Floating Fleet

You don't have to be a woodworker to build these simple floating boats.

Ages: Two to eight years
You'll Need
- Chunks of Styrofoam (appliance stores have leftover pieces from shipping boxes)
- Small blocks of wood, spools, corks, bottle caps and tops, plastic straws, cloth, string, etc.
- Glue, scissors, serrated knife

Here's How
- Any shape will work and float, so let your grandchild "design" the hull.
- Supervise as your older grandchild cuts thin Styrofoam pieces with scissors.
- You'll have to do the cutting on thicker foam pieces with the knife.
- You can create a mast, sails, a cabin, bottle cap portholes, a smokestack from a bottle top, a buoy from a cork and straw—be creative!
- You can stick things into the thicker Styrofoam or glue them onto the thinner pieces.
- Float your boats in a lake, stream, ocean, or bathtub.

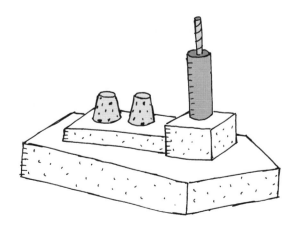

Music, Music, Everywhere

Children instinctively love rhythm and music, and your little musician will love these simple homemade rhythm instruments as he becomes the leader of your marching band.

Ages: One to six years

To "Shake, Rattle, and Roll" You'll Need
- Plastic container
- Dried beans or popcorn kernels
- Tape

Here's How
Merely put several handfuls of the beans or kernels in the plastic bottle or container. Screw on the lid and secure with tape. Start the music and clap along with your grandchild's shakes, rattles, and rolls!

To "Drum Up a Beat" You'll Need
- An oatmeal box, coffee can, or kitchen pots and pans
- Kitchen tools (plastic, wooden, and metal) for drumsticks

Here's How
- Put the lid back on the empty oatmeal box or coffee can and turn over the pots and pans.
- The smile on your budding drummer's face as she discovers different sounds will be worth any discomfort from the noise!

To "Kazoo with You" You'll Need
- Empty toilet-paper tube
- Piece of waxed paper to fit over one end of the tube
- Rubber band

Here's How
- Rubber band the wax paper over one end of the tube.
- Your biggest challenge then is to teach your grandchild how to hum (not sing) into the other end of the tube. The discovery of vibration will delight all!

94

To "Jingle Bell Rock" You'll Need

- An old pair of child-sized gloves
- Ten jingle bells
- Thread and needle

Here's How

With strong thread very securely sew the jingle bells onto the ends of the fingers (you may not want to give this rhythm toy to the child who still puts things in his mouth).

To "Tambourine a Tune" You'll Need

- A small wooden hoop
- A piece of ribbon, yarn, or string
- Jingle bells

Here's How

Wrap the ribbon, yarn, or string around the hoop, stringing on the bells as you go. Tie the ends and leave streamers. If you want to be fancy, cover the hoop first with ribbon or fabric.

To "Strum a Guitar" You'll Need

- Rubber bands and a string
- An empty tissue box

Here's How

- Wrap the rubber bands around the box and tie the string to both ends so it'll hang gently around your guitarist's neck.
- Supervise closely so that the neck string doesn't tangle or get caught on something.

To "Brush or Clap a Beat" You'll Need

- Two 3" x 4" blocks
- Sandpaper

Here's How

The blocks can be covered with the sandpaper and used to make a brushing sound. Or use them as is to clap to the beat.

To "Sing a Song" You'll Need

- Only to lose your inhibitions

Here's How

- Bellow out in full voice—it doesn't matter if you're on key or in time—and enjoy the enthusiastic response from your little ones.

Beautiful Bubble Brew

Bubbles hold a fascination for all ages!

Ages: One to eight years

You'll Need

- 6 cups water
- 2 cups dishwashing liquid (Joy or Dawn brands work best)
- 3/4 cup Karo light corn syrup
- Bubble wands: canning jar rings, funnels, plastic berry baskets, wire coat hanger shaped into a big 6" wand, plastic six-pack holder, spools, straws, etc.

Here's How

- Combine the water, dishwashing liquid, and syrup.
- Let mixture sit for four hours before using.
- Pour into a frying pan or large pan and dip in your wand for some unbelievably beautiful bubbles.
- Store mixture in covered glass or plastic containers for future use.

Note: Check out John Cassidy's *The Unbelievable Bubble Book* (Palo Alto, Calif.: Klutz Press, 1987) for further variations.

Rock Creations

Let your imaginations go wild as you and your grandchildren have fun gathering and painting rocks.

Ages: Two to eight years

You'll Need

- Rocks
- Paints and brushes
- Clear shellac (optional)
- Glue

Here's How

- Enjoy the rock hunt and the way your grandchildren can "see" things in the different shapes.
- This can be a great outdoor summer project, or cover the table with newspaper and create inside.

- Your older grandchildren might enjoy gluing rocks together to construct more complex creations.
- If you want to preserve your grandchildren's works of art, you might want to spray them with shellac when the paint is thoroughly dry. The finished rocks can then be used for everything from paperweights to doorstops.

Be sure to keep the shellac away from your grandchildren if you choose to use it; it is toxic.

Lights in the Night

When summer comes and the lightening bugs appear, help your grandchild catch a few to light up his bedroom at night.

Ages: Two to eight years
You'll Need
- Glass or canning jar
- A flashlight
- Leaves and grass clippings
- Nylon stocking, aluminum foil, or a screen
- Rubber band to hold lid down
- Fireflies

Here's How
- Fill the jar with some leaves and grass to help the bugs feel "at home."
- With your flashlight, try copying the light signals you see a firefly make—will the firefly "talk" back to you with his little light?
- Carefully catch a few bugs in your cupped hands, being careful not to squish them.
- Put several in the jar and cover the top with a screen, piece of nylon stocking, or aluminum foil in which you've poked holes (so the bugs can get air).
- Be sure you let the bugs out in the morning. Their life span is short, and all wildlife should be returned to nature.

Snow Sculpture Spritzing

With a little diluted food coloring in a spray bottle, your visiting grandchild can have great fun outside on a snowy day.

Ages: Two to eight years

You'll Need

- Snow
- Food coloring
- An empty spray bottle

Here's How

- Enjoy the fun of creating snow sculptures.
- Mix a little food coloring with water in a spray bottle.
- Turn your little one loose with the spray bottle and join in his wonderment at the instant coloring!

Funny Dough

Unlike any other dough we've recommended, this one stretches, pours, strings, and even breaks sharply if pulled quickly. It molds but doesn't hold it's shape—remember Silly Putty?

Ages: Three to eight years

You'll Need

- 1 cup white glue
- 1/2 cup liquid starch

Here's How

- Mix the glue and starch with a strong spoon.
- Add more liquid starch—slowly one tablespoon at a time—probably about 4 Tbsp. total. If you add too much, the dough will become too stiff.
- Watch your enthralled grandchild stretch, pour, string, and break the dough.
- Store in the refrigerator for lasting fun.

Caution: Children should not eat this dough.

Roots and Shoots

Potatoes, avocado seeds, carrot tops, and the bottom half of a pineapple give your grandchild a chance to see the new growth that usually occurs underground.

Ages: Two-and-a-half to eight years
You'll Need
- Any or all of the above foods and toothpicks
- Shallow pan for the carrots, glass for the potato and avocado seed, and bowl for the pineapple

Here's How
- Insert four toothpicks firmly into the sides of a potato or avocado seed about one-third of the way down (keep the rounded end of the seed facing down).
- Set the potato or seed into a small glass, resting the toothpicks on the edge of the glass.
- Fill the glass with water so that about half the potato or seed is immersed.
- In a week or so, your grandchild will witness the roots growing down into the water and the shoots growing up into the air.
- The pineapple will produce both roots and shoots if you set the lower half in a bowl of water just like you did with the potato and seed.

To grow carrot greens
- Cut the top of the carrot off, leaving about one inch of carrot and all of the fresh carrot greens.
- Set the carrot stub in a shallow pan and record the daily growth of green tops!
- Remember that plants need light to grow, so place your "kitchen garden" near a window.

Feeding Our Feathered Friends

An inexpensive, simple bird feeder can be made from a half-gallon milk or orange juice carton.

Ages: Three to eight years
You'll Need
- An empty carton
- A stapler and package tape
- Wire
- Pencil
- Bird seed

Here's How

- You'll have to do most of the construction because it requires the use of a knife, but your grandchild can be in charge of keeping the feeder filled.
- Staple the top of the carton together, then cover the "roof peak" with tape to keep the inside dry.
- Poke two holes in the middle of the front and back about two inches up from the bottom of the carton. Insert a pencil "perch" through these holes.
- About a half an inch above the perch, cut a two-inch-square flap (leaving the top intact to swing up as a "perch roof").
- Secure the "perch roof" up with some wire. It'll help keep the rain out of the seed.
- Last but certainly not least, have your grandchild fill up the feeder with the seed. Pick a spot and hang it where the feeding birds can be observed from inside the house.

Ships Ahoy!

Sailors of all ages will love making these simple boats, and we all have the makings right in our homes!

Ages: Two years and up
You'll Need
- Walnut shells or bottle caps
- Colored paper or 3x5 cards
- Toothpicks and tape
- Clay or chewing gum

Here's How
- Carefully crack open the walnuts so you have two shell halves (or use bottle caps).
- Mold a little mound of clay (or chew some gum and use it) to put in your little "boat's hull."
- Erect your mast by putting the toothpick into the clay or gum.
- Cut a triangular sail, and tape it on the mast.
- Sail away in the tub, pool or pond.

We've had great fun having races; sometimes a little puff of man made wind helps win the race!

Mirror, Mirror off the Wall

Take that small plastic mirror outside with your adventuresome grandson, and see if he can follow your maze.

Ages: Four years and up
You'll Need to Tuck in Your Suitcase
- A small plastic mirror

Here's How
- Draw a maze in the sand or on the driveway with chalk—making the path about one foot wide.
- Teach your little guy how to make the mirror reflect the sun on the ground.
- Challenge him to "shine his beam of light" through the maze without touching the sides of the path.

Blow Power Boats

It's simple to make two of these boats at the same time, and then you can have a race!

Ages: Two to eight years
You'll Need
- A half-gallon juice or milk container
- A balloon for each boat "hull"
- Tape and a paper punch

Here's How
- Slice the container in half lengthwise so that each boat has a pointed bow.
- Tape together any of seams that may have split apart.
- Punch a hole in the middle of the "stern" of the boat—a paper punch makes just the right size.
- Put the balloon in the boat and push the neck of the balloon through the hole in the stern.
- Blow it up and be ready for some pool or tub action when your grandchild releases the air in the balloon.

Remember, young children should be supervised when using balloons.

Now You See It . . . Now You Don't

Seeing things disappear and then reappear is like magic to a little tyke.

Ages: Nine to eighteen months
You'll Need
- A coffee can with plastic lid
- Knife
- Wooden beads or other smallish objects, such as wooden blocks

Here's How
- Cut an X in the top of the plastic lid.
- Let your grandchild enjoy the fun of pushing things through the slot, hearing them "clink," and then having them reappear when they remove the lid.

Note: There are many variations on peek-a-boo: hiding behind your hands or a blanket, peek-a-boo books, advent calendars, match-box secret "drawers," or the good old hide-and-seek game. Try hiding dinosaurs or other small plastic figures in your yard and going on a "dinosaur hunt" with your grandchild. They'll love the surprise element in all of these activities.

Remember the dangers of choking. Keep tiny objects away and supervise all activities closely.

Seaside Symphony

Turn the treasures from a day at the beach into a lasting memory of your grandchild's visit.

Ages: Three to eight years
You'll Need
- Driftwood
- Shells with a hole in them
- String

Here's How
- While at the seaside, take a hike to gather driftwood and interesting shells.
- Thread the string through the holes in the shells and tie them onto pieces of driftwood at different heights.
- Hang the smaller pieces of driftwood from the largest piece, creating a mobile or wind chime of shells.
- You'll remember your day at the beach every time the wind plays you a seaside symphony.

Simply Wonderful Water

Water is fascinating for all ages!

Ages: Six months and up
You'll Need
- A bathtub, outdoor wading pool, or large dishpan with about two inches of water in the bottom
- Water "toys" such as sponges to bath a washable doll, an eye dropper, a funnel, a piece of plastic tubing, an egg beater, plastic cups, a squeeze bottle, a coffee scoop, a spray bottle top, a plastic turkey baster, plastic strainer, etc.

Here's How
- Under close supervision, give your grandchild just a few "toys" at a time.
- Watch as she experiments with sinking, floating, pouring, squirting, splashing, spraying, rippling, and dripping!

Remember, NEVER leave a child alone around water.

 # Find Your Own Pot of Gold

When the sun is closest to the horizon, either in the early morning or late evening, create some rainbow luck with your little leprechaun.

Ages: Two to five years
You'll Need
- An outside watering hose
- The beginning or end of a sunny day

Here's How
- Put your little leprechaun's back to the sun and face him toward a dark object such as a brown house or stand of evergreen trees.
- Hand him the outside watering hose.
- If he can spray it upward forming an arch of water, you'll likely find your very own rainbow—and maybe a "pot of gold."

 This might be a fun time to read Don Freeman's delightful book, *A Rainbow of My Own*. See chapter 9.

Make a Leaf-Lasting Impression!

Capture the beautiful colors of fall leaves in this easy, fun activity for you and your grandchild to do together!

Ages: Four and up
You'll Need
- A brightly colored fall leaf
- A wooden board
- A piece of clean white or beige cloth
- A hammer
- Pushpins
- White glue

Here's How
- Have your grandchild place the leaf on the board.
- Cover the leaf with the piece of cloth. Use pushpins to hold the cloth in place.
- With you right there to help as needed, let your grandchild use a hammer to pound on the leaf. The color will be squeezed into the cloth.
- If you wish, you can glue the cloth to a red or yellow frame. Now you can enjoy the beauty of fall year-round!

Submerged Sights

This unique use of a flashlight will fascinate your grandchildren as you discover together the wonders of the underwater world at night.

Ages: Three years and up
You'll need
- A small flashlight
- A glass jar with a tight-fitting lid and big enough to hold the flashlight
- String
- A lake, pond, or stream at night

Here's How
- Put the flashlight in the jar, turn it on, and screw the top down tight.
- Tie a string around the neck of the jar.
- Lower your light into the water, and you'll be amazed to see what it will attract.

The "Hug a Tree" Discovery Game

A truly hands-on game that gets everyone closer to nature!

Ages: Three and up
You'll Need
- A blindfold
- An outdoor space with several snuggly trees that have accessible trunks

Here's How
- Blindfold your grandchild.
- Carefully lead him to one of the trees nearby.
- "Introduce" your grandchild to the tree, suggesting that he feel its trunk for special bumps or knots. Tell him that during the next stage of the game he will look for his tree with the blindfold off.
- When he's ready, take him back to the starting point and remove the blindfold.
- Watch as he hugs each tree, looking for his special "friend." It's remarkable how often children can find their tree!

Nuts-a-Fun and Nuts-on-the-Run

Save those nut shells and then create!

Ages: Four to five years

You'll Need

- Walnuts or peanuts
- A few marbles small enough to fit inside half the walnut shell
- Magnetic tape
- Felt scraps
- Glue
- Poster paints
- Pipe cleaners

Here's How

- Grandpa or Grandma can carefully pry open the walnut and peanut shells with a screwdriver.
- Let your imaginations go free using paint, felt scraps, and pipe cleaners. You can easily come up with eyes, ears, whiskers, tails, noses, legs, etc. Glue felt on the back of the shell, put the magnetic tape on the bottom, and you'll have a zoo of fridge magnets.
- Make some simple racing cars with the walnut shell halves. Simply decorate the shell as you wish and slip a marble underneath.
- Provide a ramp to race your "nuts-on-the-run!"
- The peanut shells provide the base for terrific simple finger puppets.

Be careful to keep nuts, marbles, and small shells away from little ones who are still putting things in their mouths.

Chow Mein Chocolate

Simple to make—and so good to eat it'll be hard to wait thirty minutes for them to harden!

Ages: Two years and up
You'll Need
- Cookie sheet covered with wax paper
- Big bowl
- 2 cups chocolate chips
- 3 1/2 cups chow mein noodles

Here's How
- Grandparents, you should microwave the chocolate chips on high for 3 minutes. Then your grandchild can take over.
- Stir the chips until smooth.
- Add the noodles to the chocolate and stir well until the chocolate covers all the noodles.
- With a teaspoon, drop in small mounds onto the wax paper.
- Refrigerate for 30 minutes to harden.

 # Who Says It Has to Be Round?

Pizza is always fun to make, but being creative with the dough makes it even more exciting!

Ages: Three years and up
You'll Need
- 2 cups flour
- 2 teaspoons baking soda
- 1/2 teaspoon salt
- 1/4 cup oil
- 1/4 cup milk
- 2 eggs
- Spaghetti or pizza sauce
- Anything you like for toppings: peppers, mushrooms, olives, broccoli, sausage, etc.

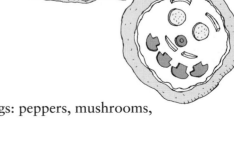

Here's How

- Mix together the flour, baking soda, and salt.
- Mix the oil, milk, and eggs together; then stir into the dry ingredients.
- Put flour on the counter and on a rolling pin, and have fun rolling out the dough until it's about 1/4" thick.
- Cut the dough into any shape you want (perhaps a dinosaur, a clown, a train?)—spread on the sauce, and decorate with the toppings to accent the features of your shape—try some cheese hair, olive eyes, mushroom ears, and pepper smiles!
- Grandpa or Grandma should bake the dough in a 375 degree oven for 18–25 minutes. The size of your pizza will determine the cooking time.

Remember the stove is operated only by Grandma and Grandpa!

Every Day Together Is Special

The parents will want to know all that happened while they were off on their "get-away weekend," so what better gift to give them when they return than a happy child and a diary of all the things you and their little munchkin did together?

Ages: All
You'll Need

- A notebook and pen

Here's How

- Keep your notebook handy and as each day progresses record the fun things you did with your grandchild, the funny or sweet things your grandchild said, etc.
- This diary will be appreciated immediately by your grandchild's parents, but it'll become an even greater treasure to pass along to the "star of the day" when he's older.

I Made These Cookies All by Myself

This simple cookie recipe doesn't require any cooking.

Ages: Three years and up
You'll Need
- 1 cup vanilla wafer cookies
- 1/2 cup grated coconut
- 1/2 cup powdered sugar
- 1/3 cup frozen lemonade or orange juice concentrate

Here's How
- Put the cookies in a sturdy plastic bag; crush them with your hands.
- In a bowl mix the cookie crumbs, the coconut, the sugar, and the juice.
- Stir well and roll into small balls.
- Roll the balls in powdered sugar.
- Refrigerate covered overnight (if you can wait that long!).

I Dream, You Dream, We All Dream of This Ice Cream

Ice cream pie, that is, especially when your grandchild helps make it!

Ages: Four years and up
You'll Need
- Vanilla wafer cookies
- 1 quart strawberry ice cream, softened
- 1 cup applesauce
- 1 teaspoon lemon juice
- 1 pint fresh strawberries

Here's How
- Line the bottom and sides of a pie dish with the cookie wafers.
- Mix the ice cream, applesauce, and lemon juice all together and pour into cookie lined shell.
- Put the fresh berries on top.
- Cover and store in the freezer.
- Let it sit out for ten minutes before cutting.

5
Visiting Your Grandchild

Uh-oh. Here come Grandpa Sam and Grandma Sally, our imaginary self-absorbed, know-it-all, done-it-all grandparents. They dump their ten bags in the hallway, plop themselves on the sofa after demanding hugs and kisses from each grandchild, and wait expectantly for couch-side service. Worst of all, these two are so eager to discuss stock options and the latest gourmet recipes that they immediately transform all opportunities for play into adult-oriented conversations.

Don't worry. We know no grandparents could be this bad. But all of us could use a refresher course on how to make sure our best efforts to become part of our grandchild's life—no matter how often we visit—can be most appreciated. What follows is our best advice to grandparents visiting their grandchildren near or far. So pack that bag of washable clothes, leave your sensitive ego at your doorstep, and read on. By the time you arrive, you'll have some ideas for making your time with your extended family as meaningful and interactive as it can be.

Grand Expectations

What do parents and grandchildren hope grandparents will be like during a visit? Young Dory Trimble from Salt Lake City, Utah, gave us her view: "Having a good time is a rule!" It's true—ask any preschool-age grandchild what they wish for when Grandma and Grandpa come, and they will undoubtedly launch into an adorable and fantastical story that includes the special treats and traditions you share. They simply want to have fun and experience all the unique aspects of you. Perhaps, too, your little ones will be wise enough to anticipate the joy of looking back on the visit with photos and mementos.

Parents and grandchildren, however, aren't the only ones fantasizing about the big event. Grandparents also have dreams and even fears about an upcoming visit. One grandparent mentioned to us her dismay at her role as "gift-giver" in her extended family. "I feel such pressure to buy things for everyone when I go," she wrote (asking not to be named), "and I really want to be more than just a cash machine in my grandchild's life." Perhaps you too feel limited by some aspect of your relationship with your children and grandchildren. These roles, once established, may seem impossible to change. Or perhaps you've made it through the important postpartum visit, but need some additional ideas to keep your relationship with your grandchild fresh during subsequent visits to their home. If so, the following paragraphs might help you recharge your batteries and take a new, positive approach.

A Recipe for a Warm and Loving Visit

What do you get when you mix two cups understanding, one cup kindness, and a generous dollop of good humor? A grandparent who's ready to accept grandchildren regardless of how grumpy or outlandish they can be.

Visiting grandchildren is unlike any other sort of family experience, and it requires that grandparents be as flexible and relaxed as possible. Grandbaby Sara might be teething, four-year-old grandson Keith might be up with nightmares each night, and your little grandtoddlers may well spend part of your visit peering at you over big toys and Mom and Dad's protective arms. Not only that, but as the visitor, you'll want to realize that you are entering your grandchild's world. The best visits, it seems, happen when grandparents offer the same respect and consideration to their grandchildren that they hope their grandchildren will grant when they stay with them.

Building this rapport will not be as easy as wiping your feet at the door or always offering to help prepare meals—in fact, these niceties have much more to do with your love and affection for a grandchild's parents. Instead, you'll want to construct, block by toy block perhaps, your role as one who appreciates and enjoys the world as it seems to your grandchild. You might start by asking gentle questions of your little ones about the routines that involve them. "Where does this doll go?" you might ask, as you help to pick up toys before lunch. "How does this work?" you inquire strategically, as you try out the unfamiliar dishwasher or coffee pot. Nick and Charlie love it when their grandparents ask how to find things around the house—and it's a great way to make a true friend of any little despot.

Perhaps the biggest bonus of establishing this respectful rapport with your littlest grandchildren is that they will begin to trust you deeply. Your priceless reward will be the moment when your grand-toddler, with wonder in his face, takes you aside to tell you a "secret" or a little story about his teddy bear—or when your school-age grandchild tells you about his favorite teacher with a shy smile. What a wonderful feeling for both of you—and a great foundation for the day when your older grandchild has more weighty matters to discuss.

Coordinating Visits with Other Grandparents

Sometimes it's hard to share time with your grandchildren. And your littlest busybodies won't benefit from an overloaded house, either. That's why we recommend that families take turns visiting grandchildren. Sure, it will be fun to have a large reunion now and again. But in general everyone will feel more relaxed and will have more quality time with those little ones if you alternate your visits.

This strategy, however, takes some coordination and cooperation not only with your grandchild's parents, but also with the other grandparents in the picture. You might have to forgo your dreams of having a big holiday get-together on the "right" day this year. Or you might gracefully suggest that your grandchild's other beloved Grandma and Grandpa visit your grandchild on her first birthday, while you send a simple, loving gift by mail instead.

We know. It doesn't sound like you're gaining much by being the "nice guy." But imagine the relief your grandchild's parents feel when they realize you're bending over backward to make your grandchild's experiences always as positive as they can be. That relief by parents is sure to be translated into appreciation and then into happy visits or enthusiastic invitations for you to come visit—and probably sooner than you think. Regardless, you'll know that you've done your best to encourage a young family to enjoy their own plans for precious family times together. That's a wonderful feeling for everyone.

Getting Messy, Getting Close

Where does your grandchild spend most of his or her time? If your grandchildren are younger than one year, your answer is likely to be "on the floor" or "in the sand or mud outside"; if they are between one and three, the answer might be "climbing into drawers," "on a tricycle," or "into your cupboards"; and if they are ages four to eight, you might respond "on a bicycle," "on play structures outside," or "drawing at a table." The point is that young children see and interact with the world in a different way than do most adults. For one thing, they're only a fraction of your height. What's important to a two- or three-foot-high person? Things on or near the floor or ground, of course. And that means that to be interesting to this lovable little person you are going to need to get down near the floor as well. Bring those comfy jeans and cuddly sweats, swear off chairs for a while—and enter the land of child-oriented love.

One thing you'll notice when you get down where the children are—besides the occasional dustbunny that a busy parent has missed (and that you should ignore!)—is that the rules can be a bit different down there. First and most important, this altitude is your grandchild's territory, and you'll want to be cautious about closing in on your little one too soon. For any child under the age of five, it's a good idea to place a toy or game between you at first so that your presence does not seem overwhelming. You might even want to bring something unique for this moment—such as a new book or a small toy your child, the parent, once had. Play with the toy or game yourself, and talk aloud or make sound effects that make it inviting. When the child joins you, continue as though nothing unusual is happening and wait for your grandchild to initiate more direct communication. After that smile, direct look, or "How's this, Grandpa?" you can play as you wish, knowing that you made the transition an easy one for your grandchild.

> Bring those comfy jeans and cuddly sweats, swear off chairs for a while—and enter the land of child-oriented love.

People who wrote to us agreed with this approach. Jennifer Strong of Penfield, New York, wrote, "Long-distance grandparents shouldn't expect hugs and kisses right away when seeing a grandchild they haven't seen in a while. The child might be wary of people he perceives as strangers. Let the child get to know you again and feel comfortable. Then the hugs and kisses will come." From Kennybunk, Maine, Delta and Peter Fuller added, "Take time to get close to them gradually so they're not frightened by a strange face." Child development experts have found that this uncertainty about unfamiliar faces can peak in many children around the age of eight months and then again at one year; but it's best to be careful with any small child. We all know that few children "follow the book" exactly when it comes to physical and emotional development.

It's a Small World, after All

Being a visiting grandparent can be much more than playing with toys on the floor, however. You'll want to acquaint yourself with many of the other places, people, and events that are part of your grandchild's day as well. Your interest and involvement in the day-to-day aspects of your grandchild's life are the essential ingredients of a dynamic friendship. These are activities that you couldn't know about without being at her home, and they will help you nurture your relationship with your grandchild when you communicate long-distance. If you know your grandchild's best buddies by name, had a funny experience at the zoo together, and can remember his or her favorite ice cream flavor, it will make your notes and phone calls that much more meaningful.

Being Memorable Away from Home

We couldn't resist chuckling the other day as we were in line to ride the swan boats at the Boston Public Garden. A visiting Grandpa who was waiting with his grandchildren was really hamming it up. "What's your name again?" he said, pointing to his giggling four-year-old granddaughter. "Don't feed the people!" he hollered agreeably to the people looking over the bridge at us. "Where do you think those ducks sleep at night?" he asked his awe-filled two-year-old grandson. Something about the way this Grandpa let it all hang out was both fun and inspiring to us. We know this is one grandparent who will spark new opportunities for learning and closeness throughout his grandchildren's growing-up years because his banter was simply irresistible to his little ones.

It may surprise you that your personality, just like this Grandpa's, is portable. Oh, we know. You think that you're toting your whole self around when you visit your youngest grandchildren. But think how much more reserved most of us feel when we're separated from our familiar home. We may feel at a loss for what to do in a community away from our own favorite museums, libraries, and local happenings. Moreover, we may need to give ourselves a pep talk before we leave so that we overcome our hesitancy to become fully involved in whatever our grandchildren dream up. Try spicing up your visits to a grandchild's home by doing a bit of homework first, and then by "putting your whole self in." You'll find yourself doing more than the hokey-pokey—whole new opportunities for closeness with your grandchildren will appear. And after all, "that's what it's all about!"

Nursery School

Preschool and daycare experiences provide wonderful opportunities for sharing. Just don't be surprised if you end up being a Grandpa or Grandma to the whole class for the day, because little ones just love the idea of having a loving senior among them. Be sure to ask the teacher if it's all right for you to join in (you're sure to get an enthusiastic response unless another special event was planned). You can then sit right down in those tiny chairs and chat along with the youngsters as you all play with playdough, art materials, or games.

Toss aside your embarrassment about how you look playing in the sandbox or giving your special bear hug at the nursery school door and revel in knowing that your grandchild only has eyes for the wonderful person you are inside. That's the magic of the love between grandchild and grandparent.

You might also take the spotlight with your grandchild during the class group, or "circle," time—if this is something that interests you both. After passing your ideas by the classroom teacher, you might read a story or sing a song (perhaps with a musical instrument) that you and your grandchild have chosen together. This way your little one will have a chance to introduce you and perform for the others with your support.

Sometimes, too, schools have special grandparent events that you might want to attend. Next time you're dropping off or picking up your grandchild at school, be sure to introduce yourself to your grandchild's teacher, if you haven't already, and ask about any parties or get-togethers to which you might come. You might even be able to fill in as a special guest for parent events if an unavoidable conflict prevents Mom or Dad from attending.

Play with the Babysitter, Too

Perhaps your grandchild has a regular babysitter, with whom you can attend a sing-along concert or story hour at your local library. Getting to know the adults who are important in your little one's life shows that you want to understand their world. Your acceptance will also help your grandchild feel more confident about his affection for this other adult—which is a great way to reassure your grandchild that it's healthy to enjoy being with people outside of the family.

Rapping with the Littlest Gang: Your Grandchild's Friends

Children grow up fast, it's true, but your under-eight grandchildren are as likely to be hippity-hopping as hip-hopping these days (thank goodness!). So trust your instincts and see if you can finagle an invitation to play. You could pop your head around the corner as your four-year-old grandchild is playing with a friend and suggest a simple cooking project (see chapter 4 for some suggestions). Or try walking around with a mask or simple facepaint design and see if your curious little ones and their friends ask to do the same. Even simply asking gently to join in their game can open the door to a fun afternoon of conversations and silliness as you add your grandparent imagination and ideas.

The respect and love you nurture by being an interested and responsive grandparent will give you access to a world you may only vaguely remember—a world of suspense, drama, and fun that revolves around events and ideas we now take for granted. You may never have dreamed that the swirly patterns made by cream as it's added to coffee would be the backdrop for such intense curiosity by your little one. You may find yourself reading stories to favorite toys while you cuddle up to your grandchild—Charlie insists that his "choo choo" enjoy all his favorite books, too. And what a wonderful feeling to be surrounded by a playgroup of little ones, all eager to make muffins or playdough. Immersing yourself in a small world is one of the richest rewards of grandparenting.

The Magic of Unconditional Love

We know, we know. This all sounds great, but some of you still feel inhibited about being childlike with your grandchild. We, too, took a while to jettison those old self-conscious feelings. But now that we have, we just can't let you lug around that outdated excuse—truly playing with grandchildren is just too much fun and too important for everyone. And if you don't believe us, believe Barb Roscoe of Fairport, New York. Her young granddaughter asked her how her diet was going before an upcoming visit. Barb replied, "I'm trying, but it looks like I'll be bringing that same old body." Her granddaughter's adorable, tinkly voice answered, "That's okay, Grandma, we love that old body!" Come on, fellow grandparents, you can do it. Toss aside your embarrassment about how you look playing in the sandbox or giving your special bear hug at the nursery school door and revel in knowing that your grandchild only has eyes for the wonderful person you are inside. That's the magic of the love between grandchild and grandparent.

Being a "Low Maintenance" Guest

"But I'm not tired yet!" protest Grandpa Sam and Grandma Sally, as their grown children politely try to usher them to bed. Oh, dear. Too bad these two haven't brushed up on their grandparenting manners. Phyllis and Chuck Curtis, of Ontario, New York, however, have the right idea. They wrote, "Go to bed early and leave parents time alone." Remember how difficult it was to find private time with your partner when you had small children in the house? When successful at garnering a private moment, parents can finally have a much-needed chance to catch up on each other's adult lives. (And you can't blame these busy parents for hoping to have even more of these moments when a helpful grandparent is around—even though this is a special time for you, too.) You might try to respect the privacy of your children and grandchildren, if you can afford to, by offering to sleep at a hotel or bed and breakfast if quarters are tight. Our family negotiated this during the postpartum visit—when both new grandparents were visiting, the grandparents arranged for other accommodations; during subsequent visits by one grandparent, the visitor stayed in the apartment's small guest room. You might even offer to play with your grandbaby at your nearby overnight place while parents have some time to themselves at home.

How long should you stay? Each family will have its own answer to this question, and it might very well depend on your culture as much as on the relationships between the family members. We were intrigued to discover, for example, that many European families we heard from had grandparent visits that lasted as long as a month or so. One possible guideline for American families, however, is given by T. Berry Brazelton, a child-development and parenting expert at Harvard University. Brazelton advises, "Regular visits for short periods are best. A three-day visit is likely to be enough. Help with housework and babysitting, [and] try to take everyone out on an excursion while you are there."[1]

Not That Surprise!

What's every new mother's deepest dread? We can tell you from our experience: it's hearing the doorbell ring. Bleary-eyed, baby in her arms, with a backdrop of dirty laundry, toys, and cluttered countertops, just about the last thing she wants is a surprise visit. Until that long-awaited day when we all confess that everyone and every home has that same disheveled look after a child's birth (and beyond!), greeting a surprise visitor—even a beloved grandparent—might just make a new parent feel anxious and embarrassed. So plan ahead with the new parents in your family, right down to whether you're bringing food to eat and what that might be. (Our freezer-stuffing family can sometimes go overboard; perhaps yours occasionally does, too?) Then they won't have to cast worried looks out the window every time a car drives by, and you'll rest easy knowing that your trip is truly welcomed.

Instead, Plan for Little Surprises

There's just something about a sticker that is irresistible to a grandchild. And don't ask us why, but those little matchbox cars are worth their weight in gold for the pleasure they bring children. As a visiting grandparent, you can make the most of the joy that results from these and other seemingly insignificant gifts. One suggestion offered by many of our grandparent writers was that grandparents could collect a few small items to give to each grandchild during the visit. Perhaps these little gifts would be given out one each day to ease a stressful time, such as while buckling a child into the car seat or when at a restaurant; or maybe you'd like to make it part of a morning or after-nap wake-up ritual. Making a sweet moment out of an awkward experience, when done as a routine or reward rather than a promised bribe, is a perfect way to say to your grandchild that you are celebrating each day you are with them.

Should I Stay or Should I Go? Handling—and Preventing—Problems

Sometimes events seem to conspire against us. In one family's experience, as soon as Grandpa arrived, little Bobby showed his first chicken pox—"just like my friend Evan's at nursery school." Within a day, the family was busy nursing two little spotted children.

What happens when children become sick, or if you fall ill during your stay? It all depends on the parenting style and personalities of the parents you're visiting. Perhaps if your little ones are under the weather, you can lend a hand with household chores, or take over the babysitter's job for a few days while Mom and Dad scramble to arrange for time away from work. But it's important that you be honest with yourself about how much child care and housework you can handle. These are physically and emotionally demanding jobs that might require more energy than you have. Let the parents know how you feel so that no resentment is fostered on either side. Even if you can't help full-time, you might do as Mary Fulreader, of Fairport, New York, suggests: create a "comfort box" for sick grandchildren that contains a few special toys and books.

If you fall seriously ill with something contagious or truly debilitating during your stay, it's probably best to head for home. No parent wants a young child exposed to anything other than the sniffles. You might talk to your little ones and reassure them that you will be fine. Promise to send fun messages and games by mail to make up for the lost time together. Hopefully you'll be able to return soon and resume the fun. Meanwhile, you can flip to chapters 3 and 7 for some between-visit ideas.

They've Got the Bad Weather Blues . . . Doo-Wah

It's been raining for days. The grandchildren are walking around like zombies whining "I'm bored" and glaring at you because they think *you're* the reason they can't go to a friend's house.

Well, who says you have to grouch along with your little grumpsters? Instead, with the Mom and Dad's blessing, try making a theme out of whatever's causing the problem. Beat back the rainy-day blues by painting with sponges or toothbrushes. Go for a walk in that rain and find items for a wet collage or building project—or some snails that can trail first through some water colored with food coloring and then track across a paper. You could even toss that little one in the tub with some safe items from the kitchen (ice-cube trays and measuring cups are always a hit) and make getting wet part of the fun.

If snow is keeping you in, you could make snowcones or do some ice-cube painting (paint with cubes of frozen tempera paint or food coloring—just watch out for stains with the latter). Cut "snowflakes" out of paper and hang them from the ceiling so they dangle at different, low levels around the room. Or join your little ones in "skiing" or "skating" around the house with cardboard skis or skates strapped on; a scarf or mittens can add to the fun. (Check out "Dazzling Snowflakes," p. 141, for another wintertime idea.)

You can even make the blues into a theme all by itself. Put on some favorite blues music and get out all blue art materials. Practice making "sad," "grouchy," and "goofy" faces with your grandtoddlers—that'll make you all smile for sure. You can top it all off with a blue snack, courtesy of food coloring. If that doesn't cure them from their grouchy ways, nothing will (except maybe the opportunity to give Grandma or Grandpa a wild hairdo with every barrette and bauble in the box—save this one for when you're really desperate!).

A Bond that Never Breaks

Melody McCall of Plainsboro, New Jersey, shared that no matter how long it has been since the last visit, "It's amazing, interesting, and wonderful to see that that deep feeling for each other is still there." With a laugh, she said we should write that "all those grandparents who are not real good at getting across the country to visit—never fear—when you do reconnect it will be as though you had just been together the day before."

Perhaps it already seems as magical to you as it does to us, but the truth remains the same: a healthy connection between grandparents and grandchildren can survive even long separations.

Knowing that this special bond exists can be an extra incentive to keep the love going between visits. Margaret Grubb of Silver Spring, Maryland, wrote, "I try to remember to always wear the same perfume when I visit the grandchildren so that they will be reminded by that scent of our being together." One terrific aspect of Margaret's idea is that it can be continued long-distance; she only has to spritz on a bit of her favorite scent and even an young toddler will realize a letter is from her Bubbie. Your own unique variation of ideas you'll find throughout this book will help you foster a growing relationship that doesn't just survive separations but makes the best of them.

We're Here . . . Again!

For grandparents who visit their grandchildren frequently, establishing traditions can seem effortless. You can take advantage of your geographical closeness and nurture the wonderful selfless nature of children by developing ways in which they can reciprocate your love. Think especially of open-ended ideas that simply give your grandchild a springboard for their own innovations. If, for example, you always have a special place in your home for a grandchild to keep their, things (and for you to hide surprises), try asking your grandchild's parents to designate a drawer or box so that you, too, might have a chance to receive delightful handmade notes from your little ones.

If you visit often, there is also the advantage of not feeling the pressure to make each moment memorable; your grandchild will be fortunate enough to remember you as part of many experiences that you'll share. But that doesn't mean that you can't enhance your visits with some exciting ideas or traditions-in-progress. We're pretty sure that no little one will mind being read to from the same special book each time you tuck her in for the night—and that shared photo album you create together will always be a favorite. Keep your resolve to energize your time with your grandchildren with new creative ideas, and you'll be remembered as the grandparent you always hoped to be.

"He Was Always There"

A friend from New York City, Susan Greenberg, wrote us this touching note: "The thing I remember about Grandpa more than anything else was his *always* being there. . . . At every school function—every play, every concert, every birthday party, every holiday—[he and Grandma] were there. When I got sick and had to be taken home from school or had to go to the doctor, if Mom and Dad weren't around to take me, Grandpa and Grandma were." There's something about the constancy of nearby grandparents that adds a unique and loving foundation to any child's life. If you've ever wondered whether your continual but not-so-showy efforts make a difference to your little one, let Susan's words reassure you. She speaks for many grandchildren whose grandparents have added wisdom and support to their everyday worlds.

Hit the Deck, Gramps!

As a frequent visitor, you're more likely to see all the moods and nuances as your grandchildren develop and grow. One sidelight to this is that you're likely to be in the line of fire at least once during a grumpy day—just because your occasionally ouchy little one feels that comfortable around you. Luckily, you'll also have had an opportunity to see your grandchild and his or her parents interact through good times and bad. Being an attentive observer to these moments will give you insight about how you might handle discipline issues. In any case, try to keep your cool, understand that this too will pass, and take action to keep everyone safe (and property intact). And ask that waiter for a doggie bag if you can holler over the din—no need to waste completely that special dinner out!

Lights, Camera, Action! Documenting the Fun

Let's face facts. Your memory, though often passable, is getting a bit loopy. And we all know that, to a child, a month is like a lifetime—and the months between visits can seem an eternity. Although the love between you will certainly outlast these trials, think of how rewarding it will be for both you and your grandchild to secure these memories with a special project.

Just Bookin' Along

You're going to read many variations of this idea throughout our book because we think a passion for the written word is something worth nurturing in grandchildren. It's also a perfect activity for a visiting grandparent and a grandchild age two or older to work on together. The activity idea is simply to create your own book of adventures depicting real or imagined things that you did with each other. (A combination of actual and fantasy is also fun—after all, that swing at the playground did seem to go up to the sun after your big push, didn't it?) You might try taking dictation of the story as it occurred in your grandchild's imagination and create pages that have one line at the bottom of a page—leaving the rest of the page for him to color. Or make the words that you copy take on a shape of their own. A spiraled tale of a snail's shell or a narrative that literally circles the moon just as your little astronaut thinks he did makes the story's writing come alive.

Video Mania

Grandparenting and pictures go together like peanut butter and jelly. We seem to be the only ones at times with hands free and the presence of mind to take along that still or movie camera. This added wisdom is especially nice during visits to a grandchild's home. Stop by nursery school early and take photos of your grandson in action, or linger after playgroup has started to get some adorable snapshots of your grandtoddler with her friends. Your grandbaby's "tummy surfing" to the theme of *Sesame Street* will be the sort of memory that few parents will stop to capture, but it will be a super addition to the family movie collection. Becoming the documentarian of what's usual in your grandchildren's home is uniquely rewarding because you know that parents often can't get those everyday moments, but will love to tell stories and see pictures of them during later years. And don't forget to include yourself in photos—with the help of your generous helper or a timer on your camera—so that you'll always be remembered as the important part of your young grandchild's life that you are.

Collecting Memories

While immersing yourself in the interests and goals of your grandchild, you might find that some patterns emerge. As a toddler, Nick had a passion for one thing at a time, for about a month at a time. Perhaps your little ones will get a kick out of colored leaves during the fall or develop an interest in the different stamps that arrive by mail. Knowing this, by being an attentive and relaxed grandparent, means that you can respond by starting a collection with your grandbuddy that really reflects his or her interests. With two pieces of wax paper and an old iron, you can preserve those leaves through the winter in a book or as a mobile dangling over your grandchild's head.

Stamps can be cut and pasted one to a page, with space left for a grandchild to extend the design onto the rest of the paper. Whatever your variation, the essence of the idea is the same: by responding playfully to your little one's interests, you can become a greater part of his or her world.

One of the most rewarding aspects of collecting with your grandchild is that the collection itself is often perfect for long-distance loving. Any small collectible that interests your grandchild can be continued as a theme. The important thing is to keep the fun going and to build on the good memories you created during your visit. Like an inside joke, these commonalities can keep a relationship between grandchild and grandparent thriving even if you live far apart.

Packing Up: Forgetful Guests Are Best

One of our favorite Grandpas was, well, messy. He had lemon drops in every dresser drawer in his farmhouse, and his barn was teeming with what we thought of as wildlife—newborn kittens in the hay, slithery bugs under every stone, and cow patties in every field. It was grandchild heaven.

Please don't get us wrong. Those cow patties cannot—and probably should not—be a part of every grandparent's repertoire at home or away. But there's simply no reason you should remember everything when you leave a grandchild's home. Try "forgetting" a well-loved scarf or some clunky shoes; leave behind a trail of fun pens, envelopes, and stickers. You'll smile all the way home imagining your little one playing dress-up or "mail carrier" with your things, and your grandchild will be thrilled to tell you over the phone about all the things he or she unearthed after you left. Forgetful herself, your little person will know for sure that she's found a kindred spirit in you.

Something You'll Never Forget

It's the last day. Time to pull back, pack up, and think of tomorrow at your home. Or is it? Instead, it could be time to cuddle up, throw things in a bag, and think of one special "gift" you received from each grandchild—something that you could make the most of with a thoughtful remembrance in return. The toothless smile from baby Randy; the exuberant hug from your feisty little Linda; the amazing city you made from blocks with growing David—if these memories touched your heart, it's time to think of a way to show your grandchild how meaningful these moments are to you. If you have some derring-do with drawing, you might try making a T-shirt for each grandchild with fabric markers or crayons. Or try leaving a warm and thoughtful note in the capable hands of a favorite teddy. Just be sure to recognize that your departure is a time for appreciating the special visit you've shared.

Looking Ahead—and How!

One creative grandparent we know gave each preschool-age grandchild a pair of "magic" toilet-paper-tube binoculars when she left their home. If they peered through the plastic wrap very, very carefully, she told them, they might be able to imagine her in her home thinking of neat things to do during their next visit together. Her playful fantasy glasses were just right for this age group. Not bound by what can actually happen, young grandchildren enjoy an imaginary world where, if you're clever enough to enter, you'll enjoy a fantastical relationship that complements and enriches those real experiences that can be limited by long distances.

You, too, can join in the fun of your grandchild's creative adventures just as this grandmother has. Let yourself loose and really come to understand your grandchildren in their environment when you're visiting. It's a wonderful world of play and learning that will bridge the miles that may separate your hands, but never your hearts.

Body Double

Maybe you'll even be allowed to take this life-sized replica of your beloved little one home with you!

Ages: Two years and up
You'll Need to Tuck in Your Suitcase
- Large sheet of paper
- Crayon or marker
- Colored construction paper
- Scissors

Here's How
- Have your grandchild lie down on the large sheet of paper and then trace all the way around your little darling.
- Cut out the life-sized body double and turn your grandchild loose with the crayons and construction paper to "clothe" and decorate the body.
- Be sure to hang it up for all to admire.

You might want to make this an annual ritual—what fun to see the growth from year to year!

Paintless Painting

Introduce your enterprising painter to the joys of no-mess, outside water painting!

Ages: Eighteen months to five years
You'll Need to Tuck in Your Suitcase
- A large paintbrush

Here's How
- Fill a large bucket or pan with water.
- Hunt for fun things to paint outside with the water such as the house, the sidewalk, rocks, a tricycle, bricks, etc.
- Watching things darken as they get wet and lighten as they dry will delight your enterprising painter!

Card Creations

Save that incomplete deck of cards for some great construction projects.

Ages: Three years and up

You'll Need to Tuck in Your Suitcase
- The incomplete deck of cards
- A handful of plastic straws

Here's How
- Cut the straws into 2" lengths.
- Cut two 1/2" slits in both ends of each straw piece.
- Slip the cards into the straw "connectors" and construct away!

Tub Tile Art

Finger painting was never so much fun, and you're going to love the way this one cleans up!

Ages: Eighteen months to five years

You'll Need to Tuck in Your Suitcase
- An envelope of unflavored gelatin
- Bag of 1/2 cup cornstarch
- Food coloring

Here's How
- Soak the gelatin in 1/4 cup cold water.
- Stir the cornstarch into 3/4 cup cold water.
- Bring 2 cups water to a boil and then slowly pour it into the cornstarch mixture, stirring constantly. Bring this to a boil over medium heat and cook and stir until the mixture is thick and clear.
- Add and stir in the dissolved gelatin.
- When cool, pour into separate containers—a foam egg carton

works beautifully—and add a few drops of food coloring to each well.

- Fill up the tub and turn 'em loose.
- Though the artistic efforts won't last, it'll be a snap to clean it all up, and with the promise that they can do it again another night, no one will mind when it's all washed down the drain!

Balloons to the Rescue

You might pull this idea out when it's raining outside and your grandchildren need to work off a little steam inside.

Ages: Three to eight years
You'll Need to Tuck in Your Suitcase
- Balloons
- Markers to decorate the balloons
- Yarn or string

Here's How
- Have your grandchildren personalize their balloons with the markers.
- With the string or yarn, create a start and finish line.
- Join your grandchildren on the floor on "all fours," and count down to the start.
- Have a blowing race to see who can make their balloon cross the finish line first—no hands allowed!

Remember, younger children can suffocate on balloon pieces. Keep balloons away from little ones who still nibble everything they hold.

Grandpa's Shaving-Cream Creations

Gleeful giggles and a memory of fun with Grandpa are guaranteed with this one!

Ages: Two to five years
You'll Need to Tuck in Your Suitcase
- Grandpa's shaving cream

Here's How
- A high-chair tray or a large cookie sheet makes the perfect table for this activity.
- You could even add a few drops food coloring to the sweet smelling, billowy mound of shaving cream.
- Let your little darling experience the smooth, irresistible feel of gliding it around the tray.
- This can be a super activity for bath time, or try finger painting on a mirror and play "peek-a-boo."
- Be sure to encourage use of fingers, knuckles, palms, fists, and toes!
- Try warming the shaving cream in a pan of hot water for a soothing experience.

Be sure the shaving cream stays out of the eyes, and thoroughly wash hands when through.

Listen, Listen, What Do You Hear?

Did you ever notice how one sense is magnified when another sense is shut out? You won't have to pack a thing to take this fun activity to your grandchild's home.

Ages: Eighteen months to five years
Here's How
- Go on a listening walk through the neighborhood together.
- As you hold your grandchild's hand, have him close his eyes and tell you all the things he hears.
- Is a bird singing, the wind whistling through the trees, a siren sounding in the distance, a church bell ringing, or a car honking its horn?

Rub, Rub, Rub

You don't have to go to Europe to enjoy making rubbings with your grandchild!

Ages: Two-and-a-half years and up
You'll Need
- Crayons
- Paper
- Objects to rub. Look for interesting textures on flat objects: ferns, leaves, keys, combs, bricks, burlap, a sea fan, coins, straw placemats, feathers, etc.

Here's How
- Lay the object flat underneath the paper.
- Using the side of a crayon held flat, rub until the object appears. Your young artists will love this project!

Wintertime Sandbox

When the snows have covered the sandbox, never fear—Grandpa's here with the ideal indoor solution.

Ages: One to five years
You'll Need
- Uncooked oatmeal or graham cracker crumbs from Mom and Dad's cupboard

Here's How
- Dust off the small summer sandbox cars and bulldozers.
- Dump the oatmeal or cracker crumb "sand" into a large high-sided cookie sheet and watch your construction crew move mountains right in the kitchen.

Inspiration from Above

Take time not only to smell the flowers with your grandchild but also to watch the clouds as they form their magic.

Ages: Two years and up
You'll Need
- A day with billowy white clouds
- Your imagination

Here's How
- Lie flat on your back with your little one.
- Let your imaginations take you into the land of billowy beauties and beasties.
- This is a wonderful springboard for off-the-cuff storytelling.

Puppets in the Palm

Puppetry provides endless hours of creative fun, and this tiny puppet is sure to delight even your antsiest grandtoddler.

Ages: One to eight years
You'll Need to Tuck in Your Suitcase
- An old cotton glove
- A small paper cup
- Yarn, paper scraps, and glue

Here's How
- Have your grandchild help you decorate the puppet face on the cup, gluing the yarn for hair.
- The glove becomes the puppet's body and the cup sits on the three middle fingers. Your thumb and pinkie become the puppet's arms.

Marvelous Masking Tape

Save the day with package or masking tape—the ultimate in toddler toys!

Ages: Six months to five years
You'll Need to Tuck in Your Suitcase
- A roll of masking, package, or drafting tape

Here's How
- You can easily make removable car or train tracks on the carpet or floor in thirty seconds or less.
- Another day, try taping a paper cape or butterfly wings on your favorite thespian; or simply give a fussy wee one a sticky ball to play with during an impatient moment in the car.

Marionettes on Stage

Any stuffed animal can become a dancing marionette with a little help from Grandma or Grandpa!

Ages: One to eight years
You'll Need to Tuck in Your Suitcase
- Stuffed animal—or just borrow one from your grandchild
- String
- Sticks or paper towel tubes

Here's How
- Suspend strings from the sticks or tubes.
- Tie the animal's arms and legs as shown.
- Then by merely tilting the stick or tubes you can teach your grandchild how to make the marionette dance.

Banana Mash Magic

Harness some of your grandchild's youthful energy to make yummy, nutritious frozen pops!

Ages: Three years and up
You'll Need
- Ripe bananas
- A large bowl
- A potato masher
- Miniature paper cups

Here's How
- Your grandchildren will love peeling and mashing the bananas into a smooth puree.
- Have your little helpers spoon the puree into the small cups.
- Freeze and they'll have a healthful, refreshing snack to enjoy.

Try this with other fruits too!

Everything's Edible

You won't have to worry about your "everything goes in the mouth" stage grandchild with this one!

Ages: Six months to two years
You'll Need Any of the Following
- Soft, almost-set gelatin
- Pudding
- Tapioca
- Yogurt
- Whipped cream
- Cooked, cooled oatmeal
- Cooked, cooled Cream of Wheat
- A bib or smock

Here's How
- High chairs or a cookie sheet in the back yard are perfect spots for this fingerpainting activity.
- Tie on the bib and listen to the squeals of delight as your grandchildren "food paint" and get gooey!

Edible Jewels

You've undoubtedly seen these in the stores, but your little ones will enjoy them even more than the store-bought ones if you make them together.

Ages: Three to five years
You'll Need to Tuck in Your Suitcase
- Cheerios or other cereals with a hole in the middle
- Miniature marshmallows
- A large plastic needle and clean, white string

Here's How
- String the various pieces of food onto the string.
- If the food lasts long enough, your "jeweler" will end up with a bracelet or necklace to wear!

Be careful that your grandchild's necklace doesn't get tangled or caught on something while worn.

Bean Bag Fun

The old-fashioned bean bag is still a winner with the younger set, so tuck a few in your suitcase before you leave home!

Ages: Two to five years
You'll Need to Tuck in Your Suitcase
- Bean bags—inexpensive or simple to make!

Here's How
- See who will be first to get a "ringer" by trying to throw a bean bag into a large kitchen pot in the center of the floor.
- Try "bean bag bocce" and see who can come closest to the first bean bag tossed.
- Set up a few tin can "bowling pins" and see who can knock over the most with one throw.
- Create a "target zone" about six feet away by outlining a large diamond on the floor with tape. Then see who can land their bag inside the diamond.

We're sure you and your grandchild will come up with more bean bag games—send us your ideas!

The "Think-a-Lot" Scavenger Hunt

Scavenger hunts can be fun with even your youngest grandchildren if you join them in making and finding a list of "something" items.

Ages: Three years and up

You'll Need
- Pencil and paper
- Bags to hold the found objects
- Your imaginations

Here's How
- Use this list or create your own such as:
  - Something that feels slippery
  - Something round
  - Something that floats
  - Something hairy
  - Something you could eat
  - Something that never grows or gets smaller
  - Something that makes a sound
  - Something that feels rough
  - Something square
  - Something that smells sweet
  - Something you can see through
  - Something you step on
  - Something green
  - Something soft
  - Something wet
- Off you go to see how many things you can find that fit the "something" description!
- This takes a lot more imagination and is a lot more fun than just hunting for a specific list of items!

Abracadabra, What's Missing?

Your little "whiz-kid" grandchild will love the challenge of this game.

Ages: Two to six years
You'll Need
- A large tray or cookie sheet
- A collection of objects—kitchen utensils, pencil, ruler, small plastic toys, anything that your grandchild can name and that will fit on the tray
- A towel or small blanket large enough to cover the objects

Here's How
- Enlist your grandchild's help in collecting an assortment of objects to use, and then arrange them on the tray.
- Give him a minute or two to "study" the tray.
- Cover the objects with the towel.
- Ask your little "whiz-kid" to close his eyes while you remove one or more objects.
- With a flourish say something like "abracadabra, peanut butter sandwiches!" and remove the covering.
- Your grandchild can then open his eyes and try to guess what you took away.
- Taking turns can be fun too.

Snow Maze

When the winter snows have fallen and you're feeling claustrophobic, take your little cherubs outside for some run-around fun.

Ages: Four years and up
You'll Need
- Boots
- Fresh snow

Here's How
- Be the first outside to stamp out a maze in the snow.
- You might build a "snow king" or "snow queen" at the end to welcome the first one who makes it through your maze.

"Chase-less" Indoor Catch

Toddlers and young grandchildren love to play catch with a caring grandparent. Here's a way to make sure the ball always comes right back.

Ages: Eighteen months to three years

You'll Need to Tuck in Your Suitcase
- A sponge rubber ball (nerf brand works well)
- 6 feet of long string
- A thumb tack

Here's How
- Before leaving home, thread the string with a large darning needle through the center of the ball and tie a knot at its end.
- At your grandchild's house, center the free end of the string at the top of an inside doorway molding, and carefully tack it down.
- With your grandchild on one side of the doorway and you on the other, toss the ball back and forth to your gleeful little one.

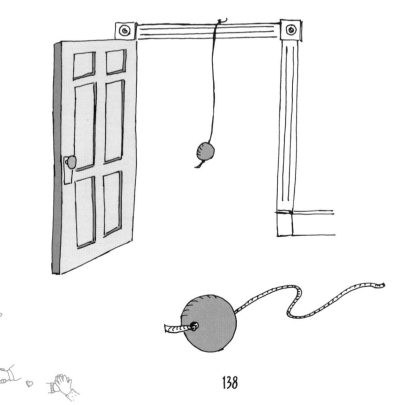

Listen Well and Then Tell

Our generation learned the art of listening from tuning in to the radio, but today's youngsters are bombarded with so much stimulation that they often don't have the ability to focus without something to look at. You can have fun while helping them develop this skill with the following games. You won't need anything except your time.

Ages: Three to eight years

Listen and Tell

Here's How
- Have your grandchildren close their eyes.
- Ask them to listen to what you are doing to see if they can tell without looking.
- Try running the water, turning on the fan, closing the door, dialing the telephone, and so on.

Simon Says

Here's How
- Remember Simon Says? Your grandchildren will love it as much as you did!
- They are to follow your instructions to "touch your head" or "bend your knee" only when these instructions are prefaced with "Simon Says."
- They'll learn to listen closely!

That Doesn't Belong

Here's How
- Have fun with categories.
- Tell your grandchildren to clap when they notice you've mentioned an item that doesn't belong!
- You might start with something simple such as: "red, blue, green, yellow, purple, mother, white, brown."
- Or try "dog, cat, pig, cow, train, donkey."
- If the grandchildren are listening well, they'll clap their hands as soon as you say, "mother" or, in the second example, "train."

What Does That Feel Like?

Learning to "feel" things and determine what they are without looking makes a great game.

Ages: Two to five years
You'll Need to Tuck in Your Suitcase
- A paper bag or pillowcase

Here's How
- Collect some objects that will fit in the bag or pillowcase and that are familiar to your grandchild such as a ball, crayon, wooden block, stuffed animal, spoon, cup, book, etc.
- With eyes closed, have your grandchild pull out one object and "feel" it without peeking.
- When she guesses correctly (with the help of a few hints from Grandpa or Grandma if needed), she can open her eyes to see!

Sticky Sock Sketch

A fun spring or summertime activity is to take an "old sock nature walk."

Ages: Eighteen months and up
You'll Need to Tuck in Your Suitcase
- Two pairs of old cotton sweat socks
- A small magnifying glass

Here's How
- You and your little cherub can put on the old cotton socks and run around outside to see what will stick to the bottoms.
- Use the magnifying glass to inspect the burrs, twigs, and treasures you've gathered.
- It might be fun to make a collage of your treasures—or to try planting some of the seeds that stick. Just put some damp potting soil in the sock, spritz with water, and set in a baking pan—keeping it moist until sprouts appear.

Dazzling Snowflakes

If you'll be visiting your grandchild during a snowy time, you might have the thrill of being the first one to introduce your curious little one to the beauty of snowflakes.

Ages: Eighteen months to five years
You'll Need to Tuck in Your Suitcase
- A piece of black paper
- A small magnifying glass

Here's How
- Chill the black paper for about twenty minutes in the freezer.
- Take your paper outside and let a few snowflakes settle on it.
- Introduce your grandchild to the wonders of snowflake crystals with the magnifying glass. Hold your breath while you look!

Peanut Butter Pinecones

As soon as your nature lover can hold a small butter spreader, she'll enjoy making this simple bird feeder and watching all the birds that come to visit.

Ages: Two to eight years
You'll Need to Tuck in Your Suitcase
- A jar of peanut butter
- A butter spreader
- A pinecone (or better yet, find one on a walk together!)

Here's How
- Be prepared for gooey fingers, but it's okay for your grandchild to lick them!
- Using the spreader, have your grandchild smear peanut butter onto the pinecone.
- Roll the cone in birdseed and hang it outside near a window for good viewing from inside.
- Be prepared to attract a few squirrels as well as birds!
- This can provide a good conversation piece when you are back home and are talking with your granddaughter or grandson. Find out who has been "visiting" the feeder since your visit!

Queen Anne's Lace Fit for Royalty

You've watched celery soak up colored water, but have you tried it with wild, feathery Queen Anne's lace? Your grandchildren will have to wait overnight to see the results, but the magical effect is worth it.

Ages: Two to eight years
You'll Need to Tuck in Your Suitcase
- Some colored crepe paper

Here's How
- Fill jars with water and add one color of crepe paper to each jar. Watching the colored crepe paper turn the water into gorgeous colors will be half the fun.
- This might be a fun time to experiment with mixing yellow and blue to make green, red and yellow to make orange, etc.
- When the water has reached a deep color, remove the crepe paper and discard.
- Enjoy an afternoon walk with your grandchildren gathering the Queen Anne's lace flowers in a field or along the roadside. These wild flowers wilt quickly, so keep your walk short.
- When you return home, immediately put the stems in the jars of colored water.
- In the morning, your little ones will be amazed to see that their feathery white flowers have turned colors.

Tea for Two

Letting the sun do the "brewing" can help your little hostess feel grown up while learning to appreciate the power of the sun.

Ages: Three to eight years
You'll Need to Tuck in Your Suitcase
- Two herbal tea bags

Here's How
- Have your little hostess fill a glass jar with two cups of water.
- Add the two tea bags, cover the jar, and set it in the sun for four hours.
- Add some ice, sugar, and lemon or lime slices if she wishes.
- Enjoy your "Tea for Two" party.

Hoops-a-Fun

Turn those Styrofoam plates into great games in the pool or tub.

Ages: Two to eight years
You'll Need to Tuck in Your Suitcase
- Two Styrofoam plates
- Tape
- A ping-pong or foam ball

Here's How
- Cut the middle out of both plates and tape the resulting "hoops" together without nesting them . . . they should look like a tire rim.
- Float in the lake or pool, or tape to the tile above the tub for basketball practice and hoops-a-fun!

Cool Cubes

Jazz up those summer drinks with fruity cubes that are easy enough for a two-year-old to make.

Ages: Two years and up
You'll Need
- Fruit juice
- Pieces of fruit: strawberries, melon balls, lemon, lime or orange slices, etc.
- An ice cube tray

Here's How
- Put a piece of fruit in each tray section.
- Pour juice over the fruit.
- Freeze until firm, pour those summer drinks, and "ice-em-up" with your cool cubes!

 # Magic Movers

Magnets hold a real fascination for every little scientist!

Ages: Two to eight years
You'll Need to Tuck in Your Suitcase

- Walnut shell halves
- Twist ties—the type with wire in the middle
- A magnet

Here's How
- Glue three twist ties across the bottom of a shell and when dry bend them up like legs.
- You can decorate the walnut halves if you wish—paint them red with black spots to create a lady bug, paint them all black to make a spider, etc.
- Have your little scientist hold the magnet under a box with the walnut creature on top of the box.
- As he moves the magnet, the creature will "magically" move right along with the magnet.

 # Tickle Pictures

This is a good game to try at bedtime because it has a calming effect.

Ages: Eighteen months and up
You'll Need
- Each other

Here's How
- With your finger, "draw" simple picture shapes, or letters or numbers for the older grandchild, on his back.
- See if he can guess what you are drawing—it just might feel so good that you'll hear, "Do it again, Grandma" even when he knows the answer!

Open the Gates and Watch 'Em Run

Indoors that is! Be sure to get down and play this one with your "little horses"; they'll love the competition.

Ages: Three years and up
You'll Need to Tuck in Your Suitcase
- Toilet tissue paper
- Shirt cardboards
- Washable marker
- Yarn or string

Here's How
- Each person takes one square of toilet paper and colors a number or name on his or her "horse."
- Set a start and finish line with the yarn or string.
- Using the shirt cardboards as fans, see who can fan his or her "horse" across the finish line first.

Heads or Tails?

Let your flipped coin be your guide on a "heads we go right, tails we go left" walk.

Ages: Two years and up
You'll Need
- A coin to flip
- A place to walk

Here's How
- Stretch those legs and discover the neighborhood while having fun with this one!
- Decide you'll take a hike, and at each corner flip your coin. If heads shows up, go right; if tails shows up, go left.
- You may discover some new sights—just remember how to get home!

Abracadabra: Power Lifter

We guarantee you'll impress your little fellows with this one, Gramps!

Ages: Three years and up

You'll Need to Tuck in Your Suitcase
- A piece of yarn about 8" long
- 1/8 tsp salt

Here's How
- Challenge your little fellows to remove the ice cube from your glass of water without getting their fingers wet!
- Lay one end of the piece of yarn on top of the floating ice cube.
- Sprinkle the ice cube with the salt and let stand for five minutes.
- Carefully yet with great flourish pronounce "abracadabra: power lifter" as you lift the ice with the free end of yarn—the other end will have become frozen into the ice cube.
- When your little fellows see how easily you do it, you'll be a real "cool" magician in their eyes!

Fun with Foaming Magic

Your bubbling budding magician can impress his pals with this "magic trick."

Ages: Four years and up
You'll Need
- Baking soda
- White vinegar

Here's How
- Have your bubbly magician stir 3 teaspoons of baking soda into a glass half full of water.
- Fill a second glass half full of white vinegar.
- Put newspaper under the two glasses and carefully pour the vinegar into the baking soda mixture to create the "foaming magic."

See Lincoln's Bright and Shiny Face?

Create a little magic as you use vinegar to shine up Lincoln's face!

Ages: Three years and up
You'll Need to Tuck in Your Suitcase
- 20 old, dirty copper pennies
- A clean iron nail

Here's How
- Have your little polisher fill the bottom quarter of a jar with vinegar and a few shakes of salt from Mom and Dad's cupboard.
- Add the dirty copper pennies and let them sit for several minutes.
- Add the iron nail to the pennies and let it all sit for about 15 minutes.
- The nail will become coated with the dirt, and Lincoln's face on the pennies will be as bright and shiny as your grandchild's!

Swinging Salt

This is a fascinating art/science project you'll want to do again and again.

Ages: Two to eight years

You'll Need to Tuck in Your Suitcase
- A small funnel
- A large sheet of black paper and a piece of construction paper
- String
- A small plastic bag of salt

Here's How
- Cut a circle out of the construction paper big enough to form a cone shape inside the funnel. Allow a small hole to remain at the very tip of the cone and tape the side shut.
- Insert the cone in the funnel.
- Tie the string around the lip of the funnel.
- Then tie three equal lengths of string onto the string around the funnel's lip and space them evenly (see diagram).
- Suspend it from a light fixture or cupboard door so that it is about 2" from the table or floor on which you've put the large sheet of black paper.
- Hold the tip of the funnel with your fingertip while your little one fills the funnel with salt.
- Take your finger away and gently push the funnel.
- The salt flowing from the swinging funnel will create an interesting pattern.
- When the swinging stops, dump the salt back in and try again . . . you'll never see the same pattern twice!

6
Heartfelt Holidays and Family Traditions

Few of us will admit, but most of us realize, that remembering childhood can now be easier than recalling what we were supposed to get at the supermarket. Why is this so? Our theory (and handy excuse) is that nature is preparing us for better grandparenting. After all, the essence of building a good relationship with a young child is remembering a bit of what it was like to be that small, that powerless, that eager about the world. Remembering the broccoli for tonight's dinner seems much less essential, don't you think?

If our theory is true, then having a selective memory gives you a special responsibility to your youngest family members, especially during the holidays. Think back to what made your family holidays special. The smells of gingerbread and the jingle of bells on stockings at Christmas; the warm glow of candlelight and happy songs of Hanukkah; Uncle Ed's incredible appetite at Thanksgiving and the clink of dishes being washed afterward; the light giggles of bewitching little merrymakers at Halloween. It's the camaraderie of good friends and family and the reassuring familiarity of common rituals that make a holiday special, and these are elements that you can help recreate for your grandchildren as well.

All Under One Roof

For most of us, holidays mean a reunion of family and friends—a long-awaited gathering of people who love each other and are seldom all in one place. Just getting caught up on the news and feelings of long-missed children, grandchildren, and friends can seem to fill an entire visit. But it can be very special as well to create some new traditions and memorable heirlooms to remind everyone of the love you share.

> Remember your roots,
>
> They will give you courage
>
> To choose your dreams,
>
> Wisdom to choose your path,
>
> And wings to fly.
>
> —*Anonymous*

Welcome, Family!

Imagine how delighted and loved you would feel if, after trekking hundreds of miles home for the holidays, you found a homemade banner on the door to welcome you. This feeling is the inspiration for our many welcome signs. Simply take a big piece of paper and draw and label a picture of everyone who is coming home. We draw them peeking cheerily out of windows in our house, or waving from airplanes, buses, trains, or cars as they pull in. You don't have to be an artist to make a heartfelt banner, and you especially don't have to be very creative to add the most important part: a "Welcome Home!" in big, inviting letters.

In our family, small notes are also left on a dresser in each grown child's—or young family's—room telling them how delighted we are that they have come. The appeal of this ritual is contagious: we started finding crayoned thank you notes tucked under our pillows after the young families returned home.

Saving Precious Moments from the Start

Don't let the memory-making stop at your front door, however. Instead, try to document the experiences and your common history throughout the visit. "The most important thing we ever shared," wrote Patricia McKenzie from Hampton, New Hampshire, "was one hour with each of four grandparents in front of the VCR camera (one at a time) as they answered a list of questions about their childhoods, families, school careers, hobbies, talents, dreams, and travels. Reflections on their own parenting trials, [Great] Depression, war, family traditions, favorite gift given and received, feelings on retirement, grandparenting, death. My ten-year-old held the camera and my seven-year-old helped ask some of the questions. This tape is now our most treasured family heirloom. We have the original in the safe deposit box and made copies for all the cousins for Christmas. Even our reticent Grandma complied and was so glad and proud that she did." To make your own video history, see the activity "Memory Movies" on page 189.

In our own family, one set of grandparents always took our photos on Mother's Day in front of a special tree at a local park. If you take a similar family photo each year, you'll see the growth of the tree as well as of the family over the years—and chuckle at how your once-tiny grandson outpaced even a blue spruce during his teens.

Signatures and handprints are other precious items to save. Have everyone sign the tablecloth after a holiday meal with pencil (for later embroidering), or with colorful fabric markers. Family groups can trace hands on tablecloths or on fabric squares for a quilt and give the result to the grandparents to save.

When You Have to Be Apart

For many of us, holidays are spent with smaller groups of family members and friends. Perhaps our children have moved far from home, or perhaps this year other commitments make it hard for some of our loved ones to come. We've had our share of these holiday experiences, too, and know that some of the energy and love you feel is refocused toward sending packages and waiting for holiday messages—especially from your grandchildren.

You can still wrap up some of that extra holiday love, however. Take the time to be creative, even with your packing materials. Cushion your box with things that can become art in the right little hands. Enclose instructions with your package about how to transform your crumpled tissue paper into a mosaic or tissue flowers; how to turn your packing bubbles into an easy-to-do "bubble print"; or how to reshape your crumpled newspaper into a papier-mâché form (see "Package Fun: Tiny Tissue Balls," p. 175, "Package Fun: Bubble Wrap Prints," p. 169, and "Papier-Mâché Inspirations," p. 172). And you can always sprinkle in among the packing some love notes from you to your little one.

Your gift card, too, can make you memorable. Our friend Gittan Tollgard, from Ekero, Sweden, told us about a Swedish custom: each gift is personalized with a lighthearted poem on a card that partially reveals the contents of the package. We have tried this, too, and it can be a lot of fun. In fact, it's an especially nice way to capture the interest of preschoolers who love rhymes—and to keep them from unwrapping everything quite as quickly as they otherwise might.

Another sure way to keep your grandchildren in mind and heart, even if they're not able to come, is to do as Nancy and Jim Van Metre of Alexandria, Virginia, have done. Nancy wrote: "I needleworked stockings for every member of the family this year. The stockings will stay at our house to be discovered whenever they visit during the holidays. No matter where they are, their stocking will be hung at our house so that they are in our minds during this time." These days, when jobs and schooling can scatter families thousands of miles apart, little gestures like this can make a world of difference to your family.

Celebrating on a Different Day

Holidays are about sharing—and good food, gifts, time, and attention are just a few of the ways we share ourselves. But it can be tricky to keep in mind as well how other family members are giving of their precious time and resources. Many young families have not one, but two sets of long-distance grandparents, and they spend much of their energy during the holidays traveling. When you were a child, holidays probably meant enormous family gatherings on the exact day, because the extended family lived nearby. Now, however, smaller groups gather because families seem to have scattered—and the celebration with family can occur many days before or after the actual holiday. In these days of stress and strain on young families, how can you help your children and grandchildren feel good about their holidays? Your children will cherish most your flexibility, generosity, and understanding. If you can, offer to help pay for the costs of traveling (our family, for example, divides the "circle-route" air fares three ways among grandparents and parents). Try to avoid thinking of Thanksgiving dinner as something that has to happen on Thanksgiving Day; instead, allow it to happen when the family can gather, even if that means you're having dinner the Sunday afterward at 10 P.M. (We've done this!) If you keep family as the focus, your time with your grandchildren and grown children will be as relaxed as you had hoped it would be—no matter when it occurs.

Staying Grandchild-Oriented

Sometimes in the midst of family togetherness, the littlest children can feel left out. One cure for this is to add a grandchild-oriented twist to whatever you do. Magdalena Knaflewska told us how they accomplish this in their family: "In Poland the big Christmas Eve dinner can't begin until the youngest child in the family sees the first star in the sky." Elly and Jean Patrick Donzey from Munich, Germany, related, "If a young family doesn't have glass tree balls, the grandparents might help the grandchildren wrap chestnuts in aluminum foil or make stars out of straw to hang on the tree." And if you haven't yet tried the tradition of allowing the youngest grandchild to find the Afikomen, a small piece of unleavened bread hidden during the traditional Jewish Passover Seder, you can design your own variation of this ritual.

> Try to avoid thinking of Thanksgiving dinner as something that has to happen on Thanksgiving Day; instead, allow it to happen when the family can gather.

Kathryn Outzen McLain from Ithaca, New York, told us that in Denmark they always celebrated Christmas for four days. "Christmas Eve dinner with the roast goose stuffed with prunes and apples was always followed by a traditional dessert—which held special appeal for the grandchildren." She added, "Tradition dictates that only one almond be put into the pudding, and the lucky one to get the almond in his dessert receives the prize of a big marzipan pig. After dinner we danced around the lit Christmas tree. My mother, Anna Kristensen Outzen, felt so strongly that her American grandchildren should know their Danish heritage that she took them all back to Denmark to retrace their roots."

Good luck charms are fun for all, so toss this in your bag of tricks for other holidays as well. For example, you might put a good luck charm under one of the plates at Thanksgiving dinner, give a basket of apples for each child at Rosh Hashanah to welcome in the Jewish New Year, or as Milanda Ha from Fairport, New York, shared with us, give grandchildren an envelope of "lucky money" for the Chinese New Year.

Helen and Peter McGroary from Donegal Town, Ireland, have five grandchildren all living in the County of Donegal. Helen shared with us that "when each one was born they wore the Christening robe which has been handed down for three generations." When Helen was a child, living in a thatched-roof cottage, preparations for Christmas always included "cleaning and whitewashing the cottage from top to bottom both inside and out—even the chimney was cleaned." (No sooty Santa for them!) She said, "We follow with our grandchildren the tradition we had as children of picking holly in the woods and then using it to decorate all over the house. On Christmas Eve after a sparse meal we, like generations before us, go to the chapel to see the 'crib.'" Though the thatched roof has been replaced with a lovely modern home and the oil lamps with electricity, you can feel the warmth of family and heritage as Helen talks of how she continues the important traditions with her grandchildren.

There is a lot of work involved in hosting family during the holidays, and children will feel needed and rewarded if they can help, too. With a dishtowel apron to catch spills, your grandchild can wash the veggies, oil and flour a pan, or knead bread dough. Grandchildren also can get a kick out of setting the table for meals. One way to make cooking even more meaningful—and distinguish the contributions of each grandchild—is to designate a special serving dish for each grandchild that holds a food they helped to make. You can even include the grandchildren during the meal with family games such as "Mealtime Fun: The Gift Wrap Rap" and "Mealtime Fun: Telephone Go Round" (both on p. 181).

What is the world coming to? In your day, children were taught to behave at the table—no elbows, no gooey mess in the hair, no singing. Right? Perhaps. More likely, however, your nostalgia is showing.

Grandchildren love to decorate their world, and holidays are a time when their imaginations are in high gear. You can harness their creative energies by enlisting their help to decorate your home, too. Have them make homemade decorations to display, help put up sturdy decorations with your assistance, or design bows for a pet to wear for the celebration. We're sure any hesitation you might have now about the results will wash away when you see the enthusiasm of your grandchild and everyone's pride in your little one's efforts.

Another wonderful way to celebrate the holidays with grandchildren is to get involved in a community or social project. Preschool-age children are acutely sensitive to the needs of others and can be surprisingly enthusiastic about serving food at a soup kitchen or simply giving coins or toys to the Salvation Army. In our family, we write a thank you letter during the Thanksgiving vacation to some unsuspecting friend or organization who made a difference in our lives during the past year.

Perhaps by now you have a bedtime ritual with your grandchild that is unique to the two of you. (If you need help getting started, see chapter 4.) Now is your chance to add a little holiday fun to that routine. Check some books out of the library about your holiday. (If you're really ambitious, you can record one of your readings and the conversation you have about it with your grandchild to bring out and enjoy next year.) Leave a little love note under your little one's pillow in a holiday shape. Or sing your grandchild's favorite holiday songs in a whisper-soft, sleepy voice as a lullaby.

Making Yourself Memorable

Judy and Dan Hays, of Fairport, New York, wrote to let us know that he collects "noses" to wear when he's reading books to his grandchildren. Sue and Peter Eberhardt, also of Fairport, told us that their son Race's grandfather "has a special 'whistle' with which he always greets Race. Since he was about six months old he always associates that whistle with Papa. Now he tries to whistle to him whenever they talk on the phone." And three squeezes of a hand means "I love you" in the family of Linda Knox, of Lynnwood, Washington. Developing your own signature style with your grandchild will create a wonderful "family tradition" between the two of you, no matter how insignificant your special way of doing things seems.

You probably won't have to dream up some way of being unique—more likely, you just have to let those little endearing quirks become apparent to your grandchild. If you have a hankering for crosswords, you might leave an easy word game on your grandchild's pillow to work on alone or with you. If you have a passion for gardening, you could start a garden together or ask your grandchild to find and sprinkle some fresh spices from your garden into your food. Or perhaps you love fishing and could have an inside joke going with your grandchild about the "whoppers" you've each caught in the past. Developing your interest so that it will be fun to share across generations, regardless of whether this interest is related to a holiday theme, is the very essence of "family tradition."

How Each Generation Feels During the Holidays

We're sure you realize that each member of your family has a unique perspective about holidays and traditions. You might be interested in our discovery, however, that each generation shares some common views. Here's what we learned from our many conversations and letters from grandparents, parents, and grandchildren.

Grandpa and Grandma: Full House and Full Hearts

Being with family during the holidays is exciting and fun. Although I often wonder beforehand if the grandkids will need to get to know me all over again, their car isn't even unpacked before the youngest, Charlie, says "Opa, come on!" and we're off on a new adventure. It's a thrill—and a relief—to realize that even though weeks have passed, we've picked up our relationship without missing a beat.

It gives me great joy to take Nick and Charlie to the shop and teach them how to build with wood many of the same projects I made so long ago with my own kids. Reading stories from careworn books also brings back a flood of memories and leads me to hope that my grandchildren will be as fortunate as my own children in the years ahead. Like most grandfathers, sharing memories with my grandchildren strengthens my resolve to make life as good for them as I can without stifling their independence, drive, and creativity. This wish always reminds me of a poem read at my father-in-law's memorial service:

—"Opa" Johnson

The Bridge Builder

An old man, going up a lone highway
Came at the evening, cold and gray,
To a chasm vast and deep and wide.
The old man crossed in the twilight dim,
The sullen stream had no fear for him,
But he turned when safe on the other side
And built a bridge to span the tide.

"Old Man," said a fellow pilgrim near,
"You are wasting your strength with building here;

Your journey will end with the ending day,
You never again will pass this way;
You've crossed the chasm, deep and wide,
Why build this bridge at evening tide?"

The builder lifted his old gray head;
"Good friend, in the path I have come," he said,
"There followed after me today
A youth whose feet must pass this way.
This chasm that has been a naught to me
To that fair-haired youth may a pitfall be;
He, too, must cross in the twilight dim,
Good friend, I am building this bridge for him."

—William Allen Dromgoole

New Grandpas and Grandmas might be surprised at the intensity of their feelings during the holidays now that there are little ones in the family. Seeing family traditions passed on to a new generation touches us deeply. These traditions might be something as simple as holding hands around the table during grace, opening Christmas stockings before Christmas breakfast, or changing a traditional nursery rhyme so it has a unique twist. (In our family, beginning generations ago, pat-a-cake has become "Pat-a-cake, pat-a-cake, baker's man, you roll 'em and you roll 'em as fast as you can, and you—throw 'em away!")

There is a special joy, too, that comes when you see your children and your grandchildren interact, and nothing warms our hearts more than to hear our children reminisce with tales about when they were kids. Not only do we learn a lot we never knew, but it's great to know that they have fond memories of earlier times. The way the grown "kids" in our family head for the shelf of family photo albums when they come home makes us glad we recorded special times.

Planning for a visit from young grandchildren over the holidays is one way that grandparents everywhere show how much they care about their littlest family members. For many of us, in fact, the anticipation about these special holiday moments starts almost as soon as the last visit is over. Our family actually keeps a file handy and pops ideas into it whenever we think of things—a special fun outing, a new yummy dessert recipe, an art project we'd enjoy sharing, the phone number of a young playmate it would be fun to have over—anything that might be forgotten amid the confusion and hubbub of the visit itself.

If you're like the grandparents we know, your concerns center on safety and the comfort of all your loved ones. You strive to look at a home's safety from a toddler's point of view (see "Special Babyproofing Concerns for the Holidays," p. 190). You also try to anticipate the needs of everyone: Will the new mom have a quiet place to rock the baby? Will the engaged couple have space to be "on their own"? And will our other son feel comfortable including his friends? Juggling grown children who are at different stages in their lives can be tricky. Planning ahead seems to help, and yet we've learned that too much structure can be invasive and stifling. Going with the flow and sharing as much planning as possible is probably the best strategy.

Holiday Parenting: Diplomacy 101

Whew. The zipper on that suitcase is straining, the box of gifts is finally taped up. Now just to make sure enough diapers, extra clothes, toys, and food are stuffed into the carry-on bag for the six-hour flight. There's an awesome feeling of accomplishment just getting out your door for a holiday visit when you're a parent, regardless of how far you have to travel. You know that you can probably get to the store if the need arises, but you also know that it will be easier for everyone if you just remember absolutely everything in the first place. Depending on your parents and parents-in-law, and the age of your children, you may need to bring a lot of baby equipment, too. The thought is enough to tire most parents, and the reality is just short of exhausting.

Hopefully, though, a pot of gold is also at the end of this journey—the loving, helpful arms of grandparents and the wonderful traditions of a parent's childhood replayed for the grandchildren's benefit. As a parent, your expectations are high, and you know they might even be unreasonable, but you've been dreaming of so many parts of this trip for weeks: coming home, relaxed "adult" conversations that last into the evening, and sitting down to a meal that you haven't even offered to help prepare. Many parents want to be spoiled again—even if just for the length of the visit.

Being spoiled like a child and being treated like one aren't quite the same, however, and parents can find themselves negotiating even within themselves how to be assertive when necessary and still be pampered a bit. These issues of independence and authority can sometimes flare over the grandchildren—especially when those little rascals are being less than perfect—and parents can find themselves in the position of juggling contradictory needs and wishes on behalf of all parties. It can be a difficult part to play. Needless to say, any understanding comments or sympathetic gestures you can give during the holidays will be invaluable to these harried parents.

Removing the "Soft Lens" of Nostalgia: Toddler Table Manners and Other Myths

You've all sat down to the beautiful table, silver shining in the candlelight. Giving a beneficent smile to your loving family, you bow your head to give the blessing over the meal, as the table groans under the weight of the "bountiful gifts." . . . Wait a minute. The table wasn't groaning a minute ago. You glance up to see two-year-old Emon teasing the dog with a piece of turkey, eighteen-month-old Sarah flipping baby cereal off her spoon with a graceful twang, and four-year-old Monica giving off a low Tibetan-monk-style drone. What is the world coming to? In your day, children were taught to behave at the table—no elbows, no gooey mess in the hair, no singing. Right? Perhaps. More likely, however, your nostalgia is showing. As we've said before, selective memory has a place in aging—it's one of the greatest perks of getting old. Who would want to remember the natural but seemingly endless tussles between parent and child? These less-positive memories are the first to go, and any gap is conveniently filled by more frequent reminiscences of when José won first prize at the spelling bee and Rebekah got a standing ovation on opening night.

The only danger, of course, is that your edited version of the past will make you more demanding of those around you than you otherwise might have been. To avoid this possibility, decide before the holidays that you will loosen up a bit and enjoy the antics of your mischievous grandchildren—and the ease of mind in realizing that you're not responsible for their behavior. You can take the time to be with a grumpy two-year-old who's driving everyone else crazy; let that eight-year-old outside to let off steam with a soccer ball and an improvised goal (with you as goalie, perhaps); and take a turn rocking with the crying baby. Your emotional distance can be an asset to everyone in the family—and will probably diffuse behavior problems more quickly than any other strategy.

Grandchild-Development Basics: The Truth Revealed

Why do grandchildren behave the way they do? Much of it, of course, has to do with their feelings during the holidays—and this, in turn, has everything to do with their ages and stage of development. Here are a few reminders about child development so you can be ready for the bundles of joy and mischief who will soon arrive.

Infants: A little change can mean a lot—or not. The old saying about infants is true: once you and your littlest ones find a comfortable routine, they grow right out of it. These rapid developmental changes may mislead you into believing that coming to visit during the busy holidays is just another experience for a little one to take in stride. For some miraculous infants, that philosophy is perfect—but not for many. Most grandbabies will be eager for familiarity among all the new sights, sounds, and smells of your home. They might seek this out by crying until Mom or Dad comes to the rescue, or by becoming unpredictable about sleeping and eating. Try not to feel disappointed, and instead offer to help in whatever way you can. We're sure you'll find some good time for cuddling and coos after your grandbaby has a chance to warm up to the new environment.

Toddlers: An all-or-nothing experience. Eighteen-month-old David is a rollercoaster of emotions and behaviors. One moment he's giving Mom an adoring smile and practicing his kisses, and the next he's mischievously dumping water out of the tub and crying alligator tears at her frustrated—and very much expected—"No." T. Berry Brazelton, a child-development expert, characterizes this period as one of "independence and negativism."[1] But it's also one of unfettered delight and interest in the world, a time when everything seems magical to your grandchild's inquisitive mind. Grandparents, even during the busy holidays (and maybe especially so), can offer to parents a welcome relief from this topsy-turvy world of endless negotiations and boundless enthusiasm. Just keep that little one busy with appropriate toys and with helping in small ways, but don't be surprised if you have a few bumps in your otherwise adoring relationship. You might think of any upsets as chances to prove you'll still love your toddler grandchild, whether cantankerous or cute.

Twos: Sulky and sweet. By age two or so, your grandchildren will be able to ask for what they need and want and tell you how they

160

feel. This is a big advantage—most of the time! The "terrible" part of being a two is simply that your little one is aware of the limitations of being little and can become very frustrated by these barriers. Our best advice for this age is to offer two (and only two) acceptable choices. "Would you like peas first, or carrots?" "Do you want to put your jacket on now or in one minute?" And the all-time favorite backup: "Would you like to do it yourself, or do you want me to help you?" The respect you show through giving choices means the world to your grandchild, and can help make these sometimes tricky—but often terrific—years into positive ones for your relationship. You'll also appreciate all the more those frequently wonderful, loving moments with your two-year-old grandchild.

Preschoolers and school-age grandchildren: Grown-up "wannabes." Preschool-age grandchildren are more capable than you might expect—remember, it's been a while since you parented one. They love to be given jobs to do with real responsibility, and they crave your admiring comments about all they can accomplish. They also enjoy having their way sometimes (don't we all!), and often this can be accommodated if you guide their occasional bossiness. Put a preschooler in charge of getting everyone to breakfast or taking orders for dessert, and you'll get a sideways grin—and a job well done. Or ask your older grandchild to choose from among a few jobs to remember and do alone each day, such as feeding a pet, wiping the table, or picking up the mail. You'll marvel at their skills and pride in themselves. This is also an exciting, receptive age for conversations about feelings and for stories about your own fears and joys growing up. Young grandchildren are often a delight and have clever insights into the world. Best of all, they still eagerly give hugs and kisses to adoring grandparents. Enjoy them!

There's a nightmare in Grandpa's closet. What's that?! To many young children, anything and everything can "go bump in the night" at Grandpa and Grandma's house. The drama of holiday stories and the excitement of being in a new place can simply be more than a child's active imagination can handle at times. These and other stressors, such as a parade of new faces and experiences, a pet who's not sure about sharing its space, and distracted, busy parents, can cause fears in all young grandchildren. Infants might respond with an upside-down schedule of feedings and sleeping. Toddlers might find themselves waking at night and being more cranky and mischievous during the day. Twos will likely cling to familiar "loveys" and be choosier. Preschoolers might be tormented by nightmares while sleeping in a new bed. And school-age children may insist that they can't get to sleep. Your consistency and comfort are the best antidotes for your grandchild's fears. Offer your kind sympathy as much as possible, knowing that this will nurture rather than spoil your little ones.

Sharing Your Time with More than One Grandchild

As your family grows, so too might your feeling that all your precious time during the holidays is spent buying gifts, preparing meals, and refereeing the wild animal grandchildren (and their nostalgic parents) in your house. Luckily, planning can make a big difference. Get on the phone before the visit with each grandchild old enough to talk and plan something simple and fun that the two of you can do together: making a sweet treat in the kitchen, putting together a new puzzle, playing "dress up" and taking photos afterward, or even "shaving" with Grandpa in the morning—with a popsicle stick for scraping the shaving cream off your preschooler's face while Grandpa does the real thing. And for your grandbabies, get your favorite rocker set up in a place that's comfortable and quiet in anticipation of some great cuddle time. Setting aside equal time for each grandchild can seem like a huge undertaking, but it's during these little one-on-one moments that true friendships are sparked and lasting memories are formed.

When a Holiday Visit Hits a Bump

It's just not fair. You've spent days getting ready. You've spent weeks planning meals and stocking the freezer. Your closets are filled with brightly wrapped gifts. And your family is now home, just as you dreamed, but after two days of catching up, the grandkids are climbing the walls (via the couch and end table); your children, now adults, are passive blobs glued to the television set; and you're working your derriere off to just keep some semblance of order in the house. Or maybe you're blessed with go-getter children who love to help, but in the process rearrange your cupboards and create an impenetrable offensive line in front of the stove. Before you let this or any other minor problem get out of hand, you might want to try some Johnson-Carlson family tricks to get everyone working toward the same goal.

Give Responsibility—and Heaps of Praise

Perhaps it's time to resurrect the Job Chart, that dreaded chore list that your children had thought was safely buried somewhere in the basement. But this time it doesn't have to carry the weight that it did when your children were young—just take up the old idea and give it a new, lighter approach. Make a list of everything that needs to be done so that the grandparents can share fully in the quality family time. Call a family meeting of your couch potatoes—or a huddle of your offensive line—and let them know that you need each and everyone's help. You can even help the young grandchildren choose from among the manageable jobs and leave the rest for the adults to either assign or just remember and do as needed. You'll be amazed at how easy it can be, and how proud your little ones are to help, especially when you tell them how "grown up" they are to be able to do so many important things for Grandma and Grandpa.

Cure the Frenetic Frenzies with Quiet, Reflective Activities

You probably remember this suspicious feeling from your own days as a parent. It's the second day of a snowstorm, the kids have been inside too long, and there's a sort of electrical current abuzz in the house as excited little ones dash in and out of doors upstairs and light feet zip up and down and round and round. You might even get used to it, except for those single minutes of dead silence that interrupt the mayhem. You steel yourself to go see what kind of mischief this absence of sound must mean—and then the squeals begin again. Let's face facts. Your grandchildren are going bananas and need something interesting to do—fast.

Luckily for you, you have a holiday to make projects extra fun. If you have some inexpensive watercolor paints in the house, try an old nursery school trick that will intrigue even older toddlers: "negative space painting" (which is just a fancy name for cutting out shapes in a paper and painting on the holey background). Or dig out your cotton swabs and use them to paint on foil or paper that you've cut into a fun, holiday-related shape.

Perhaps your grandchildren are in a more mess-making mood—or, more precisely, you're in a mood to humor their messy fun. (See our chapter 4 for some ideas to get you started.) You can give their work a holiday twist by asking them if they can tell a story about a holiday-related character that incorporates their art. You might even try decorating your home with festive paper chains that can be colored as well as assembled. Your two- and three-year-old grandchildren can do almost all of the work if you pre-cut the paper strips and pre-tear bits of masking tape for little hands.

Zap the Boredom Blues with Controlled, Active Fun

You wouldn't believe how many children wrote us to say "Grandpa and Grandma's house is where we get to watch lots of TV whenever we want." Well, grandparents, we're here to let you know that you can easily make yourself more interesting than the latest television heroes. Turn to our chapter 4 for help in getting started, then try on these holiday-theme games and boredom-busters for size. We guess they'll fit grandchildren from about "toddler" to "size 8."

A lot of popular store-bought games provide perfect backdrops for homemade variations. Remember Pictionary (picture-drawing charades)? Well, make yourself a bunch of cards with words about your holiday, team up older grandchildren with younger but verbal tots, and watch the fun begin. Or steal that Easter Bunny idea for other holidays by having a thematic scavenger hunt in the house. Let the littlest toddlers get a two-minute head start on your easily found treasures, and then let the older ones follow for the tough finds.

We wouldn't recommend trying this on teenagers and their MTV, but a two- to four-year old who's watching *Sesame Street* or *Barney* is sure to giggle if suddenly Grandpa or Grandma (or both) appears on the screen doing the "Hokey, Pokey" or acting out a story such as "The Little Red Hen." If you don't have a videocamera, we encourage you to simply surprise your little ones sometime right before their favorite show comes on by playing "Simon Says" or another active game instead.

During fair-weather holidays, take the holiday theme outdoors with a delightful spin on the "cartoon" tag of the sixties. In this version of a dash-around favorite, children are "safe" from being tagged if they can think of a character from a holiday story in time. It's a good one for your four- to eight-year-old grandchildren.

Your Most Precious Gifts: Memories and Simple Treasures

"As I look back, it seems to me that the greatest lasting gift that one could give to a grandchild is the gift of time. Time to tell memories, to play, to read, and to share your own daily life. Your grandchildren's memories of your times together will enrich their lives and keep you near them always." —Linda Knox

Ever wonder what use you would ever have for those old wire-rimmed spectacles, hat box, even those funny red, white, and blue pants you made for the bicentennial? Try asking your toddler or older grandchild what these items were used for, and you'll be in for some fun. Better yet, put that old washboard, garter belt, and darning egg in a big sack and let your grandchild reach in and guess what each item is (see "What in the World Is That?" p. 188). This easy activity brings to light how important a link you are to the life and times of your country and world as you were growing up and raising your children. But even more exciting is the treasure trove of information you can provide about your own family's history. As Jean Whiting from Ramsey, New Jersey, wrote, it's "important to tell stories about family history—particularly about people grandchildren will never know." You're the only one who can describe firsthand how gorgeous Grandma was at the prom and tell how you got caught smooching behind the school. Best of all, you can relate stories about your grandchild's parents—and know that the more sheepish your child, the parent, would be to have you tell it, the more delighted your grandchild will be to hear it. At the heart of the grandchild's glee in these stories, of course, is the idea that their revered parents and grandparents made mistakes in their time (and will make them again); in this day of the "hurried" grandchild, this is a wonderful gift all by itself.

Many tales pop up at meals or during conversations when somebody says, "Remember when?" but there are ways to make the telling more approachable to grandchildren, too. If, for example, you can think of a "call and response" version of a favorite family tale, your grandchildren will delight in interjecting a phrase at—or near—the right time (see "The Stories We Tell," pp. 187, for this and other story ideas). If this seems too tricky for you, try instead allowing your grandchild to introduce the story, say "The End!" afterward, or even to just tell after the story what they remember and enjoyed about it.

"Book 'em, Grandma!"

One way to document some of your family memories is to make a book of memories. You can buy a book to fill out (see chapter 9 for our recommendations), but it will be even more special to you and your family if you make one yourself. Adele Wright, who is from New Zealand but currently living in England with her son, has a related suggestion: a grandparent "could compile a 'scrapbook' with photos of faraway family members, with pictures of their houses, where they work, and what they do." For those grandparents who live near their grandchildren, making memories together and documenting them in a scrapbook of this kind will be yet another way to deepen your relationship and broaden the scope of all you share.

Heirlooms for Children

To a child, an "heirloom" means something given by a Grandma or Grandpa in a way that makes it seem significant, rather than something that has monetary value. You can take advantage of this unique and refreshing perspective by giving as heirlooms things that can be played with and that give your grandchild a connection to your own life. Try presenting a book or toy that was a favorite of yours or of your grandchild's parent. Take a look into your drawer and pull out an inexpensive but sentimental item—such as an old key ring from your dating days, a photo of your spouse when you were young parents, an "I Like Ike" button from your high-school days—and write a paragraph about how you obtained it, what it meant to you way back when, and why you have kept it so long.

You might also try giving your grandchild a twin of something child-oriented that you have. A small stuffed animal that is "just like Grandma's" will have more value to your grandchild than a whole box of Hummel figurines. Further, because the two loveys will need to talk now and again, you'll have a fun time keeping the two—and yourselves, in the process—in touch long-distance or through visits to the other's home. Fabienne Potestivo, from Rochester, Michigan, wrote that her mom in France and her son, Alex, both have the same stuffed "marsupilami": "I love the fact that my mom has the same stuffed animal as Alex. When they are together, they have conversations with the 'Mimi' and play, hug, kiss, and so on, with them. And on the phone, Alex, age two and a half, always asks my mom about her 'Mimi.'"

Homemade gifts are always a treat, and if your grandchild is told how the gift was made it will be especially treasured. Nancy Van Metre told us that she "has just started another tradition—I make holiday dresses for the granddaughters." If you have grandsons, you might try a bow tie, cummerbund, or patterned overalls. Lee Norton, from Penfield, New York, is also a great believer in making things for grandchildren. She says she spends a lot of time making and sending "homemade things—cards, birthday cakes, clothes, toys, and so forth," and recommends that grandparents "show the child that time was spent . . . [and that you] put love and thought for the child into the gifts."

Perhaps, too, you made something when you were a child that your grandchild would now enjoy. Check your attic for some school-made pottery, a drawing, homemade doll clothing, or other item that you made when you were young and that an adoring grandchild could appreciate. This tradition can be especially nice if you happen across something you made when you were your grandchild's age.

Good Things Come to Children Who Wait . . . Says Who?

Most cultures have a certain time during holidays when gifts are given. But the Jewish tradition at Hanukkah of giving a small token each night for seven nights is the most child-oriented we know. Perhaps we shouldn't be surprised to realize that the effect of a mountain of presents on a little person during a typical Christmas exchange is often confusion and uncontrolled excitement. It certainly is asking a lot of a young grandchild to insist that each present in a heap be acknowledged as thoughtfully as an adult might—and to stay polite and interested through all the hoopla. Instead, you might consider giving the younger set a present or two at a time over the course of a visit rather than all at once.

Passing the Torch to a New Generation

It might be difficult to think about, but there probably will come a time when your home is not the easiest place for family gatherings. Martha and Dick Crawford from Pittsfield, New York, seemed to know this instinctively. They wrote to let us know that early on they began "visiting the grandchildren at Thanksgiving and Christmas so the grandchildren can be in their own home for the holidays." In each family in which this transition occurs, it happens at different times and in different ways. You'll want to try your best to welcome your children's and grandchildren's encouragement to have holidays at another location. Think of it as a new freedom from the responsibilities of preparing for big family events. The essence of holidays—the love and sharing of families near and far during special times—will remain unchanged no matter where you celebrate.

♥   ♥   ♥

The rewards of making holidays grandchild-oriented are personal and deep—for both grandchildren and their grandparents. The children and adults whom we asked to give their earliest and fondest memories of their grandparents almost without exception recalled one-on-one activities and conversations. Anita Johannson, from Alingsas, Sweden, remembered "helping my grandmother with her baking [and] feeding her hens. She always had time for me."

The hardest part about holidays, in our experience, is that in the rush to "get things done" these relaxed and simple opportunities for memory-making can be missed. If this sounds like a portrait of your family, try to change to simpler, more heartfelt rituals.

Trust us. Taking the time during a holiday gathering to get on all fours with your grandbaby or to get as chocolate-covered as your cake with your preschooler grandchild will give you the warmest, most meaningful family memories of all.

A Grace for Always
(to be sung with hands joined)

The Lord is good to me

And so I thank the Lord

For giving me
the things I need

The sun, and the rain,
and the apple trees

The Lord is good to me.
AMEN.

—*contributed by
Leo and Anne Berard,
Yarmouth Port, Massachusetts*

Pop a Thanksgiving Turkey in the Mail

If you're not getting together for Thanksgiving, this might be a fun way to "share a turkey" and the holiday!

Ages: One to five years
You'll Need
- A piece of brown felt
- Scraps of felt in other colors
- List of things about your grandchild for which you are thankful

- **Here's How**
- If you haven't already sent your little cherub a flannel board, this might be a good introduction to the fun it can provide.
- Cut a basic turkey shape out of the brown felt.
- Cut turkey feather shapes out of the other colors of felt.
- Write brief "thankful" notes to your little one and staple them to the ends of each feather . . . something like, "I'm thankful for your hugs" or "I'm grateful you're my grandchild."
- Send these to your "little Pilgrim" and as the turkey "grows" its feathers, your grandchild will appreciate how much you love her.

Package Fun: Bubble Wrap Prints

When you send those packages, be sure to include some bubble wrap with these instructions for an easy project your little artists will love!

Ages: Eighteen months to eight years
You'll Need
- Tempera or washable fingerpaints
- Smocks or Grandpa's old shirt as a coverup
- Newspapers to protect the table
- Plastic bubble wrap

Here's How
- Paint the bubble wrap.
- Place a piece of paper over it, press, and remove.
- The result is a gorgeous design that looks like modern art.

Have a "Grape" Halloween

Just because you're far away doesn't mean you can't take part in your grandchildren's Halloween fun. Send a simple "do-it-yourself" costume and transform those tricksters into "luscious grapes"!

Ages: Four to six years

You'll Need to Send for Each Costume
- 15 purple or green balloons
- 15 small safety pins
- A grape-leaf collar and hat cut from green felt or paper

Here's How
- Parents may have to help blow up balloons, making some big for the top of the "grape bunch" and some small for the bottom of the "grape bunch."
- Knot the end of each balloon.
- When the little ones have dressed in their outdoor clothing, tell parents to carefully pin the end of each balloon onto the jacket and pants, making the "grape bunch" broad at the shoulders and narrow at the hips.
- The finishing touch is the grape leaf collar and hat!

Remember, deflated or broken balloons can cause choking and should be kept away from younger children.

Snowman in a Box

When you can't be together to make a snowman, you can still send the "ingredients" in a special kit!

Ages: Two years and up
You'll Need to Send
- An old hat
- A scarf
- Buttons and pieces of coal
- A corn cob pipe and red tinsel garland for mouth
- A carrot

Here's How
- Send the kit to your grandchild, along with this cute note and poem:

Dear little one, have fun bringing your snowman to life!

Coal for eyes and buttons,

A carrot for his nose,

Plaid scarf to warm his neck

When the icy cold wind blows!

Pipe to hold 'tween his teeth,

Stick arms to give a pat,

Pin on his tinselled smile,

Top off with his stovepipe hat!

Papier-Mâché Inspirations

A no-fail project that, though messy, is great for creating holiday decorations, puppets, or whatever your grandchild's imagination dictates!

Ages: Three years and up
You'll Need
- Newspaper torn into strips
- Balloons blown up, paper tubes, boxes, Styrofoam balls, crumpled paper tied with string, or whatever shape you want to cover
- Thin paste made with this recipe:
  - Combine 1/4 cup sugar, 1/4 cup flour, and 1/2 teaspoon alum in a saucepan. Gradually stir in 1 cup water.
  - Your job is to bring this mixture to a boil and to stir until it is clear and smooth. Then add 3/4 cup more water. While you're at the stove your grandchild can tear the paper into strips.
  - For a nice smell add 1/4 teaspoon oil of wintergreen.
- Tempera or washable fingerpaints or markers

Here's How
- Dip the newspaper strips into the paste mixture and spread evenly over the balloon or base to be covered by building up three or four layers. Use a brush or hands to smooth the strips.
- Allow to dry, then paint with tempera, fingerpaints, or markers.

Remember, keep balloons away from babies; they pose a choking hazard if deflated or broken.

 # Any Resemblance?

All ages can get in the act with this fun family game.

You'll Need
- One baby picture for each member of the family

Here's How
- Set out all the pictures without any names attached. Then see who can correctly identify the most pictures. Get ready to hear, "Doesn't he look like . . ?"

Pumpkins Aglow

Your entrance way will be the hit of the neighborhood on Halloween night if lined with "Pumpkin Luminaries"!

Ages: Three to six years
You'll Need
- Small, lunch-size paper bags
- Safety scissors
- Short votive candles

Here's How
- You'll have to show your grandchildren how to fold the bags before cutting, but once they see you do it, they'll have fun creating their own unique pumpkin luminaries.
- With the bags still flat, fold in half once lengthwise.
- Cut out half a mouth and half a nose . . . just like you used to do to make paper snowflakes!
- Fold the bag once again lengthwise and cut out half an eye and eyebrow.
- It might even be fun to round off, scallop, or spike some hair at the top.
- Set the luminaries out in a safe location and secure a small votive candle in a cup of sand at the bottom of each bag to light the way for little ghosts and goblins.
- You could use these votives inside as table or window decorations with the lights turned down.
- Your grandchildren will love the glow that shines through the unique faces they've created.

Use extreme caution with flame near young grandchildren.

An Ornament Just for Me

These might just become heirlooms, as they have in our family!

Ages: Three to eight years
You'll Need
- Traditional glass ball ornaments
- Glitter
- Pencil with an eraser on the end
- Nontoxic white glue

Here's How
- Dip the end of the eraser in the glue, and print your grandchild's name in glue on the ornament.
- Quickly, before the glue dries, have your grandchild sprinkle the glitter over the ball.
- The glitter will stick just to the glue.
- You might also wish to document the date your grandchild made her ornament.

Remember, glitter is not meant to be eaten.

 # Create a Winter Wonderland

Save the chiseling for the pros—your grandchildren will still be able to create ice sculptures unlike any you've seen anywhere.

Ages: Three years and up
You'll Need
- Freezing weather, water, and salt
- A variety of containers: plastic food containers in all sizes and shapes work well

Here's How
- Fill the containers with water.
- Set outside to freeze in the cold.
- Unmold and with dabs of water and a shake of salt as "cement" stack one shape onto another to create a masterpiece.
- Hold a family ice sculpture contest to see who can make the smallest, the largest, the funniest, the scariest, and so on.

Package Fun: Tiny Tissue Balls

Holiday gift boxes and tissue can be as much fun as the present!

Ages: Three to six years
You'll Need
- Tissue paper and glue
- Shirt cardboard or other stiff paper

Here's How
- Your grandkids will love tearing the tissue into small pieces and rolling them into tiny balls.
- Suggest they arrange and glue the small, round "tiles" of paper into their own unique pattern on the stiff cardboard backing.
- Younger grandchildren will also enjoy painting flat pieces of tissue paper onto a paper background with a mix of equal parts starch and water (keep little fingers from tasting this mixture).

Wrap It Up

When your grandchildren have had the fun of making the wrapping paper all by themselves, they'll be as excited about the paper as they are about the gift they are wrapping!

Ages: Two to six years
You'll Need
- Stampers made from half a potato into which you've carved a design for your grandchildren
- Plain paper for printing (a real thrifty and clever idea is to purchase the unprinted end rolls from your local newspaper) or cut up brown grocery bags
- Acrylic paints and brushes

Here's How
- Paint the cut side of the potato with paint.
- Stamp the paper.
- When the image no longer appears, repaint and stamp away again. This is a great, no-fail project that your grandchildren will love.

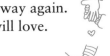

Scrap-Box Art

Holidays are times when wrapping paper, ribbons, and cards can be added to your little one's favorite scrap box.

Ages: Two to eight years
You'll Need
- Odds and ends: colored paper (tissue and construction); foil, sequins, old buttons, or cotton balls; fabric scraps and magazine pictures; and scraps of holiday glitter—tinsel, ribbons, etc.
- Provide a strong backing—cut in a holiday shape if you wish
- Glue
- Safety scissors
- Paper punch (optional)

Here's How
- Provide the materials, and let them go!
- Maybe you'll see collage paper-plate hats or cardboard "butterfly wings" emerge!

Magical Blooms

Even a grandtoddler's scribbles will be transformed into "rainbows" on these terrific watercolor flowers. They make a unique addition to any holiday table!

Ages: Eighteen months to six years
You'll Need
- Coffee filters and paper towels
- Water-soluble markers
- 1/2" of water in a cup
- Pipe cleaners or construction paper

Here's How
- Let your grandchild decorate the coffee filter with the markers.
- Cut a hole in the center of the filter "flower" and insert a 3" rolled paper towel "stem."
- Put stem in the cup of water and watch the colors move!
- Remove and let the filters dry alone. Make new stems for the dried flowers from the pipe cleaners or from rolled construction paper.

Fantasy Friends and Funny Phrases

Take the time to do this for your grandchild during busy holidays and other family gatherings. You'll be glad you did!

Ages: One to five years

You'll Need

- A keen ear and a notebook or index card file

Here's How

- Every time your little one comes up with a special word, phrase, or funny saying, write it down!
- Our adult children still enjoy hearing about the funny things they said as little tykes—their bloopers and their favorite imaginary buddies "Spoonishish," "Bobba," and "Whispitil."
- In later years your recordings will become a true treasure!

Springtime Bonnets upon Us

Hold a family May Day parade after you've all made your springtime bonnets and caps, and give out some prizes for the funniest, prettiest, biggest, most colorful, and so on—just make sure that all the grandchildren are winners in some category!

Ages: Two years and up

You'll Need

- Bonnet bases: paper plates, boxes, plastic flower pots, shirt cardboards, etc.
- Materials to decorate the hats: fabric, ribbons, crepe paper, yarn, lace, doilies, colored paper, tissue paper, etc.
- Glue, tape, and stapler (with supervision or assistance) for fixing those embellishments onto the "bonnet" base

Here's How

- Grandparents, you provide the materials and the enthusiasm.
- Your grandchildren will come up with creations beyond your wildest dreams—just be sure you have the camera loaded!
- How about starting a tradition of making a May Day parade through the neighborhood to display your hats?

 # Face Paint Fun

Whether it's for Halloween or a family circus in the backyard, your imaginative grandkids will get a kick out of this activity.

Ages: Eighteen months to five years
You'll Need
- 1 1/4 tsp. of Grandma's cold cream
- 1 1/4 tsp. cornstarch
- 1/2 tsp. water
- 1 drop food coloring

Here's How
- Mix the ingredients to make a nontoxic face paint, using a separate custard cup or egg carton section for each color.
- Create designs with your finger on that adorable little face, and have your camera ready!

 # Creative Cupids

Valentines are as much fun to make and give as they are to receive.

Ages: Two to eight years
You'll Need
- Red paper and colored pens
- Lace, doilies, yarn, ribbons
- Pictures to cut out of magazines
- Pressed flowers, sequins, glitter
- Safety scissors
- Glue and tape

Here's How
- From tracing hands to cutting hearts, the fun is in the doing.
- Just provide the materials and watch your grandchildren create!
- For extra excitement you can help your little cupids sign their cards with a "Guess who loves you?"

Springtime Nested Treats

Your grandchildren will love not only making these yummy treats, but also nibbling the finished product.

Ages: Two years and up

You'll Need

- A bowl
- Cookie sheet covered with wax paper or tin foil
- 1 cup flaked coconut
- 1 ounce unsweetened baking chocolate
- 1/4 cup sweetened condensed milk
- Small bowl of sugar
- Jelly beans

Here's How

- Grandparents, melt the chocolate in the microwave on medium for two minutes and stir until smooth.
- While you're doing this, your grandchildren can be measuring the coconut and condensed milk. You can then add these to the hot chocolate and stir until it is well blended.
- When the mixture is cool enough to be handled safely, show the eager cooks how to roll about a tablespoon of the mixture into balls and drop them onto the covered cookie sheet.
- Next, have them dip their thumbs into the bowl of sugar and then press their thumbs into the center of each "bird's nest."
- If they can stop licking their gooey fingers long enough, have them fill their nests with the jelly bean "eggs"!
- Refrigerating the nests for thirty minutes will help firm them up.
- This should make about twelve nests to help celebrate Easter or the arrival of spring.

Be sure you are the one to microwave the chocolate; it will become very hot.

Wintertime Warmers

Start some memorable traditions with warm cider and cocoa.

Ages: One year and up
You'll Need
- Powdered cider and cocoa mixes (single-serving packages work well)
- Cinnamon sticks and peppermint sticks

Here's How
- Make the cider or cocoa.
- Use the cinnamon stick to stir the cider, or the peppermint stick to stir the cocoa.
- You'll have started a yummy tradition!

 # Halloween Games

Revive some of the old favorites you used to love!

Ages: Two to eight years
You'll Need
- Apples and a bucket of water
- A paper pumpkin and paper noses with tape or tacks
- Doughnuts and string
- Bean bags and a carved pumpkin

Here's How
- Bob for apples with your little goblins just the way you used to—no hands allowed!
- Play pin the nose on the pumpkin.
- Hang some doughnuts, on long strings, from the overhead garage door tracks or the basement joists, and see who can eat their doughnut first—with hands behind your backs of course!
- Play bean bag toss into the pumpkin.
- Be sure to join in with your little competitors—they'll love it!

Mealtime Fun: Telephone Go Round

Remember playing "telephone" or "gossip" when you were young? Jazz up your holiday dinner-table conversation by playing this timeless game with your grandchildren.

Ages: Two to eight years
You'll Need
- Your family sitting around the table

Here's How
- Send a whispered message from one person to the next until it gets to the last person in the group.
- This last person—hopefully a grandchild—will then say what they heard (usually something silly!) and laugh at how the original message changed.

Mealtime Fun: The Gift Wrap Rap

Don't be surprised if your grandchildren want to make this a holiday tradition!

Ages: Two years and up
You'll Need
- Your family seated around the dinner table
- A gift appropriate for any age such as homemade cookies, a simple game, or puzzle
- To wrap the one gift in at least as many layers of different paper as there are people at the table

Here's How
- Send the multiwrapped gift around the table, having each person in turn remove one layer of paper.
- The person who removes the last wrapping can keep the gift, which ideally will be something they can share or do with the family.
- This is a good attention-getter for those chaotic moments at the holiday table, or you could play it at the beginning or end of any special meal.
- Your really hip preschoolers might even like to accompany this game with a little finger drumming or "rap" chant!

Ornamental Treasures

If your preschooler grandchild wants to make some lasting holiday ornaments, this clay recipe might be just what you need.

Ages: Three to eight years
You'll Need
- 4 cups unsifted flour
- 1 cup salt and 1 1/2 cups water
- A nail to punch a hole in the top of the ornament
- Poster or acrylic paints and a brush
- Ribbon for hanging (and optional spray shellac)

Here's How
- Combine the flour, salt, and water and enlist the help of your energetic creator to mix and knead the clay for at least five minutes.
- Watch as she molds or shapes the clay into figures or ornaments.
- Poke a hole for hanging in the top with the nail.
- Bake on a cookie sheet for one hour at 350 degrees.
- Cool thoroughly and then turn her loose with the paints.
- To preserve, spray with shellac when the paint has dried.
- Insert the ribbon and you'll have a lasting ornamental treasure!

Always be careful to use shellac, which is toxic, far from little ones.

Hug Tag

Holiday family gatherings are a great time to play Hug Tag, and that "huggable honey" of yours will be especially happy if you play too!

Ages: Two to eight years
You'll Need
- A group of at least four people—the more the merrier!
- Room to run around outside

Here's How
- Played just like regular tag, hug tag has one person who is "it" trying to tag someone else to make them "it."
- But you can't be tagged as long as you're hugging someone else!
- There is no limit to the number of people who can hug each other at the same time, but the hugs can't last too long!

Stepping Stones

Make a unique piece of garden art—and a treasured memento that your whole family will cherish as you "plant" memories!

Ages: Three years and up

You'll Need

- Old baking pans with sloping sides, or use a bottomless plastic mold, found at building supply stores, so you can create right at the spot you've chosen in the garden.
- Quick-drying concrete, the kind without stones.
- Mixing container (the lid of a plastic garbage can works well—just be sure to rinse before the concrete hardens!)

Here's How

- Prepare your mold by spraying the inside with a nonstick cooking spray.
- Mix the concrete according to the directions on the package.
- Pour the concrete into the pan, and smooth the top with a trowel or piece of wood.
- Wait until the concrete is slightly dry.
- Decorate the face of the stepping stone with handprints, leaves, shells, marbles—you might even want to write your grandchild's name and date in the concrete with a stick!
- Leave the concrete alone for at least a day or two to set.
- Turn the pan upside down, tap it, and the concrete stepping stone will pop out if you've chosen a mold with sloping sides.
- Clean it with a hose, removing all extra leaves and dirt, and set it in place for a lasting memento that everyone will enjoy.

Weave a Web of Fun

Reaching the gift at the end might just be an anticlimax to this fun game!

Ages: Three to eight years

You'll Need

- A ball of string
- Little surprise gifts or a larger holiday gift for each child

Here's How

- You'll need to set this game up when the kids are outside or in bed!
- Write each grandchild's name on a 3" x 5" card, and tie one end of the string around each card.
- One card at a time, weave a huge spider web under tables, behind curtains, and around chairs until the end is reached—where you'll hide the surprise gifts.
- When you give the signal, the grandchildren will be off, winding up their strings on their cards, climbing over and around each other and your house to find their hidden treasures.

Whistling Whizzers

Remember the old fashioned "buzz-buttons" you may have enjoyed with your grandparents? How about teaching your grandchildren to enjoy these fun toys for a jubilant New Year's eve celebration?

Ages: Four years and up
You'll Need
- Several large two-holed buttons
- 2 1/2 feet of strong thread or string for each button

Here's How
- Thread the string through the two holes, and knot the ends together.
- Center the button in the middle of the string.
- Teach your grandchild to wind up the button by slipping middle fingers through the loops formed by the ends of the string.
- Holding the two ends of the string, whirl the disk around and around much like twirling a miniature jump rope.
- When the string is tightly wound up, alternately pull hands apart and together, causing the button to spin and the vibrating string to whistle.
- Get a chorus going with several "whizzers!"

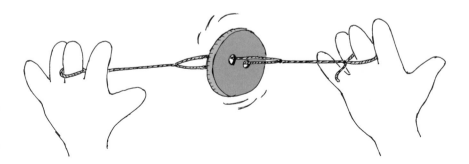

May Day Memories

Do you remember making little May Day baskets, filling them with flowers, hanging them on your neighbor's front door handle, ringing the bell, and running away as fast as you could? Share that memory with your grandchildren—it's a tradition of friendship, flowers, and fun that shouldn't be lost in their new fast-paced world.

Ages: Two to five years
You'll Need

- Spring flowers. Use whatever is growing in your area—perhaps forget-me-nots, daffodils, pansies, or just little wild violets
- Container to hold the flowers: a juice can, plastic food container, or little plastic flower pot
- Colored paper, lace, ribbons— whatever you want to use to decorate the containers
- Glue, tape, scissors, pens

Here's How

- The last day of April, go on a flower-picking expedition with water pail in hand so that the freshly picked flowers can have an immediate drink.
- Set the flowers aside while you and your grandchildren decorate your containers.
- Try a fancy lattice weave of colored strips of paper, or just wind ribbons around a base.
- Early in the morning on May First, have your grandchildren arrange the flowers in the baskets, hang the baskets on neighbors' door handles, ring the bell, and run!
- The neighbors will be thrilled with the thoughtful gesture, and your grandchildren will have May Day memories to treasure.

The Stories We Tell

Some of us feel that the best gift we can give during the holidays is the gift of family experiences. There's no better way to package our memories and love than in an interactive story. Even if you're new to storytelling, these easy-to-try formats and ideas will give you a great start to your own family traditions.

Add-On Stories

Remember this old camp storytelling game? One person starts the story, gets it to a funny climax, and passes it on. Novices might try passing after one, two, or three words instead. Some themes that grandchildren will love are:

1. Adventures in a land where people are tiny or gigantic compared to others
2. Underwater characters
3. Quests for treasure by animals who can talk

Family Skits and Puppetry

Throw a bunch of easy adverbs in a hat, divide yourselves into groups that team up the generations, and have each group pick and act out in turn an adverb for the others to guess.

Act out a favorite family story, like the time that Grandma's safety pin saved the day at Aunt Laura's wedding, or toddler Susie accidentally called the fire department.

You could also make an easy sock puppet that can visit each grandchild at bedtime and help read a favorite family story—or nibble through pretend foods in the style of Eric Carle's *The Hungry Caterpillar* (see our chapter 9). The idea is to have fun, make vivid those precious moments of the past, and begin new interactive traditions that can be carried on through generations to come.

Family Riddles and Jokes

We can't presume to know your family history well enough to suggest specific riddles and jokes here, but we know you'll agree that these slapstick moments need to be dusted off now and again. Dare yourself to be outgoing with your family—it's worth it!

What in the World Is That?

Here's an intergenerational game that will make everyone laugh!

Ages: Three years and up
You'll Need
- Go on a hunt in your attic, basement, or garage and unearth "treasures" from yesteryear such as a girdle, darning ball, old spectacles, thimble holder, etc.

Here's How
- Ask your imaginative preschooler what he thinks they might have been used for. Get ready for some silly answers, and add them to your lively family stories.

Sitting for Silhouettes

Profile the family in silhouettes!

Ages: Two to five years
You'll Need
- A large piece of white paper for each silhouette
- A lamp
- Tape and pen or pencil

Here's How
- Tape the paper to the wall.
- Have your grandchildren sit, one at a time, in front of the paper.
- Adjust the lamp so it creates their shadow on the paper behind them. Move your grandchild as close to the wall as possible for a sharp image.
- When a good sharp profile can be seen, your grandchild will have to endure the hardest part of all—sitting still for a few minutes while you trace the shadow on the paper with a pencil or pen.
- Cut out the silhouette and mount it on black paper.

Memory Movies

To get yourself thinking, or another loved one talking, try to answer questions like these:

- What is your earliest memory?
- What do you remember most about family members during your childhood? Your Mother? Father? Brothers and sisters?
- Where did you live as a child?
- What was scary to you as a child? What did you like to do best?
- How did you feel about school? What were your favorite subjects?
- What was your most embarrassing moment as a child? As an adult?
- What was the loneliest time you experienced?
- Describe popular entertainment during your teenage years. Who was your favorite movie star? What were the fashions? What was your hairstyle?
- When did you move away from home?
- What were some of your early jobs? Early loves?
- Describe the hobbies that have been the most meaningful to you.
- What have been some of the more positive changes in the world during your lifetime? Negative?
- Did you raise your children as you were raised?
- What do you hope your children and grandchildren have learned from you?
- What have been the greatest pleasures in your life? What has caused the greatest pain?
- How do you feel about being a grandparent?
- What qualities of your personality have been the most useful to you over the years?
- How do you hope you will be remembered?
- Who had the most positive influence on your life?
- What are your hopes for the future?

Your grandchild will specifically want to know
- How did you feel when I was born?
- How did you feel when my parents got married?
- Do you have any advice for me?

Special Babyproofing Concerns for the Holidays

Your home will certainly be warm and inviting during the holidays for both adults and children, and you'll want to make sure that everything within reach of your grandchildren is safe. The most poisonous holiday decorations are mistletoe and jerusalem cherry, which are highly toxic; but other plants such as holly, poinsettia, evergreen trees (if your grandchild has an allergy), and stray pine needles can also cause problems if eaten. Be careful not to use a tree preservative that contains nitrates, which if ingested can cause a blood disorder. See to it that tree lights are the new cool-burning kind and are never near your grandchild's mouth—especially the small blinking ones, which contain a chemical that is dangerous to consume. Also beware of common decorations such as angel hair, tinsel, glass, or small plastic ornaments, which are choking hazards and can wreak havoc with your child's stomach if eaten. Be conscientious during the busy gift-giving season about batteries, colognes, ribbons, and wrappings, which pose special dangers to babies. And watch any alcoholic drinks so that they aren't accidentally consumed by your grandchildren. As a special precaution, post your local poison-control center's number near your phone and be sure that you or someone in your family is familiar with first-aid and CPR techniques for children.[2]

> "When I think about my own grandpa,
> there's so much I recall.
> Like the walks we took in summer
> and the leaves we raked in fall.
> Like the sleigh rides in December,
> and the circus in the spring,
> but what I think of most of all...
> more than anything,
> is how he smiled with such delight
> whenever he saw me,
> and how he hugged me close to him
> when I sat upon his knee.
> He loved me just for being me.
> He never asked for more.
> The very way that I love you.
> (That's what grandfathers are for.)"

Arlene Uslander, That's What Grandfathers Are For

Reprinted by permission. All rights reserved.

7
More Mailbox Treasures

The symptoms are, happily, completely incurable. A feverish expectation, spontaneous dancing in the front hall, a compulsion to peek through the windows and shout, "It's coming!" A hand outreached, as if pleading for the last drop of water on some Saharan plain—or the last jelly bean in the jar—and then, as the envelope is found, a long, joyous "Yesss!"

Something magical happens when a grandchild receives a piece of mail addressed only to her. In these days when buzzwords like "self-esteem" and "whole language" can obscure what helps children learn and grow, a letter from grandparent to grandchild gets to the heart of the matter by making the child feel special and intrigued by words. There's simply no better way to show how much you care than to make your grandchild's mailbox a treasure chest where she can regularly find games, notes, and ticklers from you.

What This Chapter Is All About

We know you're going to like this idea—we all love great deals, especially as we get wiser. This chapter is the place where we offer all the creative, mailable projects you could possibly want to keep a long-distance relationship thriving. All will fit in a nine-by-twelve-inch or smaller envelope, and each is created from materials you have around the house or can purchase for less than one dollar. Best of all, even if you used one idea a week for a year, you won't run out. (It's kind of like joining an activity-of-the-week club, only here you receive all your activities at once.) So flip through, turn back, find some favorites, and get started with your first activity; we'll meet you at the end for some further guidance and encouragement!

A Final Word Before You Get Started

Most of the activities we suggest here will not need any additional materials, but a few do require that your grandchild have some basic items. On your next trip to visit your grandchildren, it might be helpful if you took them shopping and filled a small basket with "Grandma and Grandpa's Goodies," which can be pulled out to use when your fun mailings arrive. (These materials are also great to use when you are visiting.) You might want to include washable crayons; washable markers; nontoxic white glue; regular and double-stick tape; child safety scissors; nontoxic paints and brushes; a package of colored construction paper; a magnet; and a small, inexpensive magnifying glass.

 ## Sponge Playthings

These are simple to make, lightweight to mail, and fun for a little one to play with in the tub or outside pool.

Ages: Six months to three years
You'll Need
- Several small, colored sponges
- Scissors
- White glue

Here's How
- If you're not artistically inclined, just trace the outline of coloring book animals or cookie cutter shapes onto the sponges and cut them out.
- Using the scrap pieces of sponge, cut out and glue on eyes, ears, tails, etc.

Colorful Collaborations

You and your grandchild might enjoy making a nonsense picture together through the mail!

Ages: Three to five years
You'll Need
- Paper and crayons or markers
- An envelope to mail your artistic treasure back and forth

Here's How
- Begin by making a few lines or shapes on a blank piece of paper.
- Mail it to your grandchild with a message that you'd like to know what he sees in your drawing.
- Then it's his turn to add to your drawings and send it back to you.
- Now it's your turn to tell what you see in the changing drawing.
- Once again add your mark and send it back.
- The last one to add to the drawing should be sure to post it for your next visit together; it will be a wonderful conversation piece.

Ice Crystal Creations

Your little darlings won't have to play in below-freezing weather to make these ice creations.

Ages: Three to five years
You'll Need to Send
- Dark green or navy construction paper
- A small plastic bag containing two tablespoons of Epsom salts

Here's How
- Suggest that your grandchildren draw a picture with crayons on the construction paper.
- Then an adult should help them mix the two tablespoons of Epsom salts with two tablespoons of water.
- Using this solution, tell your little "crystal creators" to paint over their crayon drawing and watch the ice crystals appear.

Let the parents know that Epsom salts are enclosed. They can be harmful if eaten.

Tangram Treasures

You've probably played with these shapes yourself. Share them with the next generation; help them develop some spatial relations savvy!

Ages: Six years and up
You'll Need
- An 8" square of cardboard

Here's How
- Following our diagram below, draw and cut out the seven tangram shapes.
- You might give your grandkids a head start with drawings of a few sample tangrams you've made with the pieces.
- Rules are you must use all seven pieces and nothing can overlap.
- Wish them "Good luck!"

Paper Bag Buddies

Children love puppets. Here are some that are easy to make and mail!

Ages: Two to five years
You'll Need to Send
- Small paper bags on which you've drawn some fun faces, or some faces and bodies
- Be sure to include extra plain bags so your grandchildren can make some of their own!

Here's How
- Try adding stand-up ears, a tail, a long red tongue cut out of colored construction paper, or hair from yarn or paper curls. Let your imagination go!
- You might add to this "bag buddy" collection periodically if your little "imagineers" enjoy it as much as ours do.

Secret Codes for Special Friends

You and your grandchild can enjoy the fun of a special secret code used to send your private messages!

Age: Five years and up
You'll Need
- The key to the code (see below)

Here's How
- Send a copy of the key to the code to your grandchild.
- When you want to write a message, just substitute the lines that enclose the letter you would normally have used.
- Don't forget the dots!
- You might send your grandchild the following message:

Whirling Dervish

Your little "parachuter wanna-be's" will love this one, and it couldn't be easier to pop in the mail!

Ages: Two years and up
You'll Need to Send
- A piece of 5"x8" paper into which you've made three cuts forming 4 "blades"

Here's How
Enclose the following instructions:
- Roll the paper into a tube and twist the bottom tightly so the tube won't unroll.
- Unfold the 4 blades.
- Get up as high on your toes as you can and drop your whirling dervish.

You might also suggest that your grandchild color the inside of the blades—the colors will form a fun pattern as they twirl through the air.

 # A Love Note "Supplement"

Nearly every Sunday newspaper has a supplement that has a page for children. It invariably includes activities such as fun jokes, follow-the-dot games, mazes, or simple recipes.

Why not make it a habit to send this along to your grandchildren? They'll love anticipating the regular mail, and it would be an easy addition to your regular love notes.

Paper Plate Pals

Summertime means picnics and paper plates. Here's a super, simple-to-make project to send that plays on this theme.

Ages: Two to eight years
You'll Need to Send
- Paper plates with a triangular wedge cut out of each plate
- Some samples of what you've been able to create might also be fun to include

Here's How
- The goal is to create a creature using one plate and one triangle. It's okay to use pens, crayons, cotton balls, and glue.
- You could add a few hints for your grandchild, such as how to divide the triangle into two smaller triangles to use as ears or into thin strips for whiskers or tails.

This idea can become a lifesaver when on a plane or in a car with an antsy grandtoddler! Any paper you can cut into a circle will work, and as long as you have a pen or pencil handy, you can make some fun circle-creature creations.

Paper-Punch Pictures

This easy, no-fail, colorful project is a winner any time of the year!

Ages: Two to eight years
You'll Need to Send
- Circles punched out from different colored papers
- Shirt cardboard or a piece of construction paper

Here's How
- Tell your favorite little artist to "draw" a design on the paper with glue.
- Suggest sprinkling and shaking the colored circles on top.
- Let dry and maybe she'll send her paper-punch picture back to you. One thing is certain: she'll want you to send more circles!

 # Stamping Sponges

Your little stampers will have a blast making their very own creations.

Ages: Two to eight years
You'll Need to Send
- Sponges that you've cut into fun shapes
- Nonglazed shelf paper, or brown paper bags that you've cut open into flat sheets

Here's How
- Using cookie cutters or crayon books for sample shapes, cut 5/8" thick sponges out into fun shapes and pop them in the mail to your budding artists.
- Your grandchildren can then enjoy dipping the sponges into paints and dabbing the paint onto the paper to create their very own designs.

Balloons of Love

Everyone loves balloons, especially when they contain a message of love!

Ages: Two to five years
You'll Need to Send
- A deflated balloon with a message

Here's How
- Write a message on a piece of paper to your grandchild. Fold it and tuck it inside the deflated balloon. In order to read what you've sent, the balloon will have to be blown up and popped!
- Or write a message to your grandchild on the blown-up balloon, then deflate it for mailing—again in order to read what you've written, the balloon must be blown up.

Caution parents about the potential choking hazard of balloon pieces.

Smell and Tell

Send a science activity that will be fun to discuss over the phone.

Ages: Three to eight years
You'll Need to Send
- Little envelopes filled with things your grandchild can identify by smell—crushed mint leaves, cocoa, orange peels, rose petals, cinnamon, cloves, vanilla on a cotton ball, crushed pine needles, etc.

Here's How
- Put one "smell" in each envelope and seal it to avoid "peeking."
- It'll help keep the smells separate if you then put each envelope in a separate small plastic bag.
- Number the envelopes and keep a record of what you have put in each one so you can have fun testing your little one when you talk.

School Days, School Days

Even nursery school can be a bit frightening when September and the first day roll around. Why not start a tradition by sending an annual good luck charm to help start the year off right?

Ages: Three to five years
You'll Need to Send
- A good luck charm: four leaf clover, amulet, charm, little stone on which you've painted a happy face, or anything you decide to call a good luck charm will work just fine!

Here's How
- Let your school-bound grandchildren know that you are thinking of them and wishing them well as they venture forth into new environments.
- Suggest that they might want to carry your good luck token in their pocket as a reminder that you're always with them in spirit.

Space Shoe Shuffle

Your little one will love making "space shoes" from the aluminum foil you send.

Ages: Eighteen months to three years

You'll Need to Send
- Two big sheets of heavy-duty aluminum foil
- This could even be a good time to send some news clippings with pictures of the latest space shuttle voyage.

Here's How
- Include directions for your grandchild to mold the foil around his shoes to create "moon boots" for a pretend moon walk.
- These may not last long, but they'll be great fun while they do!

Coupons of Caring

Nearly every response we had to our questionnaires suggested one-on-one time with a grandchild. Here's a great way to plan and anticipate special times together.

Ages: Eighteen months to eight years

You'll Need to Send

- Little tickets or coupons that you have made especially for your grandchild

Here's How

- You know better than anyone else what you and your grandchild enjoy doing together, so capitalize on that knowledge.
- Write one activity you enjoy doing together on each ticket or coupon. It might be something like baking cookies, going fishing, taking an evening walk, reading a favorite story, or taking a trip to the zoo.
- Whatever it is, your grandchild can look forward to redeeming the coupons the next time you are together. The anticipation will be half the fun!

You've undoubtedly seen these coupons in stores, but believe us, the homemade version will be much more appreciated and meaningful!

Flashlight Faces

A small penlight flashlight will delight your little one, especially when you send along some paper-bag faces!

Ages: Two to five years
You'll Need to Send
- A penlight flashlight
- Small, brown paper bags on which you've drawn funny faces with bold markers
- A rubber band

Here's How
- Draw some funny faces on the bags. You might try some sleepy looking expressions, too—this makes a great bedtime activity!
- Tell your little one to insert the flashlight into the bag, and close the end with the rubber band.
- In the dark, the faces will glow as the light shines through.
- Send some extra plain bags, so your little one can create his own faces to share with you the next time you are together.

"Giggle Maker" Sock Puppets

Don't throw out those old outgrown socks—turn them into adorable hand puppets in less than a minute!

Ages: Newborn to three years
You'll Need
- Old socks
- Scissors
- Permanent felt marker(s)

Here's How

- These couldn't be easier—all you have to do is cut five finger holes through the end toe stitching.
- Draw a bold face where the palm of

your hand falls.
- Fingers then become squiggly "bangs of hair."
- Send with a love note for the grateful parents as well as your much loved grandchild!

One or two of these are "must carries" for a Grandma's pocketbook!

Mystery Sounds

Familiar sounds from your home are the backdrop to this challenging "conversation-starter" of a game.

Ages: Three to five years
You'll Need to Send
- An audiotape of sounds from your home

Here's How
- Tape sounds in and around your home (door bell, telephone, clock chimes, dog barking, birds singing, water filling a tub, sewing machine, wind chimes, typewriter, Grandpa sneezing, etc.).
- Ask your grand-children on the tape if they can identify the sound riddles.
- Set up a time to dis-cuss their answers, or have them mail the answers to you.

Felt Board Fun

The classroom isn't the only place where felt boards can be enjoyed. If you make this board for your grandchild when you are visiting, it can be the basis for wonderful communications when you are apart. Just pop some new figures in the mail whenever you think of it!

Ages: Two to five years
You'll Need to Send
- A piece of cardboard for the backing on which you've stapled or tacked a piece of flannel (old pajamas will work; a plain color is best!)
- Shapes and figures cut out of felt

Here's How
- Ask your grandchild to tell a story with his figures.
- Or suggest he create a design with your shapes.
- You might copy the figures from a favorite book you have just read together.

As an alternative, cut out pictures from a magazine, have them laminated, or cover with clear contact paper. Then glue felt to the back.

Love Note Sippers

Straws are fun, so send a few with love notes attached!

Ages: Two to six years
You'll Need to Send
- Straws slipped through some personal notes

Here's How
- Start with 3" x 5" index cards, then cut them in half.
- Cut each half into a different shape such as a heart on which you write I love you; a circle on which you draw a smiley face; or a plain card on which you write your grandchild's name.
- Then using a paper punch, poke two holes through the card—one in the upper right corner, and one in the lower left corner.
- Insert the straw and mail.

Ask a parent to tuck one into a grandchild's lunchbox!

Vest 'em Up

Indians, cowboys, robots, policeman, spacemen—you name it, you can make it!

Ages: Two to five years
You'll Need
- Paper grocery bags
- Magic markers
- Construction paper, ribbons, yarn, aluminum-foil badges
- Glue

Here's How
- Cut a vest out of the paper bag to fit your little "imaginator."
- Slit the bag up the front and cut a circle area out of the bottom of the bag to fit over the head. Cut armholes in the sides of the bag. Shortening it for a wee one is simple!
- You can either send a decorated vest or send the ideas and let your little one create his own costume.
- If the bag has writing on it, just turn it inside out.

Shape Stories

This visual method of telling a story is fun to write and will tickle your little grandchild.

Ages: One to eight years
You'll Need
- To use your imagination and write a simple story

Here's How
- Pick a shape such as a snake, a dinosaur, a train, or a doll—something you know interests your grandchild.
- Write a short story incorporating the shape by making your words literally follow that design.
- Pop it in the mail and expect requests for more stories with "twisted" plots and "circuitous" descriptions.

Wooden Puppets in Minutes

Tongue depressors, popsicle sticks, or wooden kitchen spoons make great puppets.

Ages: Six months to eight years
You'll Need
- Wooden tongue depressors or popsicle sticks
- Wooden kitchen spoons of any size
- Permanent felt markers
- Fabric scraps, yarn, and glue

Here's How
- Start by drawing a face at the top of the sticks or on the bowl of the spoon—you can do a happy face on one side and a sad face on the other!
- Create the body with fabric scraps making hats, scarves, and clothes.
- Yarn can be used to create hair.
- Be sure to enclose some plain sticks or spoons with the materials so your "puppeteers" can create some puppets of their own.

Balloons—Balloons—Balloons!

From packing material to games, don't underestimate the many possibilities with balloons.

Ages: Two to five years
Need to protect a fragile gift in the mail?
Pack some partially blown up balloons around it. They could prove to be as much fun for your toddler as the gift itself!

Need a game for two energetic preschooler grandchildren?
Make two balloon "paddles" for playing "balloon-ball" by bending coat hanger wires into ping pong paddle shapes and then covering

them with old nylon stockings. Be sure to tape the wire ends with masking tape so they won't cause scratches. Add a balloon and the fun begins!

Need a simple present to send in the mail?
Make a funny cardboard foot from a shirt cardboard by cutting a slit halfway into the middle. Send it with a deflated balloon and instruct your bouncing buddy to blow up the balloon and slip the tied end into the cardboard slit. When the balloon is batted into the air it'll land on it's feet every time!

Keep deflated or broken balloons away from babies who are still putting things in their mouths, and always keep an eye on a little one playing with a blown up balloon.

Puzzling Grandparents

Surprise your grandchildren with your smiling faces after they piece together this puzzle!

Ages: Three to eight years
You'll Need
- An enlarged photo of yourselves
- A shirt cardboard
- Glue
- Scissors

Here's How
- Glue your photo onto the shirt cardboard.
- With scissors cut it up into puzzle shapes—having the difficulty of the puzzle match the ability of your grandchild.
- Send the pieces off in an envelope with a note such as: "When you put this together, you'll see who loves you."

Picture Words

Even your littlest grandchildren will enjoy guessing what the pictures "say."

Ages: Two to five years
You'll Need to Send
- Drawings or cut outs of figures that when combined with other pictures make a word or words—a rebus.

Here's How
- The English language is filled with words that can be deciphered from a series of pictures. Some examples are:

foot + ball	missile + toe
butter + cup	chest + nuts
horse + radish	stone + wall
station + wagon	dragon + fly

- Come up with a page for your little one to guess using either drawings or pictures cut out of magazines.

Color Collections

This will make a fun activity for a toddler grandchild just learning about colors.

Ages: One to three years
You'll Need to Send
- Sheets of construction paper in red, yellow, blue, green, etc.
- Post-it notes in different colors

Here's How
- Ask your little munchkin to spread out the colored sheets on the floor and collect things on each paper that are of the same color.
- Another fun activity will be to suggest your little color coordinator pop a sticky post-it note on whatever matches the color of the note.
- When you talk on the phone, you can ask what is on each colored sheet or where the post-it notes have been placed.

Balding Grandpa Grows Hair

Kids love to watch things grow, and with this project they'll even get a chance to give "Balding Grandpa" a haircut! (With an adult supervising the use of the scissors, of course!)

Ages: Three to eight years
You'll Need to Send
- One half a teaspoon of annual grass seed
- Enough dirt in a small plastic bag to fill a 12 oz. frozen juice can
- "Balding Grandpa's" body!

Here's How
- You can either draw "Balding Grandpa" on paper or create him out of scraps of cloth—just be sure his head is cut off straight across the top where his hair would normally begin to grow!
- "Balding Grandpa" should be 5" tall.
- Have your little gardener put the dirt in a juice can, plant the seeds in the top, water well, tape "Grandpa" onto the front of the can, and set him in a sunny window.
- It won't be long before "Balding Grandpa" becomes "Hairy Gramps" and will need that supervised haircut!

Icy Icicles

A few strings in the mail can turn into not only icicles but even a conversation about stalactites in caves!

Ages: Two to eight years
You'll Need to Send
- A long string with little strings dangling down
- Instructions for how to make icicles outside a window in the wintertime

Here's How
- When the weather is below freezing, hang the "string of strings" across the outside top of a window.
- Drip water down the string a few drops at a time until icicles form.

You can follow up this activity with some fun conversations on the phone about igloos, icebergs, or even how stalactites form!

Flying Foam

Foam meat trays can be converted into great airplanes.

Ages: Four years and up
You'll Need to Send
- Foam meat trays that have been washed and cut into airplane shapes

Here's How
- Cut a plane body shape, wings and a tail from the trays.
- Make a slit where the wings should go.
- Make a slit where the tail should go.
- Mail the pieces unassembled with instructions to push the wings and tail through the body of the plane.
- Suggest contests to see whose plane can fly the highest or stay aloft the longest!

Remember Remember?

You may have called it remember or concentration, but it's an old card game favorite that even the high-tech grandchildren of today will enjoy!

Ages: Three to six years
You'll Need
- Metal lids from frozen juice containers (the kind you remove by pulling a white plastic strip)
- Stickers (two sets needed to make pairs)

Here's How
- Wash the metal lids—these have smooth edges!
- Put a sticker on only one side of each lid—making pairs.
- Send the instructions for a new twist to the old game:

- All the pieces are placed picture down on the table.
- The first person gets to turn over two lids.
- If they match, he gets to keep the pair. If they don't match, he must turn them back over and the next person has a turn.
- The one with the most pairs at the end of the game wins.

- This makes a simple fun game to add to by mail when you are separated from your wee one—just pop a new pair of lids in the mail when you think of it.
- Because they have the "ring" of money, a younger grandchild will love carrying these lids in a "dress up" pocketbook.

A Little Detective Game

Get out your old science journals, grandparents, and teach your grandsleuths how to discover who sent the parcel!

Ages: Four years and up
You'll Need to Send

- Your smudgy fingerprints on the paper and envelope
- A tiny magnifying glass
- A piece of cotton soaked in Grandma's perfume or Grandpa's shaving cream

Here's How
- You could quote the scientific fact that fingerprints and smells last and can be used to identify people.
- Send your fingerprints and the scent of your perfume or shaving cream through the mail to see if your little scientist can detect who it's from.
- Turn a few of those fingerprints into little bugs: just add some legs and eyes. and suggest you'd like your grandsleuth to send some "bug-prints" your way too.

Sprouting Beans

It won't take long for dried beans to sprout from a moist paper towel—and for your grandchildren to be excitedly telling you about it on the phone!

Ages: Eighteen months to seven years
You'll Need to Send
- Dried beans, lima beans, or corn kernels
- A paper towel

Here's How
- Have your grandchild soak the beans overnight in water and then put them on the moistened paper towel.
- If the towel is kept damp, the beans will soon start to sprout.
- Warn your little gardener not to use too much water or the beans will rot!
- When the beans have sprouted, you can discuss by phone how plants grow.

What'll Stick?

Discovering what "stickiness" is all about is good fun for your inquisitive toddler grandchild.

Ages: One to three years
You'll Need to Send
- A sheet of clear contact paper (do not remove the paper backing)
- Lightweight objects that will "stick," such as yarn, ribbon, photographs, pictures cut out of magazines, feathers, scraps of fabric, paper doilies, etc.

Here's How
- Ask the parent to tape the clear contact sheet up on a window or wall—sticky side out and down at grandtoddler level.
- Have the parent remove the paper backing and provide your envelope full of objects so that your grandchild can create and enjoy the sticky sensation.

What Is a Memory?

Help your grandchild understand the meaning of "a memory."

Ages: Four years and up
You'll Need to Send
- Part of a picture of something very familiar to your grandchild—such as your pet or your house.
- The explanation of how we carry memories in our minds even when we can't see the things we remember.

Here's How
- Cut off part of the picture of the familiar object such as the dog's tail or the roof of the house. Mail the main part of the picture one day, and save the cut-off part in a separate envelope to mail a day later.
- Tell your grandchild to draw what her memory tells her is missing.
- She'll be able to see if her memory served her well when the next day's mail arrives!

Frame It Up with Toothpicks

Toothpick construction will capture the creative energies of your clever builders.

Ages: Three years and up
You'll Need to Send
- Toothpicks

Here's How
- Wrap some toothpicks up in heavy paper so they won't poke through the envelope.
- Send off with the challenge to CREATE!
- With a little gluing on colored paper your clever builders can make unique pictures.
- Don't forget to mention using them for another favorite—3-D tinker toy toothpicks—just use cooked peas, gumdrops, or little balls of clay to join one to the other.

Be careful to keep sharp toothpicks away from smaller siblings.

 # Money Bunny

What else besides a bunny can your clever spender turn three coins into?

Ages: Three to eight years
You'll Need to Send
- A quarter, nickel, and dime

Here's How
- By tracing around her coins, see how many things your clever spender can turn the coins into before they burn a hole in her pocket!
- Perhaps she'll add ears, a face, and whiskers to the bunny; a face, black buttons, pipe, arms, and hat to a snowman; or even ears, arms, and a face to a bear!

Coins can choke a young child. Please be sure to tell parents what's enclosed if a younger sibling is at risk.

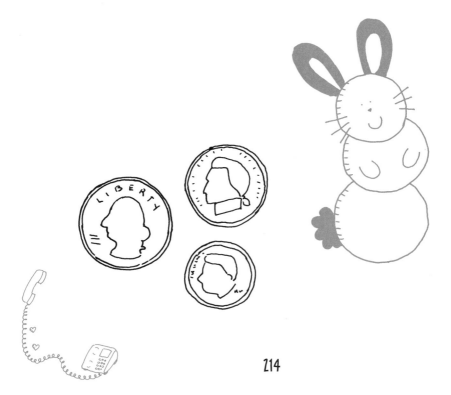

Pet Pieces

If you make these sturdy and colorful they are bound to be used again and again!

Ages: Two to five years
You'll Need
- Poster board or
  similar heavy colored paper
- Or you could use fabric to make these "pet pieces"

Here's How
- Cut out two rectangles about 1" x 4"
- Cut out two triangles about 2" x 2" x 2 1/2"
- Cut out one circle with about a 2" diameter
- Cut out one rectangle about 3" x 5"
- Cut out one rectangle about 1 1/2" x 4".
- Send these 7 shapes with the challenge: "How many different pets can you make?"

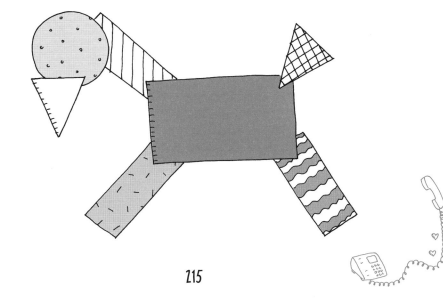

Seamstress or Tailor in the Making

Your little "wanna-be" seamstress or tailor will feel very satisfied with one of these completed projects.

Ages: Three to six years
You'll Need
- Thin cardboard
- To draw pictures or use pictures from a coloring book
- Large plastic needle
- Thick colored yarn

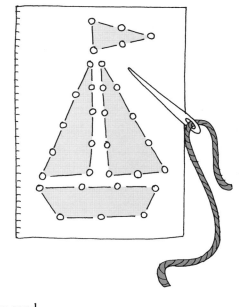

Here's How
- Draw a simple figure such as a boat, kite, or duck, but instead of making a solid line around the figure, break it every 1/2" or so with two dots spaced about 1/4" apart. You will have created a sewing or embroidery card.
- Thread the plastic needle with the yarn, and mail the package off to your little "wanna-be" to complete.
- Suggest that the yarn in the short space between the two dots be on the back of the card and the long 1/2" "stitch" show on the front side.

 # Return the Favor!

Check out the Body Double activity, p. 127 and surprise your grandchild with a life-sized poster of Gram and Gramps. It'll fold up into a large manila envelope and is sure to be a winner when opened up.

Send an Animal Zoo

This is a great follow-up activity to a trip to the zoo, and it couldn't be easier!

Ages: Two to five years
You'll Need to Send
- Pipe cleaners (3 for each animal)
- Straw cut into 1 1/2" long pieces (one piece for each animal's body)
- Construction paper

Here's How
- Send instructions to thread three pipe cleaners through one piece of straw so that the straw "body" is in the middle.
- Bend two pipe cleaners down to form the legs and feet.
- The third pipe cleaner becomes the tail and neck.
- Draw a head and face on the construction paper, cut it out, and paste them onto the neck.
- You'll be amazed at the different animals your grandchild will create!

Mysterious Mover

Turn a small piece of magnetic tape into a "magic wand," and your grandson can wow his buddies with his mysterious mover.

Ages: Three years and up
You'll Need
- Magnetic strip tape
- 3" x 5" card

Here's How
- Cut the magnetic tape into two 2" pieces.
- Cut a train, boat, or car out of the card.
- Stick one piece of the magnetic strip onto the bottom of the vehicle.
- Send along with the second strip that your little driver can use as his "magic wand."
- One end of the magnet will repel the vehicle, and the other end will attract it. For additional fun, put the vehicle on top of a cardboard box lid. Make it move, as if by magic, by dragging the "magic wand" underneath the lid.

 # Paper Doll Chains Still Captivate

Introduce your little ones to something their great, great grandparents used to make!

Ages: Two to six years
You'll Need to Send
- Some old-fashioned paper dolls and folded paper, with instructions for making more.

Here's How
- Accordion-fold a piece of paper.
- Draw a paper doll figure: paper doll, teddy bear, etc.
- Cut out, being careful not to cut through the folds where the hands and bodies must join.

Crazy Mixed-Up Creatures

Your imaginative grandkids will get a big kick out of the crazy mixed-up creatures they'll be able to create with this one!

Ages: Two to five years

You'll Need to Send

- Fun drawings of animals on 8 1/2" x 11" paper

Here's How

- You really don't have to be an artist to do these—the crazier they look, the better your grandkids will like them!
- Draw a bunch of different animals—one to a page.
- The only hitch is that the animals must be the same size at the neck and at the mid tummy sections.
- The mid-section must fall 3 1/2" up from the bottom of the page and the neck area 7" up from the bottom of the page.
- With a ruler, draw dotted lines across the page through the picture at the 3 1/2" and 7" marks—this is where your grandkids will cut each figure into three parts.
- The fun comes when all the body parts are mixed-up and then put together to form crazy creatures.
- The older preschoolers will get a kick out of mixing up the names, too. Give each section a name. Starting at the top of a figure, the head area might be called "Miss," the middle area "Susie," and the bottom area "Squirrel," "Big Harry Hamster," or "Fluffy Teddy Bear." The mixed-up names will inspire as many giggles as the mixed-up creatures!

Marching in Style

You might want to include these for all members of the marching band!

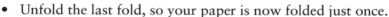

Ages: Two to four years
You'll Need
- One sheet of newspaper funnies for each hat
- A stapler

Here's How
- Fold the approximately 22" x 14" piece of newspaper in half and then in quarters.
- Unfold the last fold, so your paper is now folded just once.
- Take the outer edges of both ends of the folded edge, bringing them to the center crease line forming the two triangles. Do this one more time so they form the double 2" hat brim.
- Staple the hat brim ends.
- Suggest adding some rhythm band instruments so all can "march in style!"

Cards of Membership

Little people love to copy grown-ups, so why not supply your favorite little munchkin with a few homemade credit cards, a license, or even a "Grandpa's Grand Club" card?

Ages: Two years and up
You'll Need
- 3" x 5" cards that you've cut to be 3 3/8" x 2 1/8" to simulate a real credit card

Here's How
- Let your imagination inspire some fun cards to make and send.
- Laminate or cover with clear contact paper so they'll look like the real thing.
- We know one Grandpa who used to hold a "Papa's Picnic Pals" meeting once a month when he planned a picnic lunch with his grandchildren. You could even make a "Papa's Picnic Pals Club" card for the occasion.
- To complete the "grown-up" feeling, it might be fun to include in your package an old wallet that has plastic card sleeves.

Gelatin Jiggles

This holdable treat is simple to make, entertaining to cut out, and best of all, yummy to eat!

Ages: Two years and up
You'll Need to Send
- One large box of gelatin
- A plastic cookie cutter or two

Here's How
- Mom or Dad will have to help boil 1 1/4 cups water or apple juice and stir in the gelatin.
- Dissolve completely but unlike regular gelatin, do not add cold water!
- Pour into an 8" square pan and chill for at least 3 hours.
- Dip the bottom of the pan in warm water for about 15-20 seconds.
- Cut straight through to the bottom of the pan with the cookie cutter shapes.
- Lift out the jiggles with a metal spatula.
- These are even firm enough for those cute little hands to hold.

Flashlight Fun

A flashlight might just be one of your preschooler's favorite toys!

Ages: Two to five years
You'll Need to Send
- A small flashlight and batteries

Here's How
- Starting with her own body, ask your little gal if she can "see through" her skin to observe the bones in her fingers by shining the light through the palm of her hand.
- Use the flashlight to make "hand animal" shadows on the wall just the way we used to do on a movie screen before the homemade feature arrived!
- Tape colored tissue paper over the end of the light to give her world a new hue!
- Blink out a message to a friend in the night.

Straw Symphony

A simple but effective way to "blow your horn!"

Ages: Two to eight years
You'll Need
- Plastic drinking straws
- Scissors

Here's How
- Flatten about 1" of one end of the straw.
- Cut the flattened part into a sharp point (it'll look similar to a sharp pencil).
- Cut several straws this way—making some shorter than others and making different size "reed ends."
- Send them off in the mail with the hint: to blow your horn simply put the pointed "V" inside your mouth, just behind your lips, and blow hard.
- The shorter the straw, the higher the sound and the easier to blow.

Reflecting Painting

The fun of guessing "what's missing" and then the magic of seeing the "missing half" in the mirror makes this a terrific project!

Ages: Three years and up
You'll Need to Send
- Paper and pen
- Drawings of half of anything bilateral: a heart, a butterfly, face, person, circle, etc.

Here's How
- Fold your paper in half and draw just half of the bilateral figure, bringing the center of the figure to the fold in the paper.
- Ask your grandchild to guess what the object is.
- To find the answer, your grandchild must place the fold next to a mirror; the half-drawn image will reflect its other half, creating a whole object.
- Ask how many other reflecting pictures your little one can then draw on his own.
- For an older grandchild, you might try sending a photo of yourself that is cut in half, lengthwise. Isn't it funny how different you look when the mirror "fills in" the other half?

Wet and Wild Watercolors

These are simple to make, and grandkids will love squirting markered drawings until they become priceless watercolor paintings!

Ages: Two to six years
You'll Need
- Coffee filters
- Colored, water-soluble markers

Here's How
- Color designs on the coffee filters (be sure to send some plain ones along in the package, so your "squirter" can make some of his own too).
- Suggest that this be done outside—a super activity for a hot summer day!
- Hang the colored filters on a clothesline.
- Fill spray bottles with water and turn the "squirters" loose with their "watercolor makers."
- As they spray the hanging coffee filters, the colors will blur.
- Bathing suits might be appropriate attire for this—be prepared!

Who Needs a Magnifying Glass?

Sometimes the simplest things give the biggest results!

Ages: Two to eight years
You'll Need
- A 3" x 5" index card

Here's How
- Poke a pinhole in the middle of the card.
- Pop the card in the mail and explain to your grandchild that if he looks at something through the hole with one eye while closing the other eye, the object will seem much bigger than it actually is.
- Suggest he experiment with the same technique by curling his hand into a fist and looking through the tiny hole his fingers create.
- Pull out one of those saved paper towel tubes from the scrap box, and closing one eye, look with the other eye through the tube at the stars. Do they seem larger than normal?

Puppets in the Bath

Simple washcloth or foam sheet puppets can make for giggles in the tub!

Ages: Birth to four years
You'll Need
- Washcloths
- 1/8" thick "foamtastic" fabric, which comes in 9"x12" size sheets
- A sewing machine or needle and thread

Here's How
- Turn the washcloths or the "foamtastic" into hand puppets by sewing them into a mitt shape.
- Create faces or bodies: sew on ears, noses, tongues, hands, or feet with additional pieces of the foam sheet.
- Even your fussiest grandchild will be all smiles and giggles while getting clean.

Put on Those "Rose-Colored Glasses"

Simple colored plastic wrap can turn a grandchild's world into a magical realm.

Ages: Two to five years
You'll Need to Send
- Four 4" square pieces of colored plastic wrap—send each sheet between a piece of paper
- Four rubber bands
- Optional: a small penlight flashlight if your grandchild doesn't have one

Here's How
- Hopefully your grandchild's "scrap box" will have two empty toilet paper tubes or a paper towel tube.
- Make binoculars with the two empty tubes and a telescope with the paper towel tube by securing the squares of wrap on the ends of each tube with the rubber bands.
- Another fun thing to do is to secure a square of the colored wrap over the end of the flashlight to change the color of your grandchild's world!
- Colored cellophane will work beautifully too, but it is sometimes more difficult to find.

 # I See the Moon

"I See the Moon, The Moon Sees Me" has been a favorite family song of ours since our children were little. The moon seems to hold a fascination for young and old alike, and here's a clever way to share that interest.

Ages: Eighteen months to five years
You'll Need
- Non-toxic, glow-in-the-dark paint
- Poster board
- Double stick tape

Here's How

- Cut a moon shape out of the poster board—maybe add some stars too for a more realistic "sky."
- Paint your stars and moon with the glow-in-the-dark paint.
- Put double stick tape on the back, and before mailing cover the exposed sticky side of the tape with a piece of aluminum foil to be peeled off when the "sky" is ready to be installed on your fellow stargazer's bedroom ceiling.
- Bedtime might be more fun with Grandpa's "sky" overhead!

How about enclosing a tape of you singing:

> I see the moon, the moon sees me
> The moon sees somebody I want to see.
> God bless the moon and God bless me,
> And God bless the somebody I want to see.
>
> He picked you out from all the rest
> Because he knew we'd love you the best.
> God bless the moon and God bless me,
> And God bless the somebody I want to see.

227

Jump Through

Give your grandchild the secret to this fun magic trick so he can perform for his friends.

Ages: Five years and up
You'll Need to Send
- A copy of the pattern on the facing page, enlarged on an 8 1/2" x 11" piece of paper with the following instructions.

Here's How
- Have your grandchild challenge his friends to jump through a piece of paper.
- Following your instructions, he should carefully punch a hole with scissors through the circle at the top of the paper. Following that line, he should cut carefully across, down, back, down, across, down, etc., until reaching the circle at the bottom of the page.
- Next he should cut the remaining solid lines beginning at the edges, being very careful to stop where the lines stop.
- Voilà! To the amazement of his friends, he can spread the paper apart into a huge circle and jump through!

What Goes Through?

Discovering filters and strainers can be fun even through the mail.

Ages: Three to five years
You'll Need to Send Some of These
- A piece of old nylon stocking
- A piece of cheese cloth
- Pieces of window screening with holes of various sizes
- The bottom of a plastic berry basket
- A small plastic bag filled with a teaspoon of differently sized particles such as sugar, tapioca, rice, dried beans, macaroni, etc.

Here's How
- Number the filters from finest to coarsest.
- Suggest that your little scientist start with the finest and progress to the coarsest filter, and sift the contents of the bag through each strainer.
- Enjoy her delight and excitement when you next talk by phone!

One-Sided Wonder

Surprise your grandchild with the Möbius strip puzzle.

Ages: Four years and up
You'll Need
- A strip of paper approximately 1" x 11"

Here's How—Tell Your Grandchildren
- Make a hoop out of the strip but give it a half-twist before joining the two ends with transparent tape.
- Challenge your grandchild to draw a continuous line on the paper (without lifting the pencil off the paper).
- Your grandchild will be amazed that the continuous line has covered both sides of the paper!

Bath Tub Tiles

Colorful shapes covered with clear contact paper make a great bath tub construction toy.

Ages: One to five years
You'll Need
- Colorful paper
- Clear contact paper
- Scissors

Here's How
- Cut the paper into various shapes approximately 1" square—cut circles, triangles, moons, stars, squares, rectangles, hearts, etc.
- Peel the backing off a sheet of contact paper and position your colored shapes on top—leaving about 1" between the shapes.
- Place a second piece of clear contact sticky side down on top of the shapes.
- Cut out each shape leaving 1/2" border on all sides.
- When wet, these tub art tiles will stick to the side of the tub or tile.
- Pop them in an envelope and imagine what fun your wee one will have making funny faces, constructing buildings, or just crazy designs with your tub tiles.

 # This Sure Beats Darning!

Find a good use for those holey socks in your mending basket!

Ages: One year and up
You'll Need
- Old socks
- Felt and yarn scraps
- Pipe cleaners, ribbon, buttons, etc.
- Colored markers

Here's How
- Push the toe of the sock inside the foot and take a few stitches to hold it there—this will be a mouth.
- Let your imagination go and create some fun puppets—the zanier the better!
- Pop the puppets in the mail and be prepared to "get in the act" the next time you're visiting!

Fingers Save the Day for Our Legless Puppets

Send these puppets in the mail so your grandchild can give them legs!

Ages: Two to five years

You'll Need
- Pictures of animals or people
- Glue and cardboard

Here's How
- Cut out the figures (4" tall makes a good height), but cut off at the leg area.
- Glue onto thin poster board or shirt cardboard.
- Cut two finger holes where the legs would normally be.
- Pop your puppets in the mail.
- We know you'll wish you could be there when the puppets come to life!

From Surfacing Submarines to Balloon Boats

Send this simple toy in the mail for hours of fun and experimentation.

Ages: Four years and up

You'll Need
- Plastic straw with bendable end
- Round balloon
- Tape and scissors
- Styrofoam plate

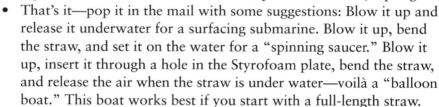

Here's How
- Cut the straw in half.
- Cut the rolled end off of the balloon.
- Insert the end of the bending half of the straw into the balloon and tape the balloon to the straw. Blow it up and if air leaks, tape again.
- That's it—pop it in the mail with some suggestions: Blow it up and release it underwater for a surfacing submarine. Blow it up, bend the straw, and set it on the water for a "spinning saucer." Blow it up, insert it through a hole in the Styrofoam plate, bend the straw, and release the air when the straw is under water—voilà a "balloon boat." This boat works best if you start with a full-length straw.

Remember that deflated balloons can choke grandkids younger than three. Be sure to alert parents if siblings may be at risk.

Here We Go Loopy Loo

Turn the straw and two simple strips of paper into a plane from outer space!

Ages: Three to five years

You'll Need to Send
- A plastic straw
- Two strips of paper—both about 1" wide. Make one strip about 8" long and the other about 11" long

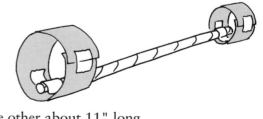

Here's How

- To construct the spaceship: Bend each paper strip into a circle and secure with tape.
- Tape one circle to each end of the straw with the ends of the straw on the inside of the circles.
- Instruct your budding astronaut to set it aloft with the smallest circle as the nose of the craft.

Kites and Grandkids Go Together

This simple kite couldn't be easier to make or send.

Ages: Two to eight years
You'll Need
- A plastic bread bag
- 3 pieces of string 20" long
- Scissors

Here's How
- Fold back the open edge of the bread bag to make a 1 1/2" cuff.
- Cut three holes (equidistant from each other) through the cuff and bag.
- Tie an end of each string to each hole.
- Bring the free ends of the string together and tie them in a knot in the end.
- Tell your "high flier" to run into the wind to set the kite aloft.

Plastic bags can be dangerous for babies. Make sure parents with younger siblings know what your package contains.

Space Capsule Landing

Send a love note to your little darling on the wings of a space capsule.

Ages: Two to eight years
You'll Need
- A 12" square piece of plastic
- 4 pieces of string each about 8" long
- Your note inside an aluminum foil pouch

Here's How
- Punch a hole in each corner of the plastic about 1/2" in from the edge.
- Thread a piece of string through each corner and knot it.
- Spread the plastic out flat and gather up the four strings so they meet in the center.
- Tie all the strings together in a knot about 1" up from the loose ends.
- Write your love note and encase it in an aluminum foil pouch. You might want to add a lucky penny or two for weight!
- Tie the foil pouch onto the end of the strings. You will have created a parachute to deliver your love note—space capsule landing style!
- Send it with the instructions to throw it up in the air before unwrapping the foil pouch.

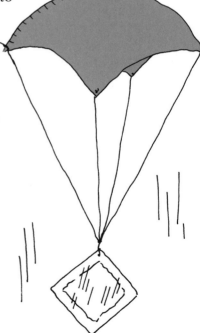

The plastic sheet and coins can choke a little one. Please let the parents know what is inside your envelope.

Puppet Pals

These finger puppets and stage are tiny, lightweight, and always handy whether on a plane or in a restaurant!

Ages: Nine months to five years

You'll Need
- The base for your finger puppets: the fingertips cut off of old cotton gloves, a 1 1/2" square of bendable cardboard, or even Band Aids!
- Tape
- Pens, yarn, fabric scraps
- Lunch-sized paper bag

Here's How
- Use the glove fingertips, wrap the lightweight cardboard around your finger and tape it, or put a Band Aid around your finger.
- Give your puppets "character" with the pens, yarn, and fabric scraps.
- Cut out a rectangle in the center of one side of the paper bag to make a "stage."
- Lights, camera, action!

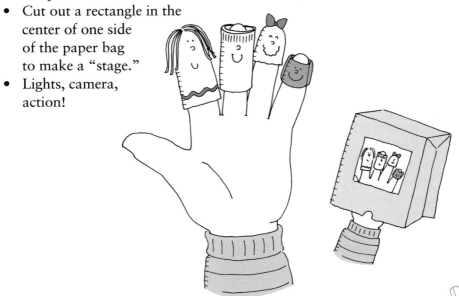

Grandloving by Mail: Creating a Lasting Language Together

By the time we're old enough to be grandparents, many of us have a hunch that young children might learn best through play. Those silly rhymes and goofy jokes we shared with our friends and family when we were kids, after all, form some of our most vivid memories. As teachers of hundreds of children whose language blossomed during our time together, Julie and I can happily and wholeheartedly confirm your suspicions: all that fun actually launches "schoolbook" learning. It's beyond question now that the way children learn to talk and write is intimately tied to the ways in which they play and form loving relationships.

What does this mean for your relationship with your little bundle or busybody? Simply that you can encourage this astonishing process of learning to speak and write through your light, fun communications. Best of all, this is the kind of sharing and learning that grandparents and grandchildren can do best.

No, we're not suggesting that you work to make that grandchild of yours a superbaby. That little one is going to be the sparkle in your eye no matter what he or she accomplishes, and that's just as it should be. But by bridging the distance between you and your grandchild, you'll both benefit. Think of how fun it will be to build a collection of favorite found objects; how your magical "decoder" will draw out many of the cryptic feelings of your grandchild; and how the bits of science that you teach through mailable experiments could spark a lifelong interest in exploration and discovery. Every time you pop one of your ideas in the mailbox, you'll know that you're encouraging the best in your grandchildren and offering the best of yourself—your personalized love—to them. It's a win-win proposition that will enliven your friendship with your little ones and make you the most memorable grandparent you can be.

Happy Grandloving, everyone!

8
Caring for Your Grandchild

If I Had My Child to Raise Over Again
If I had my child to raise all over again,
I'd build self-esteem first, and the house later.
I'd finger-paint more, and point the finger less.
I would do less correcting and more connecting.
I'd take my eyes off my watch, and watch with my eyes.
I would care to know less and know to care more.
I'd take more hikes and fly more kites.
I'd stop playing serious, and seriously play.
I would run through more fields and gaze at more stars.
I'd do more hugging and less tugging.
I'd see the oak tree in the acorn more often.
I would be firm less often, and affirm much more.
I'd model less about the love of power,
And more about the power of love.

From the book Full Esteem Ahead *(1994 by Diane Loomans with Julia Loomans. Reprinted by permission of H.J. Kramer, P.O. Box 1082, Tiburon, CA. All rights reserved).*

Taking care of a grandchild—for a weekend, summer, or even longer—is both a trick and a treat. Without the guiding presence of your little one's Mom or Dad, you'll truly be flying solo, with all the responsibility and worry of being your grandchild's primary caregiver. It may have been awhile since you had to negotiate through a day with a youngster, and both you and your grandchild may feel anxious about how the routines of meals, bath, and bedtime will work in your home. (See chapter 4 for creative ways to prepare for a grandchild's visit.) But there is a sweet reward for overcoming any apprehension: by taking the chance to express your true self and get to know your much-loved grandchild during this special time, you'll open up wonderful opportunities for creating unique traditions together.

The Lonely Ranger: Adding a Little Familiarity in a New Environment

It's seventeen hundred hours. The parents of your four visiting grandchildren told you in no uncertain terms before they left for the weekend that this is Dinner Time at their house. Okay, then. "Hup, two, three, four! Aboooouuut face! Grandchildren, line up!"

Well, that's one example of a regimen that children can depend on, but as you've probably guessed, we think you should aim for much less routine during a busy and fun visit. Instead, focus on encouraging a flexible schedule that will result in the biggest rewards for all of you—rested, healthy children. "Keep kids on a routine—familiar foods, bring own port-a-crib," wrote Joanne Slotnick of Salt Lake City, Utah (in the abbreviated style all young mothers can appreciate). Adele and Simon Wright from Scotland concur. They wrote about their anticipated first trip to visit family in New Zealand: "As a big trip to another country to visit grandparents can be quite a disruption for a baby, . . . it's a good idea to take your own travel cot. Let the baby get used to it for a week or two beforehand by having him sleep in it at home, and it can become a safe sanctuary for him in the midst of unfamiliar surroundings."

"Dearer than our children are the children of our children."

—An Egyptian Proverb

Most important, talk to your grandchild's parents before the grandchildren are left in your primary care so that your priorities match up on these and other issues. We found that stocking up on some no-fail healthy foods and trying to hold the line on bedtimes and naps (to the extent that parents do) made for a guilt-free transition. Also find the name and number of a good pediatrician in your area; ask the parents to leave a signed and dated note giving you permission to authorize medical care for your grandchild; and make sure you can reach those footloose and fancy-free parents at all times.

Outings

There's nothing like that feeling of watching the parents' car pull out the drive or their plane taxi for takeoff. It's both exhilarating and a bit nerve-wracking to think that now you and your grandchild will be one-on-one buddies for the days to come. Well, who says you need to stay home yourselves? Outings can be one way to make this close personal attention a lot of fun for your young visitors—just take along a bag with food, any diapering items, an extra set of clothes, and a few small toys for each child to make sure nothing will spoil your good experience. Some terrific outings for young children include picnics; trips to the zoo, museums, parks, or library (check the library story hour schedule); visits to a dairy farm, cider mill or to see maple syrup being made; "doing lunch"; or going to a movie. Enjoy nature outings with your little one: feed ducks, cross-country ski, bird watch, fish, collect shells, build sand castles or snowmen, or just lie in the grass and name the shapes of the clouds in the sky. Don't forget walks around the neighborhood, or as Ginny Klassen from Sun Lakes, Arizona suggested, try to make as many people smile as you can along the way. Who can resist a sunny grin and cheery "Good Morning" and the fun of counting how many people you've made happy? You know best what's going on in your area, and if you're not sure, try browsing through your newspaper or calling your local children's library or hands-on children's museum for ideas. Most of all, do a child-oriented activity that you will enjoy as much as your grandchild will; your enthusiasm will be infectious.

You might want to consider a longer trip, such as a day trip to a beach or an overnight campout at a campground nearby. Older grandchildren will enjoy even more extensive trips. See our resources at the end of this chapter for terrific travel agencies that can help you plan.

More car safety tips

It can surprise grandparents used to driving with only the hum of the engine and some classical music in the background to suddenly have the added distraction of grandchildren in the car. Perhaps you're not accustomed to getting an occasional animal cracker down the back of your neck or a sudden holler of "What's that, Grandpa?!" from a boisterous toddler. The effect on your driving can be at the least distracting, and at the worst, disastrous.

What can you do to keep your grandchildren happy and your concentration intact? First, make sure all your grandchildren are buckled into appropriate car seats or boosters, as required by the laws in your state. All child restraints in your car should be manufactured after 1981, when the federal government began requiring manufacturers to certify that their seats could pass crash tests.

Next, make sure you have some fail-safe toys and snacks within reach of your older grandchildren or within your reach so you can pass something fun to the back seat while at a stoplight. We found an especially durable and fun companion was an unbreakable mirror fastened to the front seats and facing the munchkin in the rear. Now you won't have to be the only audience for all your grandchild's antics in the car!

Last, but never least, set some ground rules for riding in Grandma and Grandpa's car. You might want to top the list with the ultimate pair of safety rules: the car doesn't move unless everyone is buckled in, and everyone puts their hands on their heads before doors are closed (to prevent pinched fingers). And be sure to include the essential dictate that "everyone gets to choose a silly song to sing." After all, not all rules have to be dreaded or difficult.

Alphabet Derby and Other Games for the Car

The call you've been waiting for has finally come. The parents are exhausted, on their last legs, and are actually anxious to hand their dynamic dynamo over to your tender loving care for a whole week. The only trick is that they said, "come and get her." Grandpa will help drive, but you hadn't thought about entertaining that angelic bundle of energy in a car seat for a seven-hour trip. Well, never fear, grandparents, you're not alone. Just skim through this section, and you'll be armed with ideas to amuse even that terrific two.

I See a . . .

This game has the advantage of endless variations. One person picks an object in the car and gives the color of the object; the others guess until someone names the object and then it's his turn.

I Packed My Trunk

This is a fun memory game. The first person says he packed something in his trunk, say, a towel; the second person says he packed a towel and something new, say a toothbrush; the third person must repeat the first two items and add a new third one; and so on.

Alphabet Derby

In this discovery game, the first person must find a word in a sign beginning with A, the next person must find a word beginning with B, and so on through the alphabet.

Dots

This activity is perfect for older grandchildren. Start with a sheet of paper on which you have drawn a square of dots evenly spaced across and up and down. Each player takes a turn to draw a straight line either horizontally or vertically between any two dots. When your grandchild is able to draw the fourth line, closing up a box, she "owns" the box and can put her initials inside it. She then gets another turn until she can no longer close up a box. When she has closed up all the boxes she can, she must still draw another line before the next person's turn begins. When all the lines have been drawn and the initials counted up, the game is over.

> "Grandparenting is a gift between two people at opposite ends of their journey."
>
> —*Anonymous*

Motel Mania

Finally a room you can make a mess in but not have to clean! If your trip with your little one involves a night in a motel, try using your imagination to make this safe but boring room a launchpad for new adventures. A pack of cards can create a city for tiny people. Hide small objects in the room and give clues—either "hot" and "cold" or riddle-like hints—until the item is found. Turn that wastebasket into a goal or a coat hanger into a basketball net and take turns playing "hoops" with crumpled newspaper. You can even play a half-scary game of "islands." Simply lay sheets of newspaper or paper towel on the rug—these become safety islands and the grandkids must cross the ocean without getting into the water.

Bathtime, if your young grandchild is comfortable in a new tub, can also be a fun time for play if you are careful to give constant supervision. Those improvised toys you think of, too, will be both memorable and fun. You might try using a straw for making bubbles, fashioning boats out of popsicle sticks, or using paper or plastic cups for pouring or for channel marker buoys.

Most of all, enjoy the excitement of your new one-night home, and be patient with unsettled feelings. Set up that portacrib, but don't be surprised if you have a visitor before the night is through. Just think of it as another opportunity for cuddling with a young person who's growing up faster than we dare admit.

Going with the Flow

Thank goodness that unfamiliar motel rooms aren't the only places where grandsnuggling is cherished. Terri Rosett from Urbana, Illinois, has memories of "sharing my bedroom with my visiting grandmother and waking up to cuddle with her in the morning. My daughter and mother also share a bedroom when Mom and Dad visit. The second twin bed in my daughter's room is known as 'Mimi's bed.'"

Remember all those "no-no's" from your parenting days? You may recall that in your time children were often taught to stay in their beds until morning, to eat what was put in front of them, and to always clean up their messes. Whether your child actually did all these things all of the time is up to you and your soft-focus memory (we'll never tell). But in any case, one of the delights of grandparenting is that you can bend many of these old-fashioned rules and not do any harm. Snuggling in bed early in the morning with a grandchild is a delight we all deserve—try it and see what fun your little one has burrowing under your comforter to make a tent or giggling quietly as you make "tickle pictures" on her back (see "Tickle Pictures," p. 144).

See what other rules you can bend, too, after checking which ones are important to your grandchild's parents. Maybe you can have an afternoon "tea" with your grandchildren with some small treats you make together—despite the common pressure to save a child's appetite for dinner. Or perhaps you can give a backrub at naptime or bedtime to help your little person relax—one way of adding a special touch to the regular, probably more independent, routine. Marta and Ed Kievitt of Fairport, New York, for example, wrote to tell us that "Dinner with Grandpa often starts with dessert!" Making your time together unique will mean adding your own spin to the ordinary daily program. Don't be afraid to make yourself an extraordinary grandparent.

Bedtime and Other Discipline Dilemmas

Ever done laps with Bruce Jenner? Well, don't feel disappointed, because you'll have your own little Olympiads around the house to chase come bedtime or après bath. Just wait until that toddler takes off naked and giggling around the house, "blowdrying" his dripping wet body while he runs as fast as his little legs will go. Laughter will be your undoing here, Grandpa—he's cute, but you'll need your full speed and strength to head him off.

"As far as I remember, my grandparents never disciplined us in any way, and we loved that about them," wrote Susanne Wullen of Canberra, Australia. We agree that grandparenting is not really about discipline. But delightful as this picture is, there will probably come a time when you won't want to chase that little one—or, for that matter, be up until all hours with an older grandchild who doesn't want to go to sleep. The solutions to these sorts of problems are seldom easy—but we do have some tips.

First, discuss with the parents what behaviors are most important to you before the visit begins. A week with a five-year-old who starts off with five trips to the bathroom at bedtime and who ends up needing two hours of bedtime stories to go to sleep could wear thin. How do you feel about bedtime routines? What is the established routine in your grandchild's home? These are issues to discuss with your grown children and your grandchild before the parents are halfway to their weekend getaway. Your job is to make sure your grandchild gets enough sleep to have fun doing all the daytime activities you're sure they'd love, while keeping bedtime as stress-free as possible. Toward this end, the grandparents we asked suggest that you follow the order of home-established bedtime events as closely as possible (bath, pajamas, toothbrushing, story, and lights out, for example), but with a twist or two—you might set aside the bedtime gear they came with and instead share your own lullabies and stories with your grandchild.

"Discipline" literally means "to teach," and if you take this approach with your grandchild you will be delighted at how much you both can learn from a difficult situation. Make sure, first, that your guidelines are clear. Do you allow candy before dinner? Is the dog allowed to snuggle up to your grandchild in bed or to beg from the table? Reinforce the good behavior at least twice as often as you cluck

(To the tune of "Over the River and Through the Woods")

Over the couch and under the bed

A toddler chase is on

Bedtime has past and they're awfully fast

And Mom and Dad are gone—oh, NO!

about the bad; give choices when at all possible (peas or carrots?); and if you need to get tough with a behavior that just won't stop on its own, calmly interrupt the fun part of the activity or tell your grandchild firmly to do something apart from you or the group for a couple of minutes.

Raising Your Grandchild

If occasional solo grandparenting is a breathtaking sprint, taking on the job of caring for a grandchild every day can be an arduous marathon. When you raised your own children, you couldn't have imagined waking at 2 A.M. to help a grandbaby fall back asleep; waiting outside a classroom for a grandchild to come out, laden with books and homework; or arguing with a health insurance company about coverage for your new dependent. Your love is unwavering, but you can feel alone—and burdened. According to a 1997 American Medical Association study, caregivers are about twice as likely as other grandparents to suffer from depression.

You are not alone. Over 4 million children in the United States, 5.8 percent of all U.S. children, are being raised by their grandparents. In these grandparent-headed households, 43 percent are headed by a grandmother with no husband. This significant minority needs the support of all fellow grandparents: two-thirds of these homes are in poverty, and half of the grandchildren in such families are under age six.[1]

Fortunately, good help is available: several agencies are working hard to answer your important needs. Below is a list of those that we believe will give you the most reliable information. Good luck, and let us know by email or letter if we can help further. We wish you strength, courage, and the ability to smile at your beautiful grandchildren at the end of the day.

Special Resources for Grandparent Caregivers

AARP Grandparent Information Center

If you're raising grandchildren, you must check out this invaluable, free resource geared just for you. The center was created "to provide grandparents raising their grandchildren with a place to call or write to when seeking assistance." It has a wealth of reliable information on everything from custody, guardianship, and adoption to immunizations, day care, health insurance, and taking care of yourself. Contact the center at (202) 434-2296. They are located at 601 E Street NW, Washington, D.C., 20049. Ask for a free subscription to their newsletter "Parenting Grandchildren: A Voice for Grandparents."

Elderhostel

This organization can connect you with other active seniors (age 55 and over) through educational and enriching outings. When you need a break from the little ones, this is the place to go. You can reach them at 75 Federal Street, Boston, MA 02110-1941; phone: 1-877-426-8056; www.elderhostel.org.

Foundation for Grandparenting

This nonprofit organization promotes the roles of grandparents and encourages intergenerational involvement. They have a newsletter, "Vital Connections," and run a summer camp for grandparents and grandchildren. See the web at www.grandparenting.org, or write to 108 Farnham Rd., Ojai, CA 93023.

Generations United

This national organization represents over 70 million Americans and promotes intergenerational strategies, programs, and policies. Its website features legislative and public policy updates, as well as sections for grandparent caregivers and foster grandparents. Contact them at 440 First Street NW, Washington, D.C., 20001-2085, phone: 202-662-4283, or visit them online at www.gu.org.

Grandparents' Rights (Self-Help Law Kit with Forms), by Tracy Truly

This is a helpful, comprehensive sourcebook for grandparents who need advice. It was updated in 1999 and is available at stores or directly from Sphinx Publishing by calling 813-587-0999.

SHHH (Self Help for Hard of Hearing People, Inc.)

One in four adults over the age of 53 is hard of hearing and finds it difficult to hear the voices of young grandchildren. This super organization has tips that can help. Conferences and a newsletter may also be of interest. Contact SHHH at 7910 Woodmont Ave., Ste. 1200, Bethesda, MD, 20814; voice: 301-657-2248; TTY: 301-657-2249; fax: 301-913-9413; www.shhh.org.

Advocacy Groups for Children

Stand for Children

This nonpartisan membership organization was founded in June 1, 1996, when more than 300,000 people stood together for children at the Lincoln Memorial. Its goal is to give all children the opportunity to grow up healthy, educated, and safe. To join or make a contribution, contact Stand for Children at 1834 Connecticut Ave. NW, Washington, D.C., 20009; phone: 1-800-663-4032; www.stand.org.

CASA for Children

CASA stands for Court Appointed Special Advocates, and it is a private nonprofit organization dedicated to advocating for abused and neglected children. "CASAs," specially trained volunteers, research the child's circumstances and interview the child's family. They provide reports and recommendations to the judge as to what is best for the child. CASA programs operate in every state, with more than 800 programs nationwide. Contact them at 1401 NE 68th Ave., Portland, OR 97213; phone: (503) 248-5115; fax: (503) 306-5618; www.casahelpskids.org.

Pamphlets and Newsletters for Grandparents

"A Grandparent's Guide for Family Nurturing and Safety."
This free pamphlet offers useful grandparenting tips. For a copy, call 1-800-638-2772 or visit their website at www.cpsc.gov.

"Creative Grandparenting Newsletter." Creative Grandparenting, Inc. 100 West 10th Street, Suite 1007, Wilmington, DE 19801. This newsletter is one of the best we've seen. Published four times a year, it includes articles that inspire, enable, and empower grandparents and caring adults to mentor children and unify families.

"Helping Every Generation Care for Kids." This super pamphlet will help grandparents make all visits safe. To get your free copy, send a SASE to The National SAFEKIDS Campaign, 1301 Pennsylvania Ave. NW, Ste. 1000, Washington, D.C., 20004.

Helpful Books on Child Development and Family Relationships

Brandenburg, Mark A. *Child Safe: A Practical Guide for Preventing Childhood Injuries.* New York: Random House, 2000. This practical guide, endorsed by the American Academy of Emergency Medicine and written by a father who is an ER physician, is excellent, as is his web site www.babyandchildsafety.com.

Brazelton, Berry T. *Touchpoints*. Reading, Mass.: Addison-Wesley, 1992. Drawing on his experience as a pediatrician, Brazelton shares his best advice in this easy-to-read reference. We like the way he organizes the developmental phases around "touchpoints" (opportunities to make connections with children)—many of his insights match our own experiences.

Callander, Joan. *Second Time Around: Help for Grandparents Who Raise Their Children's Kids*. Wilsonville, Ore.: Bookpartners, Inc., 1999 (800 895-7323). From a grandmother who is raising her grandson comes this outstanding resource for grandparents in the same situation. This book is personal, practical, and worth reading. As a friend of ours said, "I've highlighted so many parts of the book that I might just as well have dipped the whole thing in yellow paint!"

Carson, Lillian. *The Essential Grandparent*. Deerfield Beach, Fla.: Health Communications, Inc., 1996. From personal experience as a grandmother and as a psychotherapist, Dr. Carson shares her sensitive and insightful thoughts for grandparenting. Her new book, *The Essential Grandparent's Guide to Divorce*, will help families who are facing that challenge.

Doucette-Dudman, Deborah. *Raising Our Children's Children*. Minneapolis, Minn.: Fairview Press, 1997. The author explores social, legal, and emotional issues of grandparents raising their grandchildren.

Elgin, Suzette Haden. *The Grandmother Principles*. New York: Abbeville Press, 1998. With humor and wisdom, this grandmother of 10 offers her 21 principles to help other grandmothers of all ages and experience. This inspiring and information-filled book is an indispensable reference.

Eisenberg. Arlene, Heidi E. Murkoff, and Sandee E. Hathaway. *What to Expect When You're Expecting*. New York: Workman, 1996. If your memory of your own pregnancy is a little foggy, this is the perfect book to get you tuned in to the experiences of your pregnant child. Follow this with their *What to Expect the First Year*. It's a fun refresher course for seniors expecting grandchildren—you'll be surprised at the changes that have occurred since you were a parent! There's now another sequel, *What to Expect: The Toddler Years*.

Faber, Adele, and Elaine Mazlish. *How to Talk so Kids Will Listen and Listen so Kids Will Talk*, rev. ed. New York: Avon, 1999. With their friendly and self-effacing style, these two experts on communication give adults the tools they need to understand, appreciate, and garner cooperation from little ones. This is one of those books we read every year right before school started and we were in charge of a whole classroom of little ones.

Fay, Jim, and Foster Cline. *Grandparenting with Love and Logic: Practical Solutions to Today's Grandparenting Challenges.* Golden, Colo.: Love and Logic Press, 1994. A guide for the new "active and involved" grandparent for building better relationships with grandchildren. A solid, practical book of psychology that makes a great reference.

Galinsky, Ellen. *The Six Stages of Parenthood.* Reading, Mass.: Addison-Wesley, 1981. This one caught our eye because of the many anecdotes Galinsky has gleaned from parents. It's a revealing look into the lives of parents as they face the challenges of their child's developmental milestones.

Gordon, Thomas. *P.E.T.: Parent Effectiveness Training.* New York: New American Library, 1975. This is a favorite of ours, and it's one you might have discovered during your later parenting days. Gordon gives parents—and grandparents—the basic communication skills they need to help raise self-confident, capable, and empathetic young people.

Houtman, Sally. *To Grandma's House We . . . Stay: When You Have to Stop Spoiling Your Grandchildren and Start Raising Them.* N.p.: Studio 4 Productions, 1999. Practical solutions to the problems families face when the traditional roles break down.

Iovine, Vicki. *Girlfriends' Guide to Toddlers.* New York: Berkeley Publishing Group, 1999. Vicki will entertain you as well as keep you abreast of the latest in toddler trends with her survival manual. To stay in tune with your growing family, you can also read her *Girlfriends' Guide to Pregnancy* and *Girlfriends' Guide to Surviving the First Year of Motherhood*.

Kornhaber, Arthur, and Sondra Forsythe. *Contemporary Grandparenting.* Newbury Park, Calif.: Sage, 1996. Dr. Kornhaber provides a synthesis of the role of grandparents in the family and society of today. His latest book with Julia Nelson is *New-Fashioned Grandparenting*.

Kurcinka, Mary Sheedy. *Raising Your Spirited Child*. New York: HarperCollins, 1992. This book will offer lots of emotional support and positive strategies for dealing with a "bundle of energy"!

LeShan, Eda. *Grandparenting in a Changing World*. New York: Newmarket, 1993. With directness and humor, LeShan discusses negotiating the new family structures, understanding the developmental needs of children through adolescence, and how to deal with an aging grandparent.

Lindbergh, Anne Morrow. *Gift from the Sea*. New York: Random House, 1986; 1991. This little gem has spoken to me each summer as I reread it. It's as relevant today as when it was written—maybe even more so as our information and technologically overloaded lives seek simplicity and peaceful solitude. I have given this wonderful classic to my daughters to help them navigate the stages of their lives.

Satter, Ellyn. *Child of Mine: Feeding with Love and Good Sense*. Palo Alto, Calif.: Bull Publishing, 1991. This book is a breath of fresh air to all looking for clear but gentle guidance about what's important for a child to eat. When you are responsible for your grandchild's nutrition, this book will be invaluable. It will also make a great gift to parents of a new baby or toddler.

Spitz, Ellen Handler. *Inside Picture Books*. New Haven, Conn.: Yale University Press, 1999. This is an incredibly insightful and beautifully written tour of books that explore the world as children really experience it. Ellen Handler Spitz is an approachable, knowledgeable, and enthusiastic guide to the inner workings of the best children's books.

Toledo, Sylvie de. *Grandparents as Parents: A Survival Guide for Raising a Second Family*. New York: Guilford Press, 1999. A solid guidebook for all grandparents helping to support or raise grandchildren.

Weaver, Frances. *I'm Not as Old as I Used to Be*. New York: Hyperion, 1998. The guru of *The Girls with the Grandmother Faces* has produced another feisty yet poignant account of life after 70. Just as she says, "Grandmothers learn from grandmothers"—we all have much to learn from her positive attitude about aging as well as her thoughts on grandparenting.

Catalogs We Have Found Helpful

Back to Basic Toys, 313 Sunset Park Dr. Herndon, VA 20170, (800) 356-5360, www.basictoys.com offers sturdy, classic toys, and books for infants through teenagers.

Chinaberry, 2780 Via Orange way, Suite B, Spring Valley, CA 91978, (800-776-2242), www.chinaberry.com. This outstanding catalog reviews books and items to support families in raising their children with love, honesty, and joy. You'll find heartfelt reviews, complete with helpful ideas for reading to children, and if you're like us, you'll look forward to *Chinaberry* just as much as a visit with a dear friend.

Discovery Toys, 6400 Brisa Ave. Livermore, CA 94550, (800) 426-4777, www.discoverytoysinc.com features educational toys, books, games, and software for children of all ages.

Young Explorers, P.O. Box 2257, Loveland, CO 80538, (888) 876-8810, www.youngexplorers.com is a leading provider of creative, educational toys for the newborn to age 14.

Hanna Andersson, 1010 NW Flanders, Portland, OR 97209, (800) 222-0544, www.hannaAndersson.com is called the "Rolls Royce" of children's clothing. We love these cotton cuddlers because they wear like iron—and because the founder and president, Gun Denhart, has her heart in the right place: note her "hannadowns" used-clothing-donation program and the terrific maternity and child care benefits she gives her employees.

HearthSong, 1950 Waldorf NW, Grand Rapids, MI 49550, (800) 325-2502, www.hearthsong.com offers classic children's toys and project kits for building and encouraging the imagination. You'll see some old favorites!

Insect Lore Catalog, P.O. Box 1535, Shafter, CA 93263 (800-LIVE-BUG), www.insectlore.com. This unique catalog features kits and creatures to bring science to life for children—literally! We've ordered their butterfly kits several times, and we're confident you'll enjoy working with this company.

One Step Ahead, P.O. Box 517, Lake Bluff, IL 60044, (800) 274-8440, www.onestepahead.com offers equipment, clothing, and toys for infants through toddlers.

Sensational Beginnings, PO Box 2009, Monroe, MI 48161, (800) 444-2147, www.sb-kids.com caters to the newborn to age nine!

Spoiled Rotten, 7544 Fay Ave. La Jolla, CA 92037, (877) 776-4533. This children's catalog boutique carries elegant European and domestic lines for infants through 6x, as well as toys, gifts, and accessories.

The Grandparent's Toy Connection, 31 Viaduct Rd., Stamford, CT 06907, (800) 472-6312, www.toyclassics.com, having received the Parent's Choice award for the third year in a row, offers classic and award winning toys—many you'll remember having bought for your own children.

The Right Start, 5334 Sterling Center Drive, Westlake Village, CA 91361, (800) 274-8440, www.rightstart.com carries developmental toys and equipment for babies through age five.

Helpful Sites on the Web

Looking for a super catalog for children's clothing? Searching for a great resource for new moms? On the lookout for classic toys for little ones? Want to connect with other grandparents? These links might be helpful, and we hope you'll write to share your favorites with us to help us keep our web site links up-to-date!

www.etoys.com—web based toy & book retailer
www.family.com—crafts, recipes, travel, family fun
www.grandloving.com—our monthly web magazine
www.grandmotherworld.com—bimonthly newsletter
www.grandparenting.org—foundation for grandparenting
www.grandparents-day.com—history of Grandparents' Day
www.grandparentworld.com—toy reviews, articles, travel tips
www.GrandsPlace.com—help for all raising grandchildren
www.igrandparents.com—from tough issues to fun things to do
www.mommytimes.com—mom's insights into young families
www.MrModem.net—easy guide to the internet for seniors
www.mygrandchild.com—toys, books, and clothing
www.ourgrandchild.com—classic gifts for grandchildren
www.ParentTime.com—parenting & pregnancy advisor
www.seniorstore.com—products and gifts for seniors
www.SmarterKids.com—opens minds, opens worlds

www.storyseeds.com—story starters for young thinkers
www.thirdage.com—comprehensive site for seniors
www.toysmart.com—toys, books, teacher aids, furniture
www.wholefamily.com—resources for the whole family

Family Travel Agencies

Access-Able Travel Source
Looking for a travel agent to help travelers with disabilities? P.O. Box 1796, Wheat Ridge, CO 80034; phone: 303-232-2979.

Earthwatch Institute
This unusual agency sends families with teens all over the world on research projects. Call 800-776-0188 or visit the web at www.earthwatch.org.

Family Travel Forum
The forum's newsletter-style website, at www.familytravelforum.com, is a place to trade tips with other traveling families. Or write 891 Amsterdam Ave., New York, NY 10025; phone: 212-665-6124.

Grandtravel
Grandtravel offers unique, upscale trips for grandparents and grand-children: everything from camel rides in Australia to safaris in Kenya. Contact them at the Ticket Counter at 6900 Wisconsin Ave., Ste. 706, Chevy Chase, MD 20815; phone: 1-800-247-7651, www.grandtrvl.com.

Orlando/Orange County Convention and Visitors Bureau
With the Orlando Magicard in your pocket, you'll save up to $500 on your next vacation to Orlando, Florida, the home of DisneyWorld. Look on the web at www.go2orlando.com or call 800-643-9492.

Rascals in Paradise
This travel agency specializes in sending families to off-the-beaten-track destinations. Call 800-U-Rascal or visit www.rascalsinparadise.com.

Volunteer Opportunities for Grandparents

National Senior Service Corps
Over half a million members of this federal program share their time and talents to help their communities. Take a grandchild along and show him or her the rewards of volunteering! The corps is at 1201 New York Ave., Washington, D.C., 20525; phone: 202-606-5000.

9
Wonderful Books for Grandparents

We know you'll enjoy these picture books and other resources because we've loved using them in our classrooms and within our family. So, without further ado, here's our collection of favorite generation-spanning resources, new and old. Use it as a basis for your next library list—or your next trip to a favorite bookstore. You can find an even more updated list on our free web magazine, www.grandloving.com.

Children's Books That Feature Grandparents

There's no better way to enhance an experience with young children than by reading more about it. The next time you have grandchildren around, pull one of these off the shelf to share.

Bahr, Mary. *The Memory Box*. Illustrated by David Cunningham. Morton Grove, Ill.: Albert Whitman, 1992. Ages: Five and up. This is a sensitive, generous book about a young boy and his grandparents. When challenged by the onset of Alzheimer's, the grandfather and his son work together to create a special memory box. A touching and very positive portrayal that comes alive with lovely text and captivating pictures.

Barrett, Judi. *Cloudy with a Chance of Meatballs*. Illustrated by Ron Barrett. New York: Atheneum, 1982. Ages: Three and up. Grandpa tells the silly, whimsical tale of the magical land of Chewandswallow where the weather rains food from the sky.

Berger, Barbara. *Grandfather Twilight.* New York: Philomel, 1984. Ages: Baby to five years. Everyone loves this wonderful bedtime storybook. The illustrations have a soft glowing quality, and blend beautifully with the quiet story of Grandfather Twilight performing his nightly ritual.

Buckley, Helen, and **Jan Ormerod.** *Grandmother and I.* New York: Lothrop, Lee, & Shepard, 1994. Ages: One to five years. A grandchild is never too old to think of Grandmother's lap as the best place to sit for rocking and cuddling. Buckley and Ormerod continue to capture the spirit of true grandparenting in *Grandfather and I.* "Grandfather and I never hurry. We walk along and walk along and stop . . . and look . . . just as long as we like."

Bunting, Eve. *The Butterfly House.* New York: Scholastic Trade, 1998. Ages: Four to eight years. You and your grandchild can also create a butterfly house right along with this grandpa as he helps his granddaughter make a house for their larva. The joy of releasing the beautiful butterfly to freedom is one all ages will appreciate!

Butterworth, Nick. *My Grandma's Wonderful.* Cambridge, Mass.: Candlewick Press, 1992. Ages: Two to five years. From buying the biggest ice cream cone to always carrying just what a grandchild needs in her pocketbook, this book celebrates what makes a grandma special! Check out his *My Grandpa Is Amazing* too.

dePaola, Tomie. *Now One Foot, Now the Other.* New York: Putnam, 1981. Ages: Three to eight years. A quietly touching story of how the tables turn when Bobbie's grandfather, Bob, has a stroke. Bobbie teaches his grandfather to speak, eat, and walk just as his grandfather had once done for him. Note that although this is a wonderful book for grandchildren encountering this particular situation, it should be read with caution to grandchildren facing a less hopeful diagnosis for their grandparent.

Greenfield, Eloise. *Grandpa's Face.* Illustrated by Floyd Cooper. New York: Philomel Books, 1988. Ages: Four to eight years. Tamika and Grandpa share a special togetherness on their "talk-walks." She loves his changing sturdy brown face, and the double page drawings are realistic and rich with earth tones. Greenfield's *Grandmama's Joy* will bring tears to your eyes as you read how Rhondy reminds her Grandmama that as long as they have each other, that's all that matters.

Hill, Eric. *Spot and His Grandparents: An Activity Book.* New York: Puffin, 1998. Ages: Baby to four years. This delightful activity book is full of puzzles, stories, stickers, and songs. You'll love it! Other books about grandparents in the series include *Spot Visits His Grandparents* and *Spot and His Grandparents Go to the Carnival.*

Hines, Anna Grossnickle. *Gramma's Walk*. New York: Greenwillow, 1993. Ages: Four to eight years. In this lovely story, Donnie and his Gramma take a quiet, contemplative walk to the beach. The dear illustrations show the two talking closely together, with Donnie leaning over Gramma's wheelchair or holding her hand.

Johnson, Angela. *When I Am Old with You*. Illustrated by David Soman. New York: Orchard Books, 1990. Ages: Four to eight years. You can feel the love between the generations when a young grandson dreams out loud about what he'll do with his grandfather when they are both old.

Kunhardt, Dorothy. *Pat the Puppy*. Racine, Wis.: Western Publishing, 1993. Ages: Baby to two years. Fellow grandparents, this one's written especially for us! The grandparents in this wonderful texture book have all the pep we feel. Even better, your little ones will love fastening Grandma's velcro jogging shoe, feeling her shiny sunglasses, and turning the dial to watch "videos" with Grandpa.

MacLachlan, Patricia. *All the Places to Love*. Paintings by Mike Wimmer. New York: HarperCollins Publishers, 1994. Ages: All. A treasure, this heartfelt book will help you slow down and remember to pass along to your grandchildren the essence of what is important to you and your family.

McCain, Becky. *Grandmother's Dreamcatchers*. Morton Grove, Ill.: Albert Whitman, 1998. Ages: Four to eight years. A grandmother helps her granddaughter overcome nightmares and homesickness when they make a dreamcatcher of twigs, feathers, and beads. You'll find the directions for making this Native American craft on the last page.

Oxenbury, Helen. *Grandma and Grandpa*. New York: Dial, 1984. Ages: Baby to two years. This is a wonderful board book featuring Oxenbury's inimitable artwork as it depicts daily experiences with grandparents.

Rylant, Cynthia. *When I Was Young in the Mountains*. Illustrated by Diane Goode. New York: Dutton, 1982. Ages: Three years and up. A young girl describes her experiences growing up in the mountains in the care of her Grandma and Grandpa. Goode's pictures transport readers to a place where grandchildren skinny-dip gleefully in muddy swimming holes, and Grandma scares snakes with her hoe. This Caldecott Honor book is a pleasure to share with little ones, and it's also available on audio.

Say, Alan. *Grandfather's Journey*. Boston: Houghton Mifflin, 1993. Ages: Four years and up. In this lovely three-generational tale, Say's grandfather travels to the West from Japan and falls in love with his new country. Yet he still belongs to the first: "The funny thing is, the moment I am in one country, I am homesick for the other." Say's tribute won the Caldecott Medal in 1994 and is filled with beautiful paintings in delicate colors.

Shaw, Eve. *Grandmother's Alphabet.* Duluth, Minn.: Pfeifer-Hamilton, 1996. Ages: Four years and up. Tired of pictures of stodgy old grammas in rockers? This is the book for you. With luminous and detailed illustrations, Shaw captures the spirit of today's happy-to-be-me grandparents. What a wonderful message for young grandchildren!

Shute, Linda. *How I Named the Baby.* Morton Grove, Ill.: Albert Whitman, 1993. Ages: Three to six years. Join James and his family, including "Grams" and "Grandpa," as they search for the perfect name for the new baby. Shute's inclusive, warm text is as inviting as her sweet color-pencil illustrations. A thoughtful choice for an "expecting" big brother or sister.

Smith, Robert Kimmel. *The War with Grandpa.* Illustrations by Richard Lauter. New York: Yearling Books, 1984. Ages: Nine to twelve years. When Grandpa comes to live with Peter and his family, Peter has to move out of his room—and he isn't happy about it! The art of giving and true understanding comes alive with humor and delightfully realistic characters.

Williams, Vera. *More, More, More Said the Baby: 3 Love Stories.* N.p.: Tupelo Books, 1997. Ages: Six months to three years. This board book is a must for the baby or toddler in your life, for it celebrates the joy babies create among those who love them. It is the story of the love of children.

Zolotow, Charlotte. *William's Doll.* New York: Harper & Row, 1972. Ages: Three to five years. Sometimes only a grandparent knows how to respond to a young grandchild's unusual requests. In this story, William's grandma gives him the doll he's always wanted and in the process teaches him that "being yourself" is important and wonderful.

Classic Picture Books: Our All-Time Family Favorites

There's something about reading a favorite family book to a small child curled in your lap that tickles even the most reserved grandparent and delights even the most active of toddlers. Flip to this list the next time you're looking for a super gift for your grandchild or when you're browsing in the library before a visit by an inquisitive little one.

Bemelmans, Ludwig. *Madeline.* New York: Viking, 1939; Puffin, 1977. Ages: Three to six years. Remember Miss Clavel and her twelve little girls who live in "an old house in Paris that was covered with vines"? Share their adventures and the irrepressible Madeline with your grandchildren.

Bornstein, Ruth. *Little Gorilla.* New York: Clarion, 1976. Ages: Baby to three years. Ever wonder if your little one has mixed feelings about growing up? Well, this little gorilla discovers that even when he grows very big, everyone still loves him. A perfect companion for a new big brother or sister.

Brown, Jeff. *Flat Stanley*. Illustrations by Steve Bjorkman. New York: Harper Trophy, 1996. Ages: Four to eight years. This revised edition of the 1964 classic will tickle your grandchild just as it did your own children as you recall how Stanley appreciates the value of being different and enjoys the advantages of his "squashedness"!

Brown, Margaret Wise. *Goodnight Moon*. Illustrated by Clement Hurd. New York: Harper, 1947; 1977. Ages: Baby to three years. We wish we had a nickel for every time we read this book to our children. Your grandchildren too will be lulled to sleep by the soothing colors and repetitive text of the little rabbit saying goodnight to everything in "the great green room." You might also recall Brown's *Runaway Bunny*. The playful dialogue between the baby bunny and its mother makes it a perfect story for times when a child feels less secure, such as after a move.

Burton, Virginia Lee. *Mike Mulligan and His Steam Shovel*. Boston: Houghton Mifflin, 1974. Ages: Two to five years. Remember reading how Mike Mulligan and his steam shovel, Mary Anne, ended up in the cellar of the Popperville Town Hall? Burton's *Katy and the Big Snow* is another fun adventure that deserves to be shared with the next generation.

Crews, Donald. *Freight Train*. New York: Greenwillow, 1978. Ages: Baby to three years. Your grandchildren will feel as though they are moving right along with the colorful, powerful train . . . the next best thing to a real ride! Other books by Crews are *We Read A to Z* and *Ten Black Dots*.

Flack, Marjorie. *Ask Mr. Bear*. New York: Macmillan, 1958. Ages: Two to five years. You might recall reading this book to your children. Your grandchildren, too, will love Danny's hunt for the perfect gift for his mother's birthday. Another of Flack's books, *Angus Lost*, dates back to 1932, but your grandchildren will be as taken with this adventuresome Scottie dog as you and your children were.

Freeman, Don. *Corduroy*. New York: Viking Penguin, 1968. Ages: Two to five years. After a night of adventures in the department store hunting for his lost button, a teddy bear named Corduroy finds a loving home. The sequel, *A Pocket for Corduroy*, is also worth reading, as is Freeman's *Rainbow of My Own*.

Gag, Wanda. *Millions of Cats*. New York: Coward, McCann & Geoghegan, 1928; 1977. Ages: Three to six years. Though this "oldie" is still printed in black and white, your grandchildren will delight at the repetitive tale of how the lonely old couple ended up with just one cat—even though the old man brought home "hundreds of cats, thousands of cats, millions of cats."

Hoban, Tana. *Is It Red? Is It Yellow? Is It Blue?* New York: Greenwillow, 1978. Ages: Baby to three years. Hoban's photos are inspirational in their simplicity—in other words, your grandbabies and grandtoddlers will love them. If this one becomes a favorite, you might also try other Hoban books such as *What Is It?* and *I Read Signs.*

Keats, Ezra Jack. *The Snowy Day.* New York: Viking, 1962. Ages: Two to six years. Peter discovers the wonder of a snowy day. If your grandchildren like this story, read about Peter's adventures in Keats's *Goggles, A Letter to Amy, Peter's Chair,* and another favorite of ours, *Whistle for Willie.*

Kunhardt, Dorothy. *Pat the Bunny.* Racine, Wis.: Western Publishing, 1940. Ages: Baby to three years. We wore out a copy with each child, not because the quality was poor but because we read it that many times. Grandchildren will love to feel Daddy's scratchy face and put their finger through Mommy's ring. A great first activity book.

Lionni, Leo. *Frederick.* New York: Pantheon, 1967. Ages: Three to eight years. Frederick, the daydreaming mouse who collects the rays of the sun, colors, and stories to sustain his fellow mice when winter comes, is as charming today as when you introduced him to your children. Other books we recommend by Lionni include *Alexander and the Wind-Up Mouse, Swimmy, The Biggest House in the World, Fish Is Fish,* and *Little Blue and Little Yellow.*

MacLachlan, Patricia. *Sarah, Plain and Tall.* New York: Harper Trophy 1986. Ages: Seven and up. A beautiful story that teaches the value of family and the importance of each other's strengths during times of hardship. This won the Newbery Medal in 1986 and is followed by the sequel *Skylark.*

Martin, Bill. *Brown Bear, Brown Bear, What Do You See?* Illustrated by Eric Carle. New York: Henry Holt, 1992. Ages: Baby to three years. Originally published in 1967, this new version has beautifully bright colored animals to enhance the singsong text.

McCloskey, Robert. *Blueberries for Sal.* New York: Viking, 1948; Puffin, 1976. Ages: Two to five years. Your grandchildren will be enchanted to learn this timeless tale of the baby bear and the little girl whose mothers mix them up while out picking blueberries. Another of McCloskey's classics, *Make Way for Ducklings,* will win the hearts of your grandchildren as Mrs. Mallard and her ducklings (with rhyming names) stop the busy traffic as they head to the Boston Public Gardens.

Milne, A. A. *Winnie-the-Pooh.* Illustrated by Ernest H. Shepard. New York: Dutton, 1961. Ages: Five years and up. Winnie-the-Pooh, the lovable nonsensical bear, and his friends continue to win the hearts of young children, who love the musical quality of the words. And despite its few pictures, you might even get away with reading this book to your younger grandchildren if they have become familiar with Pooh through videos.

Payne, Emmy. *Katy No-Pocket.* Boston: Houghton Mifflin, 1972. Ages: Three to five years. Katy, a mother kangaroo without a pocket, asks all the other mother animals how they carry their babies, but it isn't until she meets a generous carpenter that her problem is solved.

Piper, Watty. *The Little Engine That Could.* New York: Platt & Munk, 1930; 1961. Ages: Baby to five years. "I think I can, I think I can" will be as good a lesson in positive thinking today as it was years ago. Your littlest grandchildren will want to hear again and again about the little engine that makes it over the mountain.

Potter, Beatrix. *The Tale of Peter Rabbit.* Middlesex, Eng.: Frederick Warne, 1902; 1987. Ages: Two to five years. Could you imagine a childhood without Flopsy, Mopsy, and Cottontail, the good little rabbits—not to mention the mischievous Peter?

Rey, H. A. *Curious George.* Boston: Houghton Mifflin, 1941; 1973. Ages: Two to five years. This is the beginning of a series of funny stories about the curious monkey George and his many adventures.

Scarry, Richard. *Best Word Book Ever.* New York: Random House, 1980. Ages: Baby to four years. Toddlers will love the detail, the jokes, and the many things to name in this classic. Don't miss Scarry's ***What Do People Do All Day?*** Join Huckle and all the rest as they go about their work in Busytown. The enchanting peek into the homes and workplaces of an idyllic town will teach your grandchildren about the jobs people do—and give you an opportunity to tell about your own life and work.

Sendak, Maurice. *Where the Wild Things Are.* New York: Harper, 1962; 1984. Ages: Two to seven years. Max misbehaves and is transported to a land where he gives the orders—until the smell of dinner calls him home. This is a great one to read to a grandchild who's had a mischievous day.

Seuss, Dr. *Hop on Pop.* New York: Random House, 1963. Ages: Two to five years. Our little ones "read" this book to us first. The characters have an irresistible appeal. Another of Seuss' early readers, ***One Fish, Two Fish, Red Fish, Blue Fish,*** will appeal to your younger grandchildren. The make-believe creatures and silly rhymes make it a book for all generations to share.

Silverstein, Shel. *The Giving Tree.* New York: Harper Collins, 1964. Ages: All. This classic for all ages teaches about the giving a receiving of love, a message you will want to share with your grandchild.

Slobodkina, Esphyr. *Caps for Sale . . . A Tale of a Peddler, Some Monkeys and Their Monkey Business.* Reading, Mass.: Addison-Wesley, 1968. Ages: Two to six years. Remember how the peddler tricks the monkeys into throwing his caps back to the ground in this funny classic.

Wright, Blanche Fisher. *The Real Mother Goose*. New York: Checkerboard Press, 1916. Ages: Baby to three years. Check your attic for this treasure of timeless rhymes; it's as fresh to little ones today as it was to your children—and you.

Zion, Gene. *Harry the Dirty Dog*. New York: Harper, 1956; 1976. Ages: Two to six years. Grandchildren will identify with the little white dog and his aversion to soap and water. They'll love his adventures in the sequels, too: *Harry and the Lady Next Door*; *Harry by the Sea*; and *No Roses for Harry*.

Newer Arrivals: Some Sure-to-Please Additions to Your Collection

All of us who love dipping into the children's book section of our libraries have been thrilled to see all the wonderful additions to children's literature in the last few years. Our latest discoveries have the same timeless qualities of our favorite classics—true-to-life characters; warm, captivating illustrations; and themes that speak to the interests of all children. Even better, many of these new arrivals reflect a greater awareness of cultural and racial diversity and lend a generally more inclusive tone to the stories they tell. So make room on your bookshelves for these truly wonderful "new" books. They'll be as loveworn as your children's favorites before you know it.

Ahlberg, Janet, and Allan Ahlberg. *The Baby's Catalogue*. Boston: Little, Brown, 1982. Ages: Baby to two years. This is a beautiful first cuddle book. The endearing, lighthearted narrative follows six babies through a typical day. Your littlest grandchildren will love pointing out all the familiar things and people they find.

Alexander, Martha G. *When the New Baby Comes, I'm Moving Out*. New York: Puffin, 1992. Ages: Two to five years. If your grandchild is expecting a first sibling, this book might be helpful to read. Oliver hollers about having to share his Mom and outgrown baby things with the new arrival, but he soon discovers the positive side of being a big brother.

Barton, Byron. *Airport*. Toronto: Fitzhenry & Whiteside, 1982. Ages: Baby to three years. Any grandchildren who will be flying to see you should read this book first. With bright, bold pictures and a simple text, Barton takes you through every step from arrival to up, up, and away. If your grandchild enjoys Barton's non-fiction books, check out some of his others such as *Building a House*, *Trains*, *Trucks*, *Boats*, or *Machines at Work*.

Brandenberg, Aliki. *Welcome, Little Baby.* New York: Greenwillow, 1987. Ages: Baby to two years. With sweet pictures and simple words, this book celebrates the miracle of a new life and the rapid growth that occurs during the first few years.

Brumbeau, Jeff. *The Quiltmaker's Gift.* Illustrations by Gail de Marcken. Duluth, Minn.: Pfeifer Hamilton, 1999. Ages three to eight years. This book is bursting with colorful art and words. The story celebrates how a quiltmaker's kindness and generosity can overcome difficulty. Even the selfish king is reformed and discovers that true happiness lies within. Look for the clues to quilt names hidden in the illustrations!

Carle, Eric. *The Very Hungry Caterpillar.* New York: Philomel, 1981. Ages: Two to five years. A tiny caterpillar with an insatiable appetite becomes a beautiful butterfly in this much loved tale. Your grandchildren will love the holey pages!

Carlstrom, Nancy White. *Jesse Bear, What Will You Wear?* New York: Macmillan, 1986. Ages: Two to four years. The bears are delightful, and your grandchildren will enjoy the rhythmic, rhyming wordplay. Check out the others in the series, too, including *Better Not Get Wet, Jesse Bear.*

Carter, David A. *How Many Bugs in a Box?* New York: Simon & Schuster, 1988. Ages: Two to five years. This is a uniquely designed book that young children will love. As they open the boxes, they can count the bugs from one to ten.

Clements, Andrew. *Frindle.* New York: Aladdin Paperbacks, 1998. Ages: Six to nine years. Laugh with your school age grandchildren as together you enjoy this humorous tale. Nick loses complete control of his creation as "frindle" sweeps through his school, his town, and the entire country!

Dijs, Carla. *Are You My Mommy?* New York: Simon & Schuster, 1990. Ages: Baby to two years. Your littlest grandchildren will love following the baby chicken as he talks with all the animals in his search for his mother.

Fleischman, Paul. *Weslandia.* Illustrated by Kevin Hawkes. Cambridge, Mass.: Candlewick Press, 1999. Ages: Five to eleven years. Once an outcast, the hero Wesley makes being a "geek" look cool! The splendid paintings explode with color.

Hill, Eric. *Where's Spot?* New York: Putnam, 1980. Ages: Baby to three years. Spot's mother searches everywhere for her missing puppy. Your grandchildren too can lift the flaps to hunt for Spot. Although this is our favorite of the Spot books, there are others in this wonderful "lift-up" series. You might try *Spot's First Walk, Spot's First Christmas, Spot Goes to School, Spot Goes to the Farm,* and *Spot's Birthday Party.*

Inkpen, Mick. *The Blue Balloon.* Boston: Little, Brown, 1989. Ages: Two to five years. A magical blue balloon grows and changes as you and your grandchild unfold the special pages. If you like this book, you might take a look at Inkpen's adorable *Kipper* series.

Isadora, Rachel. *I Touch.* New York: Greenwillow, 1982. Ages: Baby to two years. This book and Isadora's *I Hear* both make marvelous first books; their simple words and pictures portray objects babies will readily recognize.

Jonas, Ann. *When You Were a Baby.* New York: Greenwillow, 1982. Ages: One to three years. A wonderful reminder to the toddler or new big sibling of all the things he couldn't do as a baby that he can do now.

Lucado, Max. *You Are Special.* Illustrated by Sergio Martinez. Wheaton, Ill.: Crossway Books, 1997. Ages: Four and up. A heartwarming tale of how Eli, the woodcarver, helps Punchinello understand how special he is—marks and all. The powerful message of God's healing love and that we are all loved just the way we are is beautifully told and inspirational to all ages.

Martin, Bill, Jr., and **John Archambault.** *Chicka Chicka Boom Boom.* Illustrated by Lois Ehlert. New York: Simon & Schuster, 1989. Ages: Baby to three years. A rhythmic text accompanies bright pictures of adventurous letters playing on a coconut tree. Charlie loves where the "mamas and papas, and uncles and aunts, hug their little dears, then dust their pants."

Osborne, Mary Pope. *The Magic Tree House* series. Illustrated by Sal Murdocca. New York: Random House, 1992-. Ages: Five to eight years. In this delightful series, two young children travel through time and space to solve mysteries and learn history firsthand.

Pfister, Marcus. *Milo and the Magical Stones.* New York: North-South Books, 1997. Ages: Two to eight years. Pfister, the author of the wonderful book *The Rainbow Fish*, gives us another jewel. Your grandchild can decide whether the magical glowing stone will bring disaster or delight by choosing from the dual ending. The message that today's environmental choices will affect the future of our planet comes through loud and clear.

Pomerantz, Charlotte. *Here Comes Henny.* New York: Greenwillow, 1994. Ages: Two to four years. Grandchildren will love the nonsensical tongue twisting verse in this fun story of Henny with her "sacky" and her "chickies" with their "snacky-snicky"!

Raffi. *Baby Beluga.* Illustrated by Ashley Wolff. New York: Crown, 1983. Ages: Baby to three years. Our Charlie has pretended to be a baby beluga in the tub every night since reading this book. It's especially fun if you learn the tune and can sing the words to your grandchild. An adorable baby beluga whale and his mother play and rest in the "deep blue sea."

Rosen, Michael. *We're Going on a Bear Hunt.* Illustrated by Helen Oxenbury. New York: Macmillan, 1989. Ages: Two to six years. With enchanting illustrations and a lyrical text, Oxenbury and Rosen take us right into a bear's cave before we're chased all the way back into our beds. Get ready to hear "Again!" from your little ones as soon as you've finished.

Rowling, J.K. *Harry Potter and the Sorcerer's Stone.* New York: Scholastic, 1999. Ages: Six to twelve. From Britain comes a new classic series filled with adventure and magic as the hero, Harry, captures the imagination of young readers through each of the series of seven books.

Seeger, Pete. *Abiyoyo.* New York: Macmillan, 1986. Ages: Two to six years. This book has achieved cult status among the over-two crowd. A little boy and his father defeat the yucky (but not too scary) giant Abiyoyo by getting him to dance. It's a catchy tune that will have all tapping their feet!

Simmons, Jane. *Come Along, Daisy.* New York: Little, Brown, 1998. Ages: Baby to three. This is an adorable tale with absolutely irresistible illustrations. Little Daisy gets distracted when Mother calls, and chases a frog to a faraway place. When Mother finds her, your grandchildren will cheer.

Walsh, Ellen Stoll. *Mouse Paint.* New York: Harper Brace Jovanovich, 1989. Ages: Baby to four years. This is a whimsical introduction to colors as three white mice play with red, yellow, and blue cans of paint. When you hear those magic words, "Read it again, Grampa!" then you'll know, as we do, that you've found a winner.

Weisner, David. *Sector 7.* New York: Clarion Books, 1999. Ages: Two to eight years. Illustrator David Weisner gives us another wordless adventure to stretch your grandchild's imagination. With a marvelous mix of science and fantasy you'll travel to Sector 7 in the Cloud Dispatch Center.

Wilhelm, Hans. *I'll Always Love You.* New York: Crown, 1989. Ages: Three to six years. With sincerity and a soft touch, Wilhelm guides us through the feelings of a young boy as his dog, Elfie, ages and dies—and shows us the comfort the boy takes in having told Elfie every night, "I'll always love you." This gentle book, with its sweet illustrations, reminds us how important it is to regularly tell our loved ones how much we care.

Children's Activity Books and Other Resources for Grandparents

If you're like us, once you get a taste for being creative with your little ones, your appetite is hard to satisfy. When we need a new idea, we often turn to our collection of reliable "project starters." Here is a sampling from our shelf of favorites.

Brown, Marc. *Party Rhymes*. New York: Dutton, 1988. Even the music is included in this colorful book of twelve rhyming games. A great addition to parties, backyard games, or whenever you have three or more little ones to join in the fun. You'll also find old favorites in Brown's *Hand Rhymes*.

Cassidy, Nancy. *The Book of Kids Songs: A Holler-Along Handbook.* Palo Alto, Calif.: Klutz Books, 1986. This is a super collection of singable favorites, conveniently spiralbound and packaged with a tape to remind you of the tunes. It's a great travel companion for long road trips because the pages are so durable and the songs are such fun.

Cornell, Joseph. *Sharing Nature with Children: The Classic Parents' and Teachers' Nature Awareness Guidebook.* Nevada City, Calif.: Dawn, 1998. The games and activities in this book will help you and your grandchild smell, feel, listen, watch, guess, and imagine yourselves as part of nature.

Free Stuff for Kids. Minneapolis, Minn.: Meadowbrook, 1999. This regularly updated collection of free and up-to-a-dollar offers will keep your grandchild running to the mail box. You might even consider keeping a copy on hand for yourself and sending freebies with little added notes from you.

Goins, Beverly. *Arts, Crafts & More.* N.p.: Teacher Created Materials, Inc., 1999. Ages Five and up. When you and your grandchild are feeling stir crazy, turn to this book and their other new ones, *Exploring Nature* or *Rainy Day Fun,* for some wonderful boredom busters!

Hart, Avery, and **Paul Mantell.** *Kids Make Music.* Charlotte, Vt.: Williamson, 1993. Clapping and tapping from Bach to rock, the twelve chapters in this book will help you enjoy melody, feeling, and beat with your grandchild through singing, dancing, and playing with musical toys.

Hickman, Danelle, and **Valerie Teurlay.** *101 Great Ways to Keep Your Child Entertained While You Get Something Else Done.* New York: St. Martin's, 1992. This book will give you some novel ideas for indoor and outdoor activities that will help your little ones entertain themselves. You'll also find good travel and special occasion activities that are creative, practical, and inexpensive.

Jones, Sandy, with **Werner Freitag.** *Guide to Baby Products,* 6th ed. Yonkers, N.Y.: Consumer Reports Books, 1999. If you're anything like us, you've turned to Consumer Reports' publications for their terrific advice on all sorts of products. This is their comprehensive and invaluable guide to items you might buy for a grandchild. It even includes considerations for buying second-hand products for your little one.

Kamen, Milton. *A Grandparent's Book*. New York: Berkley, 1987. This book, when completed by you, makes a beautiful gift for your grandchild. The questions you will answer will give your next generation your life story—their heritage, their background, their roots.

Katzen, Mollie, and Ann Henderson. *Pretend Soup and Other Real Recipes*. Berkeley, Calif.: Tricycle, 1994. This delightful visual cookbook will help your preschool-age (and older) grandchildren take part in an essential family activity—and it's a great resource for grandparents looking for easy recipes to try with little ones.

Keeshan, Bob. *Family Fun Activity Book*. Minneapolis, Minn.: Fairview, 1994. Television's "Captain Kangaroo," who has always said the greatest gift an adult can give a child is time spent together, has compiled over one hundred simple activities for grownups and children ages three and older.

Lansky, Vicki. *Games Babies Play: From Birth to Twelve Months*. Deephaven, Minn.: Book Peddlers, 1993. In this small volume, Lansky has collected some of the best fingerplays, songs, and movement games to do with your littlest grandchildren. It makes a super gift to a new family and a wonderful reference to pack for those early visits to your new grandchild.

Levy, Judith. *Grandmother Remembers Songbook: Heirloom Songs for My Grandchild*. Illustrated by Judy Pelikan. New York: Workman, 1992. Lovely little illustrations border each page of this book of forty songs—many of which you'll recall from your own childhood. The music is easy to play on the piano, and lyrics are included. This book is intended to be given as a gift from a grandparent to a young grandchild.

Lewis, Valerie, and Walter Mayes. *Valerie & Walter's Best Books for Children: A Lively, Opinionated Guide for Listeners and Readers from Birth to Age 14*. New York: Avon Books, 1998. This book is extensively cross-indexed with a 114 page index of nearly 1,000 themes which the more than 2,000 books reviewed contain. It has concise, fun-to-read reviews.

Miller, Karen. *More Things to Do with Toddlers and Twos*. Chelsea, Mass.: TelShare, 1990. An excellent book for grandparents or anyone working with children ages eighteen months to three years. All of Miller's creative ideas are based on a solid understanding of toddler behavior and development. As in Miller's first book, *Things to Do with Toddlers and Twos*, we especially like the way she uses found objects to create toys.

Ninkovich, Thomas, and Barbara E. Brown. *Family Reunion Handbook: A Guide for Reunion Planners*, 2d ed. San Francisco, Calif.: Reunion Research, 1998. A super guide to planning your family get-togethers.

Oppenheimer, Joanne, et al. *Toy Portfolio 1999: The Best Toys, Books, Videos, Music and Software for Kids*, 6th ed. New York: Harper Perennial, 1999. Ages: Infant to ten years. This indispensable guide reviews over 1,000 expert-and kid-tested products and will help you pick just the right gift for your grandchild.

Orr, Clarice Carlson. *The Joy of Grandma's Cooking: A Treasury of Recipes and Stories from the Heart*. Lincoln, Neb.: Dageforde, 1999. Orr is a masterful storyteller, and it is a delight to browse through her collection of favorite recipes. Reading this book, with its nostalgic tales and chapters like "Grandkids' Favorites," is like having a cozy chat in a warm kitchen.

Prelutsky, Jack. *The 20th Century Children's Poetry Treasury*. Illustrated by Meilo So. New York: Random House. 1999. Ages: Two years and up. Prelutsky has selected over 200 poems from 137 of his favorite poets. Share with your grandchild the best of verse from each decade of the 20th century along with So's whimsical watercolors.

Silverstein, Shel. *Where the Sidewalk Ends*. New York: Harper, 1974. Ages: Five years and up. Don't miss this treasure—your grandchildren and you will both melt and laugh at the marvelous poems and illustrations. Fans of Silverstein's will also enjoy his *Falling Up* and *A Light in the Attic*.

Uslander, Arlene. *That's What Grandmothers Are For*. Chicago: Chicago Spectrum, 1996. Sometimes a poem is just what grandparents need, and Uslander has a gift for creating touching, sincere poems for families to share. If you like this little book, you might also look for her *That's What Grandfathers are For*. They both make wonderful presents for grandparents.

Weaver, Mary. *365 Fun-Filled Learning Activities*. Holbrook, Mass.: Adams Media Corporation. 1999. Ages: Three to seven years. Weaver, a teacher, offers some wonderfully creative ways you and your grandchild can play together while developing learning skills.

Notes

Special Delivery: A New Grandloving

1. Judith Waldrop, "The Grandbaby Boom," *American Demographics* (Sept. 1993); AARP, *2000 Statistics Update*, research.aarp.org; "(Not So) Grand Times," *American Demographics* (Mar. 1998), citing research from Roper Starch Worldwide.

1. Nine Months and Counting

1. Ellen Galinsky, *The Six Stages of Parenthood* (Reading, Mass.: Addison-Wesley, 1990), 31.

2. Anne Morrow Lindbergh, *Gift from the Sea* (New York: Pantheon, 1975), 66-67.

2. The Postpartum Visit

1. Ellen Galinsky, *The Six Stages of Parenthood* (Reading, Mass.: Addison-Wesley, 1987), 62.

3. Love Across the Miles

1. *Early Childhood Experiences in the Language Arts*, 4th ed.: *Emerging Literacy* (Albany, N.Y.: Delmar, 1990).

5. Visiting Your Grandchild

1. T. Berry Brazelton, *Touchpoints* (Reading, Mass.: Addison-Wesley, 1992), 436.

6. Heartfelt Holidays and Family Traditions

1. T. Berry Brazelton, *Touchpoints* (Reading, Mass.: Addison-Wesley, 1992), 166.

2. Arlene Eisenberg, Heidi E. Murkoff, and Sandee E. Hathaway, *What to Expect the First Year*, 2d ed. (New York: Workman, 1992).

8. Caring for a Grandchild

1. U.S. Census, July 1, 1999.

Index

1, 2, 3 . . . How Many Do I See? 90

AARP Info Center, 246
Abracadabra, What's Missing? 137
Abracadabra: Power Lifter, 146
adoption, 22
advocacy groups for children, 247
Ahoy, Matey-There's Treasure! 57
album of your home before visit, 60
Alphabet Derby, 243
Animal Zoo, 217
Any Resemblance? 172
Arms of Love, 32
art: materials to have for visits, 66;
    our philosophy about, 1-2
audio tapes, 42-43; guessing game,
    203; poems and songs on, 52;
    sound bingo game, 51; telling
    stories on, 43, 50
automobile safety. *See car safety*

babyproofing, 190
badge, for big brother or sister, 34
Balding Grandpa Grows Hair, 209
Balloons of Love (note inside), 199
Balloons to the Rescue (race), 129
balloon activities: All This from One
    Balloon, 89; balloons as box
    padding, 206; balloon doll, 207;
    boats, 102, 234; homemade
    paddles and, 206-7; note inside,
    199; race, 129
Balloons, Balloons, Balloons, 206-7
Banana Mash Magic, 134
Bath Tub Tiles, 231
bath time activities: ball game, 143;
    painting, 128-29; puppets, 225;
    sponge toys, 192; tiles, 231
Bean Bag Fun, 135
Beautiful Bracelets, 76

Beautiful Bubble Brew, 96
Bedtime Stories from Afar, 50
bedtime, 244-45
behavior issues: giving choices, 245;
    relaxing about, 244; reinforcing
    good behavior, 245
Big Brother/Big Sister Badge, 34
binoculars, homemade pretend, 226
bird feeder, homemade, 100
boat activities: Blow Power Boats,
    102; Grandpa's Floating Fleet, 93;
    Ships Ahoy, 101
Body Double, 127. *See also Return
    the Favor!* 216
books on child development and
    family relationships, 248-51
books, children's, featuring
    grandparents, 255-58
books, classic children's, 258-62
books, homemade: adventure, 47-48;
    Crazy Mixed-Up Creatures, 219;
    making with your grandchild,
    123; photo storybook, 52; recipe,
    47; story, 47. *See also journals,
    stories*
books, newer children's, 262-66
books, children's activity, 266
boxes, for dramatic play, 83
boxes, homemade: activity, 46; as gift
    for new sibling, 28
Brazelton, T. Berry, 119, 160
bubble recipe, 96

Capturing Daydreams and New
    Discoveries, 16
car games, 90, 242: Alphabet Derby,
    243; Dots, 243; I Packed My
    Trunk, 242; I See a..., 242
car safety, 241-42
Card Creations, 128

Cardboard Box Creations, 83
Cards of Membership, 220-21
caring for your grandchild, 239-54:
    documents and info you need, 240;
    outings, 241; resources, 246-47
CASA for Children, 248
Cassette Connections, 52
cassette tapes. *See audio tapes*
catalogs, our favorite, 253-54
"Chase-less" Indoor Catch, 138
Chief Correspondent, 51
Chow Mein Chocolate, 108
Christmas activities: ornaments, 174,
    182; wrapping paper, 175
clippings: of meaningful quotes, 35;
    newspaper, during pregnancy, 16
codes to send to grandchild, 54, 195
collections, 124-25
Color Collections, 208
color mixing activity, 75
Colorful Collaborations, 193
computers, 43-44
cooking: chokable foods, 69; for
    grandchildren, 68-69; with
    grandchildren, 67, 86. *See also*
    recipes
Cool Cubes, 143
Coupons of Caring, 201
Crazy Mixed-Up Creatures, 219
Create a Treasure as You Record, 33
Create a Winter Wonderland, 174
Creative Cupids, 178
Creative Curls-84

Dazzling Snowflakes, 141
discipline. *See behavior issues*
Doggone Good Goodies, 87
dolls, homemade, 36
Dots, 243
drawings: with Epsom salts, 193;
    fanciful, to exchange, 193
Dress-Up Drama, 81

Edible Jewels, 135
Elderhostel, 247

email, 43
equipment for grandchildren, 61-63
Every Day Together Is Special, 109
Everyone Loves Being Welcomed
    Home, 30
Everyone Needs a Baby-36
Everything's Edible, 134

Face Paint Fun (recipe), 178
Fantasy Friends and Funny Phrases,
    177
fax, 43
Feeding Our Feathered Friends, 100
Felt Board Fun, 204
Find Your Own Pot of Gold, 104
Fingers Save the Day for Our Legless
    Puppets, 233
fireflies, catching and releasing, 97
Flashlight Faces, 202
Flashlight Fun, 222
flashlight, activities using: Flashlight
    Faces, 202; Flashlight Fun, 222;
    Submerged Sights, 105
Flying Foam (airplane), 210
"Follow Me" Footsteps, 91
Forget-Me-Not, 57
Foundation for Grandparenting, 247
Frame It Up with Toothpicks, 213
From Surfacing Submarines to
    Balloon Boats, 234
Fun with Foaming Magic, 147
Funny Dough, 98

Galinsky, Ellen, 6, 20
gardening: sending seeds, 57; Roots
    and Shoots, 99; garden stones,
    183. *See also nature*
Gelatin Jiggles, 221
Generations United, 247
gifts: during pregnancy, 7-10; during
    visit to grandchild, 119-20; for
    grandchild to give baby, 15, 31;
    for new baby, 32; for new big
    sibling, 34, 36; for parents after
    birth of baby, 35; game for finding

gifts, 184. *See also holidays*
"Giggle Maker" Sock Puppets, 202
glue recipe, 74-75
good luck charms: for grandchild,
    200; for pregnant mom, 17
Good Night, Grandma and Grandpa,
    52
Grandpa's Floating Fleet, 93
Grandpa's Shaving-Cream Creations,
    130
Grandparents' Rights, 247

Halloween activities: costume, 170;
    games, 180; luminaries, 173
Hand in Hand, 82
handprint cast, 76
Hands or Feet of Dough, 76
Hanukkah activity: homemade
    wrapping paper, 175
Have a "Grape" Halloween, 170
Heads or Tails? 145
Here We Go Loopy Loo (straw and
    paper spaceship), 234-35
holidays, 149-90: activities, 169-89;
    babyproofing, 190; celebrating
    elsewhere, 167-68; celebrating on
    a different day, 152; dangers of
    high expectations, 159; decorating
    with grandchild, 154; creating
    traditions, 155; documenting the
    fun, 150; doing project with
    grandchild, 155; enlisting family
    help, 163; games, 164; how
    grandchildren feel, 160-62; how
    grandparents feel, 156-58; how
    parents feel, 158-59; long-dis-
    tance, 151-52; making time for
    each grandchild, 162; memorable
    gift cards, 151; rituals from other
    countries and families, 153-54;
    simple gifts, 165-67; spreading
    out the gift-giving, 167; staying
    grandchild-oriented, 153; using
    packing materials for art, 169,
    172, 175; welcome banner, 150
Hoops-a-Fun, 143

"Hug a Tree" Discovery Game, 106
Hug Tag, 182

I Dream, You Dream, We All Dream
    of This Ice Cream, 110
I Made These Cookies, 110
I Packed My Trunk, 242
I See the Moon, 226-27
Ice Crystal Creations, 193
icons in this book, 2-3
Icy Icicles, 209
illness during visit, 120
injury, avoiding, 10-11
Inspiration from Above, 132
It's a "Houzzle"? 56

Jokes and Riddles to the Rescue, 58
jokes to send, 58
journals: about visit with grandchild,
    for grandchild, 48; for parents,
    70; for pregnant mom, 16; Love
    Soup, 72
Jump Through, 228-29

Keep It Going, 85
Kitchen Kaboodle, 86
Kites and Grandkids Go Together,
    235
Knead It, Roll It, Squish It, 74

Lights in the Night, 97
Lindbergh, Anne Morrow-13
Listen Well and Then Tell, 139
Listen, Listen, What Do You Hear?
    130
listening, active, 6
Little Detective Game, 211
long-distance activities, 191-238;
    materials grandchild should have,
    192. *See also individual activities*
Love Note "Supplement," 196
Love Note Sippers, 204
Love Soup, 72

Magic Movers, 144
magic tricks: foaming magic, 147; ice

cube lifting, 146; invisible messages, 49; magnet tricks, 144, 218; paper hoop, 228-29; shining pennies, 147

Magical Blooms, 176

Magical Colors, 75

Magical Music Drawings, 92

mail. *See long-distance activities*

Make a Leaf-Lasting Impression, 105

Marching in Style, 220

Marionettes on Stage, 133

Marvelous Masking Tape-133

May Day activities: baskets, 186; bonnets and parade, 177

May Day Memories, 186

Mealtime Fun: Gift Wrap Rap, 181

meetings, gentle first, 63

Memory Movies, 189

messes, preparing for, 2

miniatures, collecting with grandchildren, 66

Mirror, Mirror, Off the Wall (games with sun and mirror), 101

miscarriage, 11-12

mobile, for baby, 15

Money Bunny, 214

motel room activities, 243-44

movies. *See videos*

Music, Music, Everywhere, 94-95

music: drawing to, 92; homemade instruments, 94-95; passing down lullabies, 31; wind chimes, 103; with straws, 222

My Family Loves Me, 52

Mysterious Mover, 218

Mystery Sounds, 203

nature: Balding Grandpa Grows Hair, 209; bird feeder, 141; coin flip walk, 145; cloud watching, 132; dying Queen Anne's lace, 142; finding seeds, 140; hug a tree, 106; ice sculpting, 174; icicle making, 209; leaf impressions, 105; listening walk, 130; sending seeds, 57; scavenger hunt, 136; snow maze, 137; snowflake catching, 141; snowman, 171; sprouting beans, 212; sun tea, 142

New Year's activity: Whistling Whizzers, 185

newsletters: family, 51; for grandparents, 248

newspaper: clippings during pregnancy, 16; hats, 220; sending activities from, 196

Now You See It, 102-3

One Lucky Baby-17

One-Sided Wonder, 230

Open the Gates, 145

Ornament Just for Me, 174

Ornamental Treasures, 182

outdoor games. *See nature*

Package Fun: Bubble Wrap Prints, 169

Package Fun: Tiny Tissue Balls, 175

paint recipe, 73

painting: rocks, 96-97; with food, 134; with gelatin, 128-29; with mirror, 223; with spaghetti, 80; with string, 78; with water, 127

Paintless Painting, 127

pamphlets for grandparents, 248

Paper Doll Chains, 218

Paper Plate Pals, 197

Paper-Punch Pictures, 198

papier-mâché Inspirations, 172

Passing of the Tunes, 31

paste recipe, 74-75

Peanut Butter Pinecones, 141

Perfect Paints, 73

Pet Pieces, 215

pets and grandchildren, 64

phone calls, 37-42: asking open-ended questions, 40; keeping list, 40; phone gadgets, 42; saying goodbye, 40-41

photos: as puzzle, 207; baby photo game, 172; for memory game, 213; in calendar of visit, 72; in

"goodnight board," 52; in "I love you" book, 52; in placemat, 50
Picture Words (rebus), 208
playdough recipes, 74, 98
Pop a Thanksgiving Turkey in the Mail, 169
pregnancy, 5-18: gifts for baby, 9; gifts for dad, 7-8; gifts for mom, 7-10, 16; helping siblings during, 12-14; how grandparents can prepare during, 10-11; parents' feelings during, 5-7
Pumpkins Aglow, 173
Puppet Pals, 237
Puppets in the Bath, 225
Puppets in the Palm, 132
puppets, homemade: bath, 225; finger, 233, 237; flashlight, 202; glove and cup, 132; marionettes, 133; shadow, 222; sock, 202, 232; wooden, 206
Put on Those "Rose-Colored Glasses," 226
Puzzle Just for Me, 55
puzzles: Little Detective Game, 211; of your home, 56; Pet Pieces, 215; photo, 207; secret message on blank, 55; What Is a Memory? 213
Puzzling Grandparents, 207
Rainbow "Rags," 79
raising your grandchild. See caring for your grandchild
recipes: Chow Mein Chocolate, 108; coconut "nests," 179; dog biscuits, 87; food necklaces, 135; frozen fruit pops, 134; fruity ice cubes, 143; gelatin shapes, 221; Happy Face Pancakes, 88; ice-cream pie, 110; no-bake cookies, 88, 110; pizza, 108-109; stir sticks, 180; sun tea, 142
Reflecting Painting, 223
relaxing: about food issues, 68-69; about messes, 1-2, 69-70
Remember Remember? 210-11

Return the Favor! 216. See also Body Double, 127
Rock Creations, 96-97
Roots and Shoots, 99
routines and rules: being flexible about, 240, 244; importance of for grandchildren, 60
Rub, Rub, Rub, 131

Sawdust Sculptures, 85
School Days, School Days, 200
science activities: filters, 230; glow-in-the-dark moon and stars, 226-27; Mobius strip, 230; pinhole magnification, 224. See also nature; magic tricks
Scrap-Box Art, 176
Seamstress or Tailor, 216
Seaside Symphony, 103
Secret Club Codes of Yore, 54
Secret Codes for Special Friends, 195
Secrets in Wax, 49
See Lincoln's Bright Face? 147
Self Help for Hard of Hearing People, Inc. (SHHH), 247
sewing cards, 216
Shape Stories, 205
shaving with popsicle stick, 162
Shhh . . . Baby's Sleeping, 31
Ships Ahoy, 101
sibling issues, helping with esp. after birth of new baby, 25-28
signs: baby's sleeping, 31; to welcome family home, 30;
Simply Wonderful Water, 104
Sitting for Silhouettes, 188
Smell and Tell, 199
Smiles from under the Spaghetti, 50
Snip and Send, 16
Snow Maze, 137
Snow Sculpture Spritzing, 98
Snowman in a Box, 171
Sounds Like Somewhere I've Been, 51
Space Capsule Landing (parachute and note), 236
Space Shoe Shuffle, 200

Spaghetti Painting, 80
Sponge Playthings, 192
Springtime Bonnets upon Us, 177
Springtime Nested Treats, 179
Sprouting Beans, 212
Squish-and-Wiggle Painting, 78
Stamping Sponges, 198
Stand for Children, 247-48
Stars of the Show, The-55
Stepping Stones, 183
Stick To It! 74-75
Sticky Sock Sketch, 140
stories for grandchild: about parents,
   67-68; add-on, 187; family riddles
   and jokes, 187; family skits and
   puppetry, 187; round robin, 85;
   shape, 205; with blanks for filling
   in, 58
Stories We Tell, 187
straw and pipecleaner animals, 217
Straw Symphony, 222
Submerged Sights, 105
Suspended Animation-15
Swinging Salt, 148

Tangram Treasures, 194
tape: bracelet activity with, 76;
   masking, 133
Tea for Two, 142
telephone. See phone calls
Thanksgiving activity, 169
"Think-a-Lot" Scavenger Hunt, 136
This Sure Beats Darning, 232
Tickle Pictures, 144
tie dye activity, 79
Time Capsule of Treasures, 33
Together Stories, 58
Toy Bag or Box Treasures, 30
travel agencies, for families, 254
travel games: Card Creations, 128.
   See also car games, visits to
   grandchild
Tub Tile Art, 128-29

Valentine's Day activity: making
   valentines, 178

Vest 'em Up, 205
videos, homemade: filming
   grandchild, 124; playing games
   on, 55; questions to ask, 189;
   tour of your home, 55
visit, first postpartum, 19-36: and
   adoption, 22; at different time
   than other grandparents, 23;
   bonding with baby, 20; grandfathers' feelings, 22; helping other
   grandchildren, 25-28; respecting
   parents' privacy, 20; supporting
   parents, 21, 23
visits from grandchild, 59-110:
   activities to try during, 71-110;
   art materials to have on hand, 66;
   equipment you may need, 61-63;
   notes in child's suitcase, 71; pets
   and grandchildren, 64; sending an
   album before, 60
visits to grandchild, 111-48: activities
   to try, 127-48; being an easy
   houseguest, 118; being
   child-oriented, 112-15, 118; being
   memorable, 115-16;
   coordinating visits with other
   grandparents, 113; documenting
   the fun, 123-25; enlivening the
   last day, 125-26; experiencing
   grandchild's world, 116-17;
   frequent visits, 122; gentle first
   meetings, 114-15; grumpy
   children, 120-21; illness, 120;
   leaving treasure behind, 57, 125;
   what grandchildren want, 111;
   what grandparents hope for, 112.
   See also visit, first postpartum
volunteering with grandkids, 254

Want to "See" What? 72
water activities: garden hose
   rainbows, 104; painting with
   water, 127; Simply Wonderful
   Water, 104; spraying colored
   coffee filters, 224. See also boats
Weave a Web of Fun, 184

Wet and Wild Watercolors, 224
What Does That Look Like? 140
What Goes Through? 230
What in the World Is That? 188
What Is a Memory? 213
What'll Stick? 212
Whistling Whizzers, 185
Who Needs a Magnifying Glass?
    224
Who Says It Has to Be Round?
    108-9
Wintertime Sandbox, 131
Wintertime Warmers, 180
Wooden Puppets in Minutes, 206
woodworking: Creative Curls, 84;
    making boats, 93; Sawdust
    Sculptures, 85
Words of Wisdom, 35
Wrap It Up, 175

Warm Thanks to Our Contributors

Barnes, NY, 46
Bates, FL, 42
Carlson, MN, 21, 22, 67
Coonan, NY, 67
Crawford, NY, 60, 167
Curtis, NY, 11, 59, 118
Denhart, OR, 39
Dickens, NY, 25
Donzey, Germany, 153
Eberhardt, NY, 23, 155
Fuller, ME, 8, 115
Fulreader, NY, 120
Gordon, NH, 59
Graham, NY, 24
Greenberg, NY, 122
Grubbs, MD, 47, 66, 122
Ha, NY, 153
Hansen, VA, 46

Hays, NY, 24, 155
Hill, NJ, 23
Jackson-Smith, WI, 65
Johannson, Sweden, 168
Johnson, NY, 156
Jones, NY, 60, 65
Kievitt, NY, 244
Kirkpatrick, New Zealand, 47, 61
Klassen, AZ, 241
Knaflewska, Poland, 153
Knight, NY, 12
Knox, WA, 66, 155, 164
McCall, NJ, 121
McGroary, Ireland, 153
McKenzie, NH, 45, 150
McLain, NY, 153
Miller, NY, 10
Norton, NY, 166
Perlowski, FL, 8, 46
Potestivo, MI, 166
Rawlingson, New Zealand, 42
Roscoe, NY, 118
Rosett, IL, 244
Rothermel, ME, 8, 37, 41, 48, 69, 70
Shaw, UT, 29, 59
Slotnick-Trimble, UT, 6, 111, 240
Smith, WA, 39, 69
Strong, NY, 114
Tollgard, Sweden, 151
Uslander, IL, 190
VanMetre, VA, 152, 166
Whiting, NJ, 165
Wilbur, MA, 6, 68
Wright, Scotland, 165, 240
Wullen, Australia, 245

. . . and to the over 300 others who shared their great ideas.

Share *Grandloving* with a grandparent!

Use the handy order form on the next page or send us your name, address, phone number and e-mail address with a check or money order made out to:

Heartstrings Press ♥ 20 Birling Gap, Suite BOF ♥ Fairport, NY 14450

Grandloving sells for $16.95 plus $4.00 postage.
New York State residents please add sales tax.
Call (800) 262-1546 for quantity discounts.

We'll be delighted to personalize and sign your copy—just let us know to whom you would like to have your book inscribed.

"Come on, Grandma, let's make memories!"

Share *Grandloving* with a friend!

♥ Postal orders   Heartstrings Press
20 Birling Gap, Suite BOF
Fairport, NY 14450

♥ Phone orders   (800) 262-1546

♥ Fax orders   (716) 223-4789

♥ Email orders   Sue@grandloving.com

♥ Inquire for quantity discounts

If you know of any day care centers, schools, church groups, service clubs, community organizations or hospital childbirth or grandparenting classes that might want to offer Grandloving *as a fundraiser, please contact us.*

	# Copies	Cost
Grandloving $16.95	_____	_____
Shipping & handling		
$4.00 for the first book		_____
$2.00 for each additional	_____	_____
NYS Residents please add tax		_____
Total paid to Heartstrings Press		_____

❑ Check   ❑ Money Order

Yes, please sign and personalize my copy by writing:

_____

Mail to:

Name _____

Address _____

City _____ State _____ Zip _____

Telephone (_____) _____ Email _____